Praise for
Welcome to the Goddamn Ice Cube

"As both a storyteller and a stylist, Braverman is remarkably skilled, with a keen sense of visceral detail . . . that borders on sublime. But her ability to draw readers into heart-pounding action sequences—from the "perfect wave" of a sled dog team bounding across the snow to the disorienting rotor wash of tourist helicopters in a whiteout—is what makes the book so courageous and original as both a travel narrative and a memoir of self-discovery."

—*New York Times Book Review*

"Determined to become tougher, the author ventured into the unforgiving wilds of far-north Norway and Alaska. . . . Braverman discovered violence, beauty, love—and her true self. Her gorgeously written narrative is the perfect hot-weather escape."

—*People* magazine

"[A] remarkable memoir, a coming-of-age tale set largely on the Norwegian tundra—where she trained sled dogs—and in Alaska. . . . Braverman's clear, firm voice holds the story together. . . . It's amazing to watch as she develops backbone and grit, determined not to let anyone or anything stand between her and the ice landscape she loves so much."

—*Entertainment Weekly*

"Stimulating empathy in our readers might not be our most intentional mission when we set out to tell our stories, but it might just be our most valuable. *Welcome to the Goddamn Ice Cube* is gorgeous, moving and universally resonant. But most of all, it's important."   —Huffington Post

"[A] thoughtful meditation on a lifelong attraction to the cold."
                              —*Boston Globe*

"Braverman is a lyrical, understated writer. . . . This unusual memoir will resonate with anyone who has ever chased a dream through a thicket of difficulty."   —*Star Tribune* (Minneapolis)

"Hilarious and heart-wrenching."   —*Dallas Morning News*

"This book could be described in a dozen different ways—hero's journey, coming of age tale, travelogue, character portrait, elegy of place—but no description would get at the root of this book, which is about gender and violence and belonging, but most of all about being human and learning to live—and trust oneself—in a world where things aren't always safe."   —*Brevity* magazine

"In a new book, Blair Braverman describes a life spent obsessed with the frozen north, and the sexual violence she encountered in that male-dominated world."   —*The Guardian* (UK)

"Blair Braverman confronts hostility and harassment in her memoir of adventure in the wilderness." —*New Republic*

"There's strength in Braverman's pared-down prose, and it makes the few times she does confide her desires, frustrations, and fears more powerful for holding back. It's a deeply nuanced approach, making *Welcome to the Goddamn Ice Cube* a strange, remarkable memoir."
—A.V. Club

"*Welcome to the Goddamn Ice Cube* is a stunning piece of work. Braverman lays herself bare, exposing all of her desires, her insecurities and her triumphs in a compulsively readable tangle of raw nerves, brutal honesty, self-deprecation and biting wit."
—*Maine Edge*

"[Blair Braverman's] easy, lyrical prose makes this search for identity and self a worthwhile read." —*Publishers Weekly*

"[Braverman's] external experiences are extraordinary . . . but it's what happens internally that both sets this memoir apart and gives it universal resonance. . . . Characters, adventurous spirit, and acute psychological insight combine in this multilayered debut."
—*Kirkus Reviews* (starred review)

WELCOME TO THE GODDAMN ICE CUBE

WELCOME TO THE GODDAMN ICE CUBE

Chasing Fear and Finding Home in the Great White North

BLAIR BRAVERMAN

ecco

An Imprint of HarperCollinsPublishers

This is a work of nonfiction. The events and experiences detailed herein are all true and have been faithfully rendered as remembered by the author, to the best of her ability, or as told to the author by people who were present. Some names, physical descriptions, and other identifying characteristics have been changed to protect the privacy and anonymity of the individuals involved.

HarperCollins books may be purchased for educational, business, or sales promotional use. For information please e-mail the Special Markets Department at SPsales@harpercollins.com.

A hardcover edition of this book was published in 2016 by Ecco, an imprint of HarperCollins Publishers.

FIRST ECCO PAPERBACK EDITION PUBLISHED 2017.

Designed by Suet Chong
Title page photography by Tyler Olson/Shutterstock, Inc.

Library of Congress Cataloging-in-Publication Data has been applied for.

ISBN 978-0-06-231157-3

21   OV/LSC   10

For Arild

We are on a set, and the set makes us all actors.

—CHARLES BOWDEN

WELCOME TO THE GODDAMN ICE CUBE

PROLOGUE

I'M SICK," SAID MARTIN.

He sat hunched in a folding chair before the bonfire. It was St. Hans's night—midsummer—and the sun hung small and orange over the northern horizon, like a sullen child not quite willing to leave the room. Across the fjord, a line of tiny fires flickered between the water and the hills.

"I'm sorry to hear that," I said.

Martin pushed himself up and came to stand before me. "Did they tell you?" he said. "I bet they didn't tell you. Didn't want to scare you away, a nice *pia* like yourself. You don't even know what it's like. I'm going to die soon. If God has a heart, I'm going to die soon."

I was looking at the fire behind him, I realized, and made myself look up at his face. He was maybe sixty. His body seemed full of bones.

"I can't even fuck a woman," Martin said. "I'm going to die soon, and I can't even fuck a woman. Yeah, just drink your cider. Drink it while you can. You don't know what it's like to be in pain." As if on cue, he stiffened and moaned, biting his lip hard.

Then he caught his breath. "I could have fucked you," he said quietly. "Once in my life I sure could have fucked you."

He seemed to expect a response, so I tried to think of one. Fear seemed appropriate—a show of being intimidated. The proper gift for a dying man. Could he have fucked me? It made me tired to consider.

I thought of another man, the day before, who had wrapped his arms around me from behind. *Treasure*, he'd whispered, *you're north of the moral circle now.*

"Let me show you," said Martin. With white hands he fumbled the button of his canvas pants. Behind him, sparks rose toward the blue sky.

"You don't need to show me," I said. "I believe you."

"No, you don't," said Martin. "Look." He pulled down his waistband to reveal two curving, white hip bones and a colostomy bag, half full. He prodded the bag with his fingers so that it sloshed.

Across the fire, Martin's son and daughter-in-law were kissing, their legs entangled: Erling in black leather with a stiff mustache, Berit dressed from head to toe in a pink leather motorcycle suit. I'd heard rumors about her—that she was Sami royalty, the daughter of the man who owned more reindeer than anyone else in Sápmi, what used to be called Lapland. Their two toddlers rolled in the sand.

Another man, Rune, was down by the water with an armful of sticks, half bent over, his free arm extended toward a piece of driftwood. It was Rune who'd invited me to the bonfire—a party, he'd promised. A good time. Now he stood frozen, watching Martin. He seemed to have forgotten what he was reaching for.

Martin tugged his pants lower, revealing pale, hairless genitals. "You see what I have to live with?"

"All right," said Berit, looking up from her husband. "She's seen it."

Martin zipped his pants. "I just want her to understand."

"You like the cider?" Rune had come back over and stood beside me. "There's five more. I got them just for you—the others drink beer, but I thought maybe you don't like beer. Maybe we can start the salmon now. You like salmon, true?" He was talking more than usual, and slurring. He kept glancing at me and then glancing away.

"Who is she?" said Berit. "How did you find her?"

It was a fair question, and the hard answer—the real answer—stretched back fifteen years and four thousand miles, through blizzards and open tundra, smothering ice caves and the pulsing northern lights, many nights alone and some, unmercifully, not. I was a twenty-four-year-old girl from California, camped in a tiny village in the Norwegian Arctic. I had lived here once before, and it had helped me restore some lost courage. Now I'd come back, years later, and I needed that courage more than ever. I just didn't know how to get it. The truth was that Rune had found me because I was hoping that somebody—anybody—would.

The simpler answer was that Rune had found me at the local shop, and I'd found the shop because of a wool sweater, six years earlier. At the time I was a student at a local folk school, eighteen years old and learning to dogsled. I had come to the Arctic for adventure, but I also carried with me a circular logic: If I could be safe in this land, maybe I could be safe in my own body. If I could protect my body, maybe I could live in this land. So far, though, I was not doing anything right. To start with, I had no wool sweaters, and wool sweaters in the Northland were of nearly religious significance. If it was thirty below and you were cold, it was your own fault because your sweater wasn't wool. Or if your sweater was wool, then maybe your shirt wasn't, maybe your bra wasn't. I didn't own any wool at all, so I went to the nearby shop in hopes of finding some.

THE OTHER STUDENTS AVOIDED THE SHOP. It was a square white building below the church, perched on a spike of land that jutted into the fjord. Inside, the shop was decorated with out-of-date promotions for chocolate and lottery tickets, and crowded with necessities—milk, potatoes, yarn, fishing line, socks—everything except condoms, which the shopkeeper knew from experience that nobody wanted to buy at their *near-store*. Beside the counter was a single table, where locals gathered for hours to sip sour coffee and polish the dramas of their lives. "You go in there," a classmate had warned me, "and everyone looks up, and they just *watch* you."

I was used to people watching me. I went to the counter and asked the aging shopkeeper—Arild, his name was—where I might find a wool sweater. Not here, he told me. My best bet would be to hitchhike to Tromsø, then a two-hour trip if I caught the ferry right. I thanked him and walked back to the school, stopping to linger on the beach, disheartened. So I'd be sweaterless. I wasn't brave enough to hitchhike alone.

Across the fjord, sharp white mountains softened near the shore, sloughing into low mounds like melted wax. Like most communities in northern Norway, the twenty or so homes that made up the village of Mortenhals were spread on the thin strip of land between mountains and fjord, along a beach dotted with fat wooden rowboats and wooden racks for drying cod. The fish would be served with bacon grease, a delicacy, while their heads were ground into protein flour and sent to Africa. From one rack hung two dead crows, tied by their feet with string, whose wings reached toward the sand.

By the time I got back to my cabin, there were three wool

sweaters folded on the front step, and a note from Arild saying that his daughter had moved away and wouldn't miss them. I took the gift, wrongly, as a sign of particular friendship, and from then on always looked forward to my errands at the shop as visits to an ally in this strange frozen world, though we greeted each other with little more than nods. For Christmas I gave him a calendar of American national parks, which hung behind his counter for the rest of the year.

So when I returned to Mortenhals six years later in snowy June, I had some expectation of a reunion—exaggerated, I'm sure, by the fact that Arild was the only person I still knew on the peninsula. I found him behind the shop, carrying a sack of pellet feed to his sheep. I felt giddy: here was a person from my old life, right in front of me. Arild squinted and hoisted the sack on his hip.

"I've come back," I said, grinning.

"Yes so," he said. "You have."

We looked at each other. Arild readjusted the feed sack and shuffled some snow from his boots.

"I wanted to ask you," I said, suddenly shy. "Can I sleep in the old house by the water? I'm traveling through. I'll just be here a few days." People called it the Ghost House; it had been empty since World War II. I felt certain that Arild would agree.

"It got torn down," he said. "Sheep got in the basement."

"Oh."

A seagull landed nearby and started hopping toward us.

"No point standing in the cold," said Arild. He bluff kicked the seagull, shifted the sack with a slight groan, and turned back toward the barn. "I'm sure I'll see you around."

"Sure," I said. "See you around."

It was quite warm, actually.

I walked the beach slowly, wondering what I had been expecting. Too much, apparently. Now I had come back and I was alone. My flight home wasn't for another two months, and I had begun to think that this whole Return, which had seemed so vital from a distance, was maybe a bit of overkill. What was I proving, again? That I had not been scared out of the north, that I could come back and belong? I'd been looking for a home in Norway—somewhere with roots, somewhere I could come back to—since I'd first lived in the country at age ten. But now, after two weeks of sleeping in unfamiliar towns, catching rides with truckers at gas stations, I was reluctant to keep moving.

I went into the woods and found a place to camp, in a clearing scabbed with snow. I laid out my tent, my sleeping bag, and my stun gun, which I was vaguely afraid to touch. The next morning I didn't want to go back to the shop, but I was hungry. There were men at the coffee table. "There's the girl," Arild told them. And to me: "I drove all over last night, looking for you. I was going to offer you a bed and a taco."

So I sat down. After all, despite what I'd said about passing through, I had nowhere to go. But also, this particular land felt safe to me—not just Mortenhals, but the whole Malangen peninsula on which it lay, and the wilderness around it. I had survived a year among these mountains, had watched them turn white and glow under the northern lights and thaw in spring into crumpled tinfoil. There were worse places to be than Arild's coffee table.

The heart of Mortenhals's social scene, the coffee table had room for six people to sit comfortably, a thermos of fresh coffee, and a stack of small plastic cups. The cups were thin, and grew soft in contact with the hot coffee, so most people had their own mug that they kept on a shelf and never washed. There were sugar cubes in a cardboard box, and although there was a small tin with a coin slot that said Coffee: 5 Kroner, nobody ever paid. Most of the coffee drinkers were men, because most of Mortenhals was men, and they seemed pleased by the company of a young woman.

Though I came to meet many of them in those first days, the man I saw the most was Rune. Rune had a thick remarkable swoop of gray hair and beard that left just his eyes visible. When he smiled, his eyes squeezed shut. Maybe he was slow, or maybe just lazy, but he'd apprenticed as a carpenter in his youth, lived with his parents until they died, and promptly stopped woodworking. Instead, he hung around the shop and did odd jobs for Arild in a reluctant, dreamy way. In return, Arild kept Rune fed during the second half of the month, after his welfare ran out. In the coming weeks, Arild would call me to the window: "Look at Rune's idea of work." Rune would be leaning against a fence post, watching the sheep escape from their pasture one by one as he rolled a cigarette with practiced fingers.

"WHERE I FOUND HER? She went to the folk school," said Rune, taking the easy way out. "Six years ago. I remember her," he added, which seemed doubtful.

"So you drive sled dogs," said Berit.

I nodded.

"My neighbor has dogs and they've even learned not to eat reindeer," said Berit. "I bet your dogs can't do that." She began tearing open single-serving packets of marinated salmon, releasing bursts of dill-scented air, and rewrapped the fish in tinfoil. Her daughter walked up to the bonfire and stood with her head dropped back, looking up at the flames. Then she placed one foot on a burning log and stepped forward into rippling air.

Berit snapped in Sami. When the girl didn't respond, Erling walked over and picked her up, somewhat lackadaisically. Her pink rubber boots were bubbling at the toes. The girl looked at her boots, then her father, and tightened her face to sob. But her cries were preempted by a moan so loud and guttural that she whipped around, startled.

Martin had fallen from his chair and lay on his side, legs curled to his chest. He moaned again, then took a handful of coarse sand and squeezed it through his fingers. "Morphine," he whispered.

"I'll get it," said Berit.

Erling put down the girl, who returned to the fire. "It'll go over, Dad," he said to Martin. "It'll go over soon."

"Fuck you," said Martin.

"Why don't you drink more cider?" Rune asked me. He lifted my can and shook it. "Finish this and I'll get you another one."

I finished my drink and opened the next gratefully. Berit came back with a syringe and injected it into Martin's forearm. He moaned again, then sat up and climbed back into his chair.

"What are you looking at?" he said to me. "I could have fucked you."

That summer, in the days leading up to St. Hans's, the season had changed quickly. One morning the lakes were frozen and the fields bare, and in what felt like an hour the landscape sprouted into a plush green, the meadows yellow with thigh-high dandelions where there had been ice days before. I'd been in Mortenhals for two weeks, but I did not want to leave. One day I walked up into the mountains, where I drank from a creek with cupped hands, after first checking that there were no sheep upstream. The water was sweet and piercing cold. It made my knuckles ache. It tasted *healing*, I thought, and then I corrected myself, embarrassed at my own emotion. The water was water. The place was a place. It was no more healing than a kiss to a bruise.

The men at the table called me *pia*—girl—or else city-*pia* or the Journalist. "The only time we had a journalist here," one man told me, "he went back to Tromsø and wrote an article about how we're all just horny men looking for womenfolk."

Was that accurate? I asked.

"No!" he said, and they all laughed.

Another time, a visitor stopped by. I could tell he was a visitor because he was thin and paid for his coffee. "You understand that we may not talk to you so much," Arild told him, "because there's an American girl here and we tend to talk to her about things." In fact, I realized, I had quickly become as regular a presence as Rune.

I felt that the village came to know me. One night I woke at midnight to two teenage boys—assistants at the folk school—inviting me to go fishing on the fjord. They showed me how to cast and reel, and when the boat's motor broke I sat on the bow and watched them yank the pull cord time and again, feeling motherly as we drifted slowly out to sea. The sun was bright, but pearls of dew formed on our bodies and the boat. We were all shivering. Around 4 A.M. we drifted over a sandbar and I jumped out, and one of the boys did, too, and we all pulled the boat to shore. Back at the dock, another boy stood surrounded by older men; they were customers of the neighboring shop, in the village of Sand, so I did not know them. Apparently the boy had been found messing with someone's boat, and the men had confronted him. "You pedophiles!" the boy shouted, trying to unnerve them. "Let him go," said one of the men. "I was like that once, too." I walked home soaking wet and did not go back to sleep.

Arild was up early. He'd begun to assign me jobs. He received orders from distant relatives to plant flowers on their family graves in the churchyard, and these orders he delegated to me, for a salary of ice-cream bars and open-faced sandwiches.

The job—the fact of having a role—pleased me. I trudged up the hill with an armful of pansies in plastic tubs and handwritten names on scraps of paper, then walked the rows of headstones until I found one of the names. Depending on how much the relative had paid, I planted up to three pansies in an arrangement. The newest grave did not yet have a headstone; Edel Kristoffersen, Arild's mother, had died just a month before at the age of ninety-nine. Arild planted the flowers on his mother's grave himself.

Arild's grief was at once impenetrable and blatant. Even on his best days, he was the most doleful person I had ever seen, with a hanging head and enormous eyes, bright white lashes like a cow's, delicate feathers of hair that looked as if they had turned from blond to white with very little fanfare. He usually wore a T-shirt with a charging elephant on it, its ears cut off by his suspenders, and when he had a cold he tied a scrap of fabric around his throat so that people would ask how he was feeling. He rarely smiled, except with his sheep, and his air in the shop was simultaneously perky and morose. "Just ask, and I'll tell you we're out of it," he liked to say.

But Arild was savvier than he came across. He knew to give shoplifters the best service, and that liars would believe anything you told them because they had the best imaginations. He knew how to quiet a toddler with a sugar cube dipped in coffee, and to take a few bars from a box of new chocolates so that people would think their friends had tried them first. He called his oldest customers "young man" and children "geezers" and he called almost everyone else by the formal you, *De*, which had gone out of style a century before.

People called him a gossip, but Arild might say, rather, that he kept track of folks. He had delivered pellet feed all over the Northland for over a decade, and prided himself on knowing customers better after six months than other drivers did who'd been at it for years. That, combined with the social spiderweb centered around his coffee table, meant that he knew or knew of almost everybody. Once I watched two truck drivers stop in for a quick soda. Arild enticed them to sit down for a half cup of coffee—"Put on the coffee, Blair"—and set about trading names with the drivers, faster than I could follow. Both men lived hours away, but within six minutes Arild informed the first that his neighbor's mail-order bride was in fact Mongolian, not Thai, and that his father must have been a fur trapper, which meant that he knew Ronny Grape and Tor Are Magga, which, by the way, had he heard they were dead? After the astonished men left and Arild made sure they had driven away, he beckoned me to lean closer. "It's a good thing I didn't say much about that man's father," he whispered, though we were alone in the shop. "One time I delivered feed to his farm, and as I was lifting a sack from the truck it started to slip, and before it even fell the guy said, 'I want a new sack.' Just like that: 'I want a new sack.' Talk about revealing your character! That was fifteen years ago, but you understand, that's not the kind of thing one would forget."

A few days later, as I left the shop midafternoon, Arild called out to me. "Blair," he said, "who do you think showers more often, me or Rune?"

"What?" I said.

"I think I shower more often," he said, and hesitated. "By the way, if you're interested in tasting whale, stop by here around six and you can try some. But if you're busy, there's no need. Just stop by if you feel like it, around six."

When I came back at six he was closing up the shop, pulling silver foil over the meats and locking the front door. "You're here," he said. "Come up." From the back room of the shop, we climbed a narrow flight of stairs to his second-story apartment.

With the exception of the kitchen, and a rocking chair before the TV, most of the apartment seemed not to have been touched in years, or maybe decades; the lace-draped side tables and grand-motherly couches gave the distinct impression of being unused. A baby doll in a hand-embroidered dress, perched on the mantel, was fuzzy with dust. Arild glanced around, as if just noticing his surroundings. His wife, Anne Lill, he explained, lived in the larger house next door.

The kitchen counter was covered with cutting boards and bowls. A pan on the stove bubbled with gravy, and another with disks of black meat and caramelized onions in a pool of butter. From the oven Arild pulled a baking sheet lined with sliced potatoes.

"I enjoy cooking," Arild remarked, moving a cutting board to the sink. "But I have to cook for myself. Anne Lill is always on a diet."

He took a plate from the cabinet and arranged it with meat and potatoes, drizzling the gravy in an artful spiral, then looked over at me. "Get a plate," he said. "What, city-*pia*, you think I'll fill your plate for you? They're in there." I filled my plate and followed him down a hallway and out onto a roof patio. There was a table set up with two chairs, a white tablecloth, and a pitcher of milk. Arild sat down and started eating.

Though I enjoyed the company of the men at the table, and found their attention flattering, it was different to be here alone with Arild. On the patio, with a slight breeze and the faint calling of seagulls, above the now-empty shop, the meal felt oddly significant—a first date, loaded with expectation. But maybe, I told myself, the expectation was mine. A projec-tion, or paranoia. So far everything seemed okay. Besides, I was hungry, having subsisted mostly on bread and ice cream since arriving in Mortenhals. I picked up my knife and sawed off a sliver of whale.

The meat was delicious, rich and crusty but giving way to a tender center. It was harder to get whale these days, Arild told me, after he finished chewing. It wasn't long ago that whalers came through the fjord often, dragging minke whales up onto the beach at Sand. Big fat things, just enormous. Their bodies draped over the decks of ships with head and tail trailing in the water on either side. A dozen men could stand on a whale with pitchforks, cleaning it all at once. You could ride your horse down, strike a deal, and leave with a fifty-kilo strip of bone-free meat to last your family through winter. Whale had always been poor-man's food. Now you had to know where to get it. Arild got this particular whale-beef from Lofoten—he'd heard rumors of it and sent down an order. He liked to do things the old way. In fact, he said, he had a showcase of sorts, a testament to the old ways, in the form of his family shop in its original building, just behind the barn. The Old Store was locked up, its windows boarded, but inside, the shop was exactly as it had once been, complete with shelves full of wares—a perfect time capsule from the 1950s. A museum? I asked, and he brushed off the question by taking a swallow of milk. "One has many plans," he said.

We finished our food and ate second servings and then cut up strawberries and ate them with spoons in bowls of heavy cream. The strawberries were small and red and tasted almost too strongly of strawberry. It was because of the light, Arild said. Summer berries, they got sun all day and all night, and it changed them.

He led me inside and turned on the television, but when he saw that the news was about mass murderer Anders Breivik, he turned it off again. "Listen," he said. He had to tell me something. He knew that Rune would invite me to a St. Hans's bonfire on midsummer's night, three days from now. There would be another man there, and I should be careful around him. That man was not harmless. Strange things happened on St. Hans's night. I should be careful.

Feeling both relieved and disappointed that the evening was over, I thanked him for the food and the warning. "You can wash the dishes before you leave," he said.

WHEN THE SALMON WAS HOT, Rune and I pulled it apart and ate the pieces with our fingers. Martin declined his fish and leaned over to vomit mucus on the ground.

"Something's not right," said Berit. She closed her eyes. "I have a terrible feeling."

"Your Sami sense?" said Erling.

Berit nodded. "There's something really bad here. A bad spirit."

"Your Sami sense is sexy," said Erling, after a while. He reached his hand into Berit's pink leather crotch and began rubbing.

"Don't shock the American," said Berit.

I stood up and went closer to the fire. It was warm on my face, and my cheeks felt tight with the heat. Along the beach the other fires were dying out, but anyway they were unspectacular; the sky was bright as noon. In this northern summer, the sun drifting its slow laps around the sky, the longest day of the year wasn't St. Hans's. It was July.

"You're cold?" said Rune. "I'll keep you warm." He put his arm around me. "I can always keep you warm."

I had hoped he wouldn't do this.

"Don't be angry," he said, "that I didn't touch you until now."

Behind us, Berit and Erling were making out. The children stood in the grass, throwing rocks at each other. Martin had slumped from his chair again and lay on his back, arms and legs spread, looking up at the blue sky. He was almost smiling.

I stepped away from Rune.

"You're such a good girl," he said. "When I win the lottery you can live with me. Here on Malangen. I'll take such good care of you." His head was low on his shoulders. "I'll carve wood for you and give you everything you need."

There were soft moans behind us, but I couldn't tell whose they were. It was late, suddenly. All I wanted was to watch the fire.

Rune, his head somehow even lower, reached out one hand and patted me limply on the breast.

"I think I'll go home now," I said.

Martin lifted his head off the sand to watch me leave. "But, Blair," he said in English. "The night is still young."

CHAPTER ONE

I'VE SPENT MORE THAN HALF MY LIFE pointed northward, trying to answer private questions about violence and belonging and cold. By the time of my visit with Arild, I had come north—to Norway, to Alaska—again and again. I left once, too, and promised myself that I never had to go back. Arild would have liked that. "Six times she came, and once she left," he could have told his customers, as if it was a riddle. He liked to make people wonder. He liked to know more than he said.

The seventh time I came north was because Arild invited me to turn his Old Store into a museum. After the summer was over, after I flew back home, after Martin was buried by the church on the hill:

> I need a person to have the Old Store open on
> weekends during the summer, as I upon finishing work
> have no remaining energy to do it myself. If that sounds
> exciting you are wholeheartedly welcomed to work there
> (SMALL SALARY). As you know I have reasonable
> accommodations for you. Probably there will be no need

> to open every day and you can take walks in beautiful
> Malangen or borrow a car if that is what you prefer.
> Since you wrote to me I understand that you have
> not been victim to one of the many shooting episodes at
> schools in the USA.

I wrote that I would arrive the next May. And so we slipped back into each other's lives, out of convenience, out of necessity. The Old Store seemed like an excuse to keep asking my questions, a way to come back to Norway and face them head-on. I didn't know that it was part of the answer.

On my first night back in Mortenhals, I hardly slept. Outside the window, in the bright gray sky, seagulls dipped and called all night, and I kept jolting awake, blinking against the light. Arild had given me a small bedroom above the front door of the shop, and its contents were unfamiliar: a table covered with jars of paintbrushes and shards of broken glass; a short orange bed with a mattress of rough-cut foam. Lying in the bed, my knees bent to fit, I felt comfortably blank. So here I was again. At one point I walked to the bathroom and looked out the window to see that the sheep had escaped from their pasture and lay in mounds around the diesel pump. I rubbed my eyes and went back to bed.

Midmorning I woke to murmured voices drifting through the floor. I made my way down the steep turquoise stairway, bracing my hands against the low ceiling to keep from tumbling forward, and came into the back of the shop. The air smelled like bacon from the flies that sizzled in the overhead lights. Arild and Rune sat at the table with a man they called He the Rich One. Arild glanced up from his newspaper, *Northern Light*, to pour me a cup of coffee. The front-page headline read, Never Again Getting a Foreign Tattoo.

"Do you remember she American girl from last year?" Arild asked He the Rich One. "She's returned."

"I've never seen the like," said He the Rich One.

"I know," said Arild. "She's eating me out of my home."

He the Rich One leaned forward on his elbows and gazed at me. He was large and tan with silver-brown hair combed straight back from his square face, the top four buttons of his shirt open to reveal a hairy brown chest. He'd made his fortune in slaughterhouses and sausage factories, and spent his winters tanning in Spain, surrounded by—he bragged—booze and ladies. He the Rich One had a house a few kilometers from Mortenhals, with running water and even a washing machine, but he called it a cabin. None of his neighbors had a problem with the washing machine. They had a problem with calling something a cabin when it was a house.

The people of Malangen were poor, but they lived, as they frequently and inaccurately reminded each other, in the richest country in the world, with a generous welfare system to boot. As such, their poverty was less about need than class, less about money than the facts that they were both northern and rural. *Northern* meant uncivilized. While southern Norwegians took pride in their restraint—they rarely made eye contact on the street, arrived precisely on time, and spoke a cosmopolitan dialect that resembled Danish—northerners were loose and vulgar. They cursed, slurred their words, joked often about death and sex, and gauged time loosely: "I'll meet you Wednesday, after three cups of coffee." Theirs was the Norway of witchcraft, storytelling, and incest, not minimalist furniture and the Nobel Peace Prize.

Rural meant long memories. How much had changed, really, since fifty years ago—or even a hundred—when the same families had lived on the same farms? The men of Malangen had been sealers and whalers, coming home from months on the Arctic

Ocean with heaps of furs, baby polar bears to sell in Europe, and as much slimy, black sealmeat as their families could eat. They lined their skis with sealskin. They twined rope of walrus hide. They greased their saws with fish oil. They made liquor of birch sap and on the coldest winters they froze away the water to strengthen it. Women came to the peninsula to help with the haying, fell in love, married, and ran the farms when their husbands drowned at sea.

Then came electricity. Then came roads. Then came oil. Somewhere to the south, Brigitte Bardot raised a fuss and the seal-hunting industry collapsed, diminished to a single dark-gummed teenager selling flippers with his grandpa on a city dock. Men found other work: on oil rigs, in a factory that made Styrofoam boxes for exporting salmon, as cruise ship guides in the same waters where they had once hunted. The winters grew warmer, the summers longer. Forests spread over fields and up the mountains like a rising tide.

Everyone knew that He the Rich One was feeling wounded that year. He had owned a meat store in Storsteinnes, which was an hour's drive away, and a big enough town to have a grocery store, a government liquor store, and a bank. He made his brother the manager. But another employee stole money from the register for months, until finally the store went bankrupt. Arild couldn't believe that a person would be oblivious for that long about his own shop. That he wouldn't notice. Not that Arild was complaining; he had his eye on the chest freezer that He the Rich One would be getting rid of.

"I understand why you want it," He the Rich One said. "It's *jo* a nicer freezer than you've ever had."

Arild hummed. It wasn't in his practice to contradict customers.

"It was a nicer shop than this, too," said He the Rich One, turning to me. "Seven hundred square meters." He looked sad. "But it didn't have a pretty girl like you in it."

"The freezer," said Arild.

He the Rich One shook his head. "You can't afford it."

"No," agreed Rune. "He can't afford it."

Arild picked up his newspaper. Then he seemed to change his mind. "You must help yourself to your purchases," he said abruptly. "I have to show *pia* her museum. If you want to see her, then you must shop more often at your local near-store." He stood and started limping toward the door. He had a bad knee, from jumping out of trucks, but at the moment his limp seemed exaggerated.

"Anyway," called He the Rich One, "the freezer wouldn't fit through your door frame."

"Yes, it would."

"No, it wouldn't."

"We'll see about that," said Arild, closing the door behind him.

Outside the clouds hung low, so that only the bases of the mountains were visible. The air was full of moisture; though it wasn't raining, the road glistened. I followed Arild past the diesel pump—the sheep were gone—and around the barn, to a small courtyard with a flagpole. Two lambs trotted after us, bawling. Arild had discovered their mother dead the week before, the lambs curled atop her body. The sight hurt his heart. Now he fed them warm milk five times a day—a task, he said, that would soon be mine. If I wanted it.

Toward the water, white and tall, was the Old House—the heart of Mortenhals, where Arild had been born and intended to die. It rose as high as the flagpole, its walls worn but freshly painted. But if the Old House looked grand in its age, the Old Store looked simply shabby. Its walls were covered with chipped white paint, and its windows, some of them broken, papered with cardboard. Three millstones rested in the overgrown grass by the cement steps, beside an empty beer can, and the steps themselves shifted under my weight. Arild inserted a skeleton key and wrestled the knob with both hands to open the door.

We stepped into a chill. The room was grayish, all colors dulled into a narrow range of wood and metal and faded labels. I could see, through a pile of crates and boxes, how the shop had once stood: a main room with an L-shaped counter, painted green, which separated the shopkeeper from his customers. The walls behind the counter were lined with shelves, and the shelves with wares: shoes, soap, condensed milk, liquor bottles, plastic buttons, glass jars with the word *Norway* on them, which, Arild said proudly, were in high demand among hipsters on the Internet. From the ceiling dangled mittens, wooden ice skates, meat grinders, horseshoes, lanterns, bicycle gears, buoys, cowbells, and a copper teakettle. The effect was that of a jungle, dense with low-hanging vines, and I found myself ducking even though there was room to stand. To the right of the door, a potbellied stove wore a gold crown and a name tag that said: THE OVEN EL-VIRA. The stove was not original to the shop; Arild had purchased it recently from an artist in Tromsø, and it was she who named it Elvira, and painted the crown gold.

Arild glanced at me. "It's dirty work for a city girl."

"I like it." I waded over to a window and peeled off its cardboard shade, releasing a beam of light. A dead songbird lay on the windowsill. The air pulsed with dust; I waved my hand and watched ripples swirl through the room.

From a wooden box, Arild lifted a photo of the shop as it had once been: a small white building, covered with metal signs for tobacco and cardamom. Arild still had the signs in his basement. Soon we could hang them in their original places, he said, hefting an antique riveter in one hand. "And when the time comes, we'll use this instead of nails. One thing that's nice is that you need a special tool to get the rivets out. That way nobody will be able to steal the signs."

"But you know everyone," I said. "Who would steal from the Old Store?"

Arild stared at me for a long moment. Then—"No one. Of course not." He hummed again, louder, as he set the key at the edge of the counter. "Remember to lock the door when you leave."

MY FIRST YEAR IN NORWAY I'd been ten years old, living with my parents in Oslo, where my father, an anti-tobacco researcher, evaluated a proposed smoking ban. I went to school in a rich part of town, but spent my days in the attic with the other outlanders—a dozen or so Pakistanis and Somalians and Russians—doing things like making cauliflower soup for those students who had no food at home. A Russian girl named Natasha became my closest friend, though we spoke no language in common; together we explored the wide clean streets of the city, took buses to the ends of their lines, ice-skated in Vigeland Park after dusk. Norway seemed like one of the safest places for little girls to be, and we took to our freedom wildly. At the time, in the late '90s, mothers still left babies outside shops in their strollers, confident that if the infants fussed, they would be cared for by passersby.

I was an only child. Back home, in Davis, California, our house abutted an overgrown bird sanctuary, where goslings chattered in the spring and teenage boys hid magazines that my mom told me not to look at. I spent much of my childhood outside, mashing eucalyptus leaves into fragrant paste or cracking pomegranates with rocks to eat the sour seeds, a process that could swallow an entire afternoon. My favorite game was to flood an anthill and then stand on it as long as I could, as the ants swarmed up my feet, my ankles, my legs, looking for high ground. There were thousands of them, a black mass. They tickled like crazy. I'd stand still as long as I could bear it, then spray them off with the hose and watch them swim in the resulting puddle, dark specks that barely dented the hard surface of the water.

Davis was hot. Much of the year baked in a perpetual brown summer, and by the time April rolled around, the sidewalk burned blisters on my bare feet. Each June, as soon as school let out, my mom and I would pack up the station wagon and drive six hours north to Whidbey Island, where my mother's family lived. My summer days were spent on beaches and in the woods, painting sticks and picking blackberries, catching crabs and eels in tide pools and toting them around in buckets till the tide came in. My mother was happiest on the island. She was a nature lover, a poet; she walked barefoot for miles and fed bald eagles by hand. When she had announced plans to marry my father, her parents sat her down to express their concern. She thought it was because he was Jewish. But no: "Do you really think you can be happy," they asked, "if you marry a New Yorker?"

"The thing is," she'd later say, "they were right." It wasn't that the relationship was bad, far from it. My father had a particular sense of humor; he chuckled at his own thoughts, and I often pressed my ear to a wall to hear my mother laughing hysterically, brought to tears by his near-secret language of jokes. But it was true that his lifestyle overlapped very little with hers. He grew up in the Bronx and the Lower East Side; he worked every day of the week, coming home to read me bedtime stories—Robert Louis Stevenson, Robinson Crusoe—before going back to the office until three or four in the morning. Although we sometimes went camping as a family, my father rarely spent time in nature on his own initiative; he'd unroll his chessboard on the campground table, sipping coffee from a thermos and battling invisible opponents. I liked to sit on his lap and watch his quick hands move across the board. He let me hit the timer, which made a satisfying thump.

It was because of my dad that we lived in California, and my mom never forgot it. When he took the job in Davis, he'd promised her it would only be for two years. Now, where were we—ten, twelve? Every August, as she and I drove back over the California border, she'd start to cry, and then she'd apologize, and then she'd worry aloud about the effect on her daughter of having a mom who cried and apologized. I didn't think the effect was bad. She was being honest, and her tears made sense to me: she loved land almost as much as people. Anyway, I spent my whole childhood knowing that my real home was still to come. I could like Davis, sure—but I knew better than to love it.

And then my father was offered a sabbatical. And he took it in Norway, the country of my mother's roots. And just like that, I had a place to love.

After the year was over, I remained obsessed with Norway, and with northern latitudes in general. Years ago, it had snowed in Davis, a veil over the grass that dissolved by midmorning, and the whole world had seemed foreign, thrilling: the north was like that, a thousandfold. My mom collected books about Alaska, and I'd go into her office when she wasn't there and sit cross-legged on the green carpet and flip through the pictures. Black-and-white photos of villages by the sea, the wide velvet of a caribou migration, Samoyeds hauling freight sleds over sea ice. I imagined myself skiing toward the pole, staving off bears with a warning shot. I slept with a stuffed husky named Anna and a stuffed polar bear named Erasmus. I read a dozen children's books about the Iditarod; as I got older, I moved on to Farley Mowat and Gary Paulsen. Sometimes my dad joined me. I'd started reading my favorite books to him at bedtime, rather than the other way around.

> *The temperature was a perfect ten below. The sun was bright, everything was moving well, and the dogs had settled into the rhythm that could take them a hundred or a thousand miles . . .*

"Hold on," my dad interrupted. He was sitting on a cushion by my bed. "Do you have any idea how cold that is? Ten below zero?"

"Yeah," I said

"No," he said. "It's *extremely* cold. It's *unbelievably* cold. It's much, much colder than anything you've experienced. It's so cold that—" He hesitated. He was delighted. Here was a twofer: a learning experience for his daughter, and an amusing phrase—*a perfect ten below*—that he could add to his arsenal, to be deployed at opportune moments from here on out, forever. *Gee*, he'd say, putting on sunscreen at the beach. *This is nice, but if only it were a perfect ten below.* And if anyone asked him the temperature—

"It doesn't sound that cold to me," I said. "It sounds fine."

I was incredibly jealous of Gary Paulsen.

Somehow, my connection to the north, my *belonging* there, was as real to me as any part of my fledgling identity. My name was Blair, I was good at drawing, I was meant to be a polar explorer. In fact, I felt that in my heart, I already *was* a polar explorer, even if nobody else recognized it. My conviction was heightened by the idea that I had come close—had lived in Norway, albeit the urban Southland—and was untempered by the reality that the nearest I'd been to any sort of truly polar experience was the still, fluorescent cavern of an early morning ice rink, where I practiced figure skating—a sport I'd chosen, in part, because it was cold. And until I grew up, I wasn't sure how I would get closer.

Then, in tenth grade, during third-period economics, the school counselor announced over the intercom that she was looking for students to study abroad for a year. At lunchtime I went to her office for paperwork. By the time school let out, I had it all planned. I would go back to Norway. I would find a way to belong. My parents, though skeptical at first, came around to the idea. Norway, they recalled, was a good place for a girl.

I was a quiet teenager, but I wasn't shy. I was what local mothers called "a good Davis kid" and my classmates called "sheltered," a babysitter and honor-roll student who taught Jewish religious school and learn-to-skate classes, who got along well with adults and followed all the rules. In short: a perfect candidate for cultural exchange. Determined to do things right, I studied brochures and booklets with useful tips: *When in doubt, ask, "Can I help you with that?"* The brochures recommended calling the host parents "Mother" and "Father" in their own language—*Mor* and *Far* in Norwegian—and limiting contact with my own family to one phone call a month. I could do that, no problem; if it would help me build a home in Norway, I could do just about anything. Now all I had to do was wait to find out where exactly that home would be.

In late spring, the phone rang, an east coast number. I answered it in the kitchen. The man on the other end explained that the exchange organization had found me a family. His voice sounded vaguely familiar. I heard my parents pick up the other line.

"In Kirkenes," he said. "You probably haven't heard of it. It's a very small town, the northernmost town in Europe. It's very isolated. No sun at all in the winter. It's, uh, barren."

I couldn't speak.

"I'm sorry," said the man. "We couldn't find anything more hospitable."

"No, no." I had found my breath. "That's—that'll be really good. That's great."

"It's—great? Are you sure it's great?"

I nodded, then caught myself. "Yeah. Yes. Absolutely."

"Blair—" said the man.

"Hold on," said my dad from the other line. "Robert?" Somewhere far away, I made out stifled giggles. "Robert," said my dad, "it's not working. She wasn't supposed to like it. Hold on," he said again. He covered the receiver, said something to my mother. Then he ran into the room. "Honey," he said, his voice brighter. "April Fool's!" It was too late to hide my disappointment: I would not get to live in the northernmost town in Europe. My parents took me to dinner to apologize.

When I finally learned, just after my sixteenth birthday, that I'd been placed with a family in the southeastern town of Lillehammer, just a few hours from Oslo, I was too excited to feel let down. I packed my warmest clothing, including a powder blue parka bought specifically for the trip. I studied maps of the region. I looked at a photo of my host parents—my new Norwegian family, along with their daughters—and practiced in my head. *Mor*, I thought. *Far*. As it turned out, they would meet my greeting with uneasy silence, and so I realized almost immediately after arriving in Norway that to use such intimate language was a mistake. But by then I felt too embarrassed to acknowledge my misstep, and so Hilda and Ragnar Selbo would be Mor and Far for the next ten months.

Lillehammer burst from a lake on a single mountainside, so that all directions hinged on slope: the school downhill and to the right of the ice rink, the ski trails uphill and to the left of the cobblestoned town center. Mor and Far's red house was uphill and to the right of the church, adjacent to a forest that extended, as I imagined it, into an endless wilderness. As I unpacked in my new bedroom, I tried to shrug off my nervousness. So things had started out a little awkward. So what? Here I was. Maybe it would take a while to get to know each other, but with time, I would become part of the family. I would go to school. I had already decided that I would forsake English for the year, and speak only Norwegian, forcing myself into a language I had never really learned as a child. I would ice-skate and cross-country ski and laugh at inside jokes with my host sisters. Maybe I would even meet a boy.

But something felt wrong from the first night, when Far sat me down and detailed how he would punish me if I broke his rules, and something clenched in my rib cage even as I nodded along. I would feel that tightness each time I walked through the living room and he watched me pass with an expression not yet familiar to me—I wasn't used to men appraising my body—and I felt it again weeks or months later when he came up behind me and stroked my ass with his hand. I felt it a thousand times at a thousand moments—from a glance, an expression, a lift of his chin. I felt it when he remarked one evening, after I declined to sit beside him on the couch, "Your parents must be abusive for you to have turned out like this." Or when he reminded me daily that blood was thicker than water, that I was not his daughter. I felt it when he made that sound like a threat.

Something felt wrong again and again, and yet I could never say for sure, even to myself, what it was. I was never even confident that it existed. Maybe people did things differently in Norway. Maybe I was misunderstanding his Norwegian.

The walls in my bedroom had a pebbled texture, one I can still feel if I think about it; often, as I lay awake at night, I'd trace my fingers over the wall. I don't know why. I developed a lot of habits that year that I couldn't explain. I kept track of—sensed, pictured—where everyone was in the house at any time: Mor boiling potatoes in the kitchen, Far watching a beauty pageant on TV. There was a mudroom by my bedroom that opened into the backyard, and it comforted me when I knew that I was closer to that door than Far was to me. I occasionally practiced climbing out of my bedroom window, too, and left the window cracked open even as the nights grew colder, stopping only when my bedside water glass shelled with ice. The bedroom door had no lock, though I wished for one. Maybe the cold was a kind of lock.

Early in the year, I found a path that led past the backyard. It wound steeply uphill, snaking around bushes and scraggly trees, and finally flattened out toward the cap of the mountain, dissipating into bouldered terrain. The first time I followed it I was nervous, and stopped where the path petered out; but the next time I brought some gingersnaps and a blanket and spent a delicious few hours spread out on a rock, catching sunlight on one of fall's last warm afternoons. When I couldn't stand another moment in the house, all I had to do was go uphill and to the right, and I'd have a world of my own. The mountain wasn't peaceful, but it was all-encompassing, and on subsequent afternoons as I wandered farther I felt the tightness in my chest dissolving. The thing about being outside, I realized, was that I had to be alert—to landmarks, to weather, to dusk—and yet that alertness on the mountain restored whatever it was that alertness at home had drained. Pretty soon I started playing, spinning in circles before wandering myself lost. Getting lost didn't seem like the worst thing. I could wind between trees, an explorer, thinking I could be anywhere. But the game was rigged; the mountain led downhill, and I always found my way back to the house.

One day, soon after the first snow, I came back to the house at dusk. I heard happy shouts as I approached, and stepped from the woods onto the white lawn to find the family waging a snowball fight. A chunk of snow hit my cheek and dripped into my collar. It came from May, one of my host sisters, and she shrieked at the clean hit. Pretty soon I was laughing with all of them, slipping on the snow as I ran, scooping up damp handfuls and flinging them at Mor and my host sisters. It occurred to me how much I liked them—how much I had, in avoiding Far, distanced myself from a family with whom I could, for instance, engage in snowball fights. This was all I had wanted. And here was Far himself, laughing with us, looking so happy and small compared to how I saw him in my mind's eye. Maybe, in the shock of transition, I had been too quick to judge. Maybe it was up to me now to bridge the distance.

I caught one of my sisters with a snowball, then Far, and sprinted toward the entryway to hide. But when I turned around, Far was walking toward me, twisting a perfect snowball in his hands. He had me cornered. I stepped forward and held his gaze, amused at my own small-scale valor, anticipating snow down the back of my neck. A trial by ice to earn my place as temporary daughter.

But instead, upon reaching me, Far pulled open the neck of my jacket and slipped a hand down the front of my shirt. There was ice, yes, something cold crushed onto my throat, but I hardly noticed it against the electric pressure of his hand. A brief, funny feeling—his fingers against the tops of my breasts, pressing down, my collar strained tight around his forearm. He withdrew his hand, caught my eye again, and backed up a few steps, slowly. Then he turned and ran back to the yard, calling—"I got her for you! May, I got her!"

It was a snowball fight, I thought, tugging on my bra to loosen the ice that was melting there, the memory of his hand still imprinted on my skin. A snowball fight.

Nothing had happened.

A week or so later, my father e-mailed to say that he needed to talk to me. He would call today, while I was at school. He needed me to pick up. The curtness of the note, and the fact that it was unexpected, frightened me. I thought maybe someone was sick.

When my phone buzzed in class, I ducked out of the room and into a next-door science lab, which was dim and empty. Since no one was there to stop me, I climbed up and sat cross-legged on a lab table, the act of rebellion easing my nerves about the call. My father cut to the chase. He'd heard that a friend was worried about me. His voice was tight—angry.

I thought I knew what he was talking about. After the snowball fight, I'd written to a friend at home, asking, *Is it ever*

okay for a grown man to touch under my shirt without asking?
She'd been unsure. It depended on the circumstances, she suggested, citing, for example, a visit to a doctor. I thanked her, but felt dismayed; I had hoped that she would say no, it was never okay, and that then I might have clarity to support my own apparent bias.

I could have confided in my parents, but until I knew for sure whether Far was "bad" or not, it would be embarrassing to suggest as much. For one thing, though it was hard to put my finger on why, my worries—my feelings about Far, my unarticulated fears about what he might do—felt deeply private, at least where my parents were concerned. To cast doubt on an adult in such a way seemed to require solid evidence, not just feelings. More important, my parents had worried that sixteen was too young to go abroad, and I'd spent months petitioning them as to my readiness and maturity, doing extra chores as a contribution toward the cost of the exchange, which—another worry—was already paid for. To be only two months into the year, and already struggling, would only prove their doubts right.

And now my father was on the phone, and his voice frightened me. I thought of how far away he was, and how little connected us: I could open my hand, drop the phone, and all connection would be lost. Then I could be alone. If I was alone, I wouldn't have to think.

"Blair," said my father, "are you safe?"

The question seemed huge.

It was the first time I'd heard my dad's voice in weeks. That hadn't been his choice—my parents would have loved to talk to me daily, to send letters, to visit. It was out of respect for me that they didn't. I'd asked them to give me space, to let me explore without them. I'd wanted to follow the guidelines, to do things right.

On the drive to the airport, my father had given me a cartoon he'd drawn on yellow legal paper. In the picture, a long-haired girl sat on a throne, flanked by two bulldogs with spiked collars and bared teeth. The bulldogs' collars were labeled with my parents' initials. He said that when I was in Norway, I should think of myself as the princess on the throne. My parents were my bulldogs; they would always be there to protect me. I could sic them on anyone. I'd packed the drawing carefully, so as not to bend it. Now it hung by my bed, taped to the pebbled wall.

"Blair," repeated my father—my angry, loving, beloved father. "Are you safe?"

Was I safe? Far had never threatened me outright, never even raised his voice. I had not seen him harm anyone. What could I say—that he looked at me funny? That he'd stuffed some snow down my shirt? He was an authority, and though I was open in theory to questioning authority, Far would first need to do something that I could unequivocally peg as wrong. But it was myself, not him, that I doubted.

Since childhood, I had held a panicked dread of getting into trouble. I so craved my parents' approval that I wanted it to extend to things beyond my control: that my life be good, and devoid of sorrow. That was what they wanted for me—or rather, *from* me. I felt acutely what my mom often remarked: that a parent was only as happy as their least happy child. If I complained, they might be disappointed in me for more reasons than one.

Was I safe?

"Yes," I said.

"Oh, good." My father was relieved. He could chat, he said, but since I'd ducked out of class to answer the phone, I should probably go back. My father took school very seriously. We hung up.

It was quiet now, in the science room. I lay back, feeling the cold of the lab table through my shirt. I didn't have to hear my father's voice anymore. He was so far away.

A SOUND ROUSED ME FROM MY CLEANING—something repetitive, sharp and grating, coming from the direction of the shop. I locked the Old Store, checking the door behind me, and walked back toward the road. When I came around the corner I found Arild on his knees, sweat pearled on his forehead, sawing a large hole through the back wall of the shop. He the Rich One watched with his arms crossed. Behind them, resting on two pallets, was a shiny new freezer.

CHAPTER TWO

THE DAYS PASSED QUICKLY INTO A RHYTHM. In the mornings I sat at the coffee table, listening. The customers talked weather, or argued about the ways they were and weren't related, or discussed the relative merits of Thai versus Russian mail-order brides. Often they made fun of each other. Mostly, though, they just told stories. "Remember that time he Trond lost a baby polar bear in Tromsø?" a man might say to the table at large, as if incanting a chant. "Trond, he was glad with the drink. He took a ship down from Svalbard with a baby ice bear in a cage, and he put the cage out on the dock—"

"He was going to sell it," someone interrupted. "But when he went back to the ship to get his flask, the bear opened its cage and ran off down the street. A cop came over and started yelling at him to get the bear—"

"So he Trond, he handed the cop his spirits flask. And he left the cop standing there, with his thumb in the mouth of the flask!"

At which point, chuckling, the coffee drinkers refilled their mugs for another round.

"Wait," I said. I couldn't help it. "What happened to the bear?"

Six heads swiveled toward me. "I don't know, girl," the first man said. "That's the end of the story."

I learned quickly that the stories rarely ended on a conclusive note. They started and stopped on the terms that decades of retelling had choreographed them to start and stop. A century-old tale was fresh as yesterday, and yesterday's news well-worn as myth: often, stories set two hundred years ago began with the words, "Remember that time——?" and people would nod because, in a way, they did. In their stories, time collapsed.

Sometimes the men glanced at me while they spoke, and I got the impression that they were performing, in part, for my sake. I started talking back to them, keeping pace with the teasing as best I could. There was a rhythm to it, and it felt good to catch on, like joining in the chorus of a song. One day a cocky man, upon learning that I was American, started speaking to me in ever-louder English, showing off for his friends. Everyone else knew that I spoke Norwegian, but I indulged the man, answering his questions demurely as the table grew quiet. Finally he asked me, with a wink, "Why you sit here and listen to all these boring manfolk?"

"Well," I answered, in perfect Norwegian, "it's good for weeding out the fools."

The man gaped, then blushed red, as everyone broke into raucous laughter. They'd be reminding him of this moment for years, and with their laughter I felt a new welcome. "She'll become a Northlander yet," someone said, pouring me more coffee, and my own blush gave way to pride.

Sometimes Arild sat at the table, but more often he sat behind the counter and supervised from a distance, speaking up when he had some quip or insult or blandly cutting remark to add to the conversation. When customers asked where he'd found me, he was quick on the draw. "It's one of those sex websites," he said. Or, "She likes old men."

The men groaned, then glanced at me. But I would only smile.

At first Arild's remarks had bothered me, but after a few days I decided they were innocuous. Arild only ever made such jokes in the shop; they struck me as somewhat clumsy attempts to impress the men at the table, a group he was simultaneously part of and separate from. I decided that the least I could offer was public loyalty, smirking rights before his customers. In the apartment, at night, we were friends, chopping meat for stew and washing dishes, sitting and regarding the news. There was none of the tension that I expected between an older man and a young woman, nothing of the sort that was reflected in Arild's jokes, that I imagined crossing the minds of the customers and of Anne Lill next door. On my second night, as I'd walked toward my bedroom, Arild had remarked from his rocking chair, "Just so you know, I'm not *like that*." It took me a while to understand what he meant. But when I did, I was grateful.

So it was no problem to play into the jokes, to flirt with the table at large, so long as I could slip away when I needed to. I sat and listened and teased, and in the early afternoons, when I'd drunk so much coffee that my knees were trembling, I went to work in the Old Store. I usually left around the time Anne Lill, who worked mornings as a janitor at a nearby retirement home, arrived at the shop to help out.

Entering the Old Store felt like entering another world, but not in the ways I'd anticipated. The air smelled like damp wood and carried a chill that even the warmest days couldn't dissipate, so that stepping through the door felt like submerging in water. It was also strangely quiet: even with the door wide open, the outside sounds of seagulls and sheep and distant chainsaws were muffled to near silence. Instead the rooms seemed to shimmer with their own frequency. In the Old Store, even when I was alone, I never felt stillness. Things shifted in the corners of my gaze: dust rising before a window, a satin dress rotating on its hanger, a white moth caught behind glass. The floor wasn't quite flat, and walking across it made me dizzy, as if I were at sea. Every interior sound was magnified, so that a broom against the floorboards sounded like wind through a field, and a record winding down in the next room was as insistent as breath in my ear. First I moved the cabinets, the boxes and bicycles, into the basement of the Old House, and then I started on the shelves, arranging wares and polishing off dust. The room brightened in color as it moved back in time.

"Did you lock the door?" Arild asked each time I came back from the Old Store. I assured him I had, though he'd never tell me what, exactly, he was afraid might happen.

When I finished with the Old Store for the day, I walked along the shore or through the mountain village, the cluster of farms a few kilometers inland from Mortenhals. Then I'd return to the shop and help Arild and Anne Lill close down for the night, clearing the table and hauling boxes of apples into the walk-in cooler. Sometimes Rune still sat at the picnic tables outside. "Rune," Arild said, "go home." Familiar words. Then he'd hand me a recipe for whale or reindeer stew or haddock and instruct me to meet him upstairs. I took my time in the dark shop, picking out all the ingredients, plus extra onions and margarine. We cooked together—me boiling potatoes, Arild dipping slabs of meat in flour and pepper. If Rune hadn't left by the time the food was ready, I'd call out the window for him to join us.

There was always plenty of food. Arild made extra and froze it in cartons to give to local bachelors, since otherwise, he noted, they'd eat open-faced sandwiches for all four meals of the day. Besides, he took great pleasure in feeding leftovers to birds, tossing scraps of meat out the window at the crows and seagulls that came to the sound of his voice. This in particular Anne Lill disapproved of. Seagulls were a nuisance, crying at all hours of the night. Their primary usefulness, as many believed, was that their bodies could be stuffed with foam and used as discreet buoys for illegal salmon nets. "In Lofoten," she told Arild, "people steal their eggs, boil them, and put them back in the nest." Arild thought this heinous—boiled gull eggs should be eaten on toast, not discarded. He had sympathy for the gulls, the crows, and the creatures of the land, and felt a kinship with his late mother, who had once in her final years waded chest deep into the icy fjord to free a seabird caught in a net that she'd spotted from her window. Anne Lill wasn't unsympathetic; she was just practical.

It was along this divide—practicality versus sentimentality—that most of the couple's differences hinged. Anne Lill was soft-spoken and scrupulous, with a keen sense of justice, and loath to indulge the drunks and bachelors whom Arild tended. When she disliked someone it was difficult for her to contain herself, and she often opted to leave the room rather than be falsely civil. She kept order in the shop with an air of fierce resignation, patrolling the aisles with a flyswatter; and, when amused, she broke into a brilliant, contagious smile that turned down the corners of her mouth. When she could, a few times a year, Anne Lill engaged in the Norwegian tradition of South-trips, escaping with friends for a few days on the sunny beaches of Turkey and Spain. Once she'd made it as far as Florida, where she visited Disney World. It was there that she encountered the most beautiful sound of her life: crickets singing in the grasses outside her hotel window, day and night. She found their music oddly moving. After her South-trips, Anne Lill returned tanned and fortified, ready for a few more months of dreary work and cold.

Arild's escape came closer to home: he liked long drives, and he invited me along. Almost anything was a worthy reason: a half-empty sack of lamb formula, a question for an acquaintance, a particularly clear sky. He'd send me to the shop for ice-cream bars and sodas and we'd drive along the winding roads and get to know each other. I was surprised by how comfortable I felt, sitting cross-legged in the passenger seat, bumping over the pot-holes and gaps in the neglected roads, watching the fjords flow by and open into new fjords. Wherever we went, people knew Arild, and he knew them even better. He stopped to check in on widows and widowers, bringing surprises of frozen fish or pack-aged cake. He'd brief me on their lives before knocking on the door. "This man," he whispered, "doesn't like to go to the out-house in winter, so he shits in grocery bags," pulling from his pocket a handful of bags that he intended to leave behind as a surreptitious gift. Or, "He still thinks the Nazis are here." He liked everybody, but he liked knowing their dirt, too—who was a liar, who was a thief. And he was unabashed in his admiration for folks he deemed competent—the women with their hand-spun sweaters and homemade *lefse*, the men who built their own grillhouses or repaired vintage cars. "One has to admit, she was *talented*," he would say for days after a visit, over scrambled eggs or across the coffee table or as we chased escaped sheep back into the pasture. During visits he kept careful track of what people needed, whether it was a new belt or a refrigerator or just hu-man company, and he did what he could to provide it. He was the shopkeeper. That was his role, as surely as he never denied his customers their groceries just because they couldn't afford them.

At one time, shopkeepers in the Northland had been *neskonger*—kings of the small capes that peppered the fjords and isles, their shops simultaneously gossip mills, welfare sys-tems, and meeting places for travelers along the sea road. In communities without a school, the church a day's row away, the shop was everything. Arild's great-grandfather Johannes Kris-toffersen built his eponymous shop at the age of nineteen, after the land's previous owners drowned en route to a baptism; he later passed the shop on to his son, who changed its name to Johannes Kristoffersen's Descendants. Arild inherited the business from his own father, Kristoffer Kristoffersen. At that time, the shop was one of many; before cars became common, villagers traveled between any number of markets on tractors and horseback. But now shops were dying, closing, as business grew too thin, as loyal customers and owners died off and their children moved on to more interesting lives in the cities.

Often, on our drives, Arild pointed out dead shops. They were everywhere once you developed an eye for them. There was a dead shop burned on a hillside, a dead shop crumbling by a dead ferry dock, a dead shop perched on a rock by the sea. They were squat buildings with peeling paint, their windows cracked and dirty. Sometimes Arild pulled over and peered through the edges of the glass to look for equipment or wares that could be used or sold. Dead shops were depressing, but they could be a boon. It was from dead shops that Arild had gotten his grocery signs and industrial shelves and, most recently, a thousand pairs of shoes from Finnmark. Arild thought that particular shop had died because it was too far from the Russian border, where there happened to be a lively trade in shoes: "Those Communist countries, if they made an ugly shoe in 1945, they're still making it now." He arranged the shoes around the coffee table so that visitors couldn't help but admire them: soccer cleats, gladiator sandals, disco-glitter stilettos. A few women came back multiple times a day, just to see if they'd missed anything.

Arild's shop was still alive, which was about as optimistic as the old man got, at least publicly. He'd fallen on hard times before, about a decade earlier, when his oldest son, Henning, was helping him and they hadn't kept track of the books. Things got so bad that he couldn't afford shipments: each night he'd count out the cash from the register, then drive to the city to buy milk and bread to restock what he could. But the customers had saved him—they'd stayed loyal even when his shelves were nearly empty. Now the shop comforted him. Along with the sheep and a small RV park behind the barn, it made a meager living but a respectable legacy.

We got back from our drives late, usually when one of us remembered that we needed to nurse the lambs. The bright sky gave no hints to the hour, but sometimes a wall of fog would be rolling down the fjord from the north. I'd heat milk while Arild tinkered in the barn. They were solid things, the lambs, already fat and whining, and sometimes they murmured in their throats while they drank. Afterward, Arild and I nodded good night to each other, and I'd curl into my small bed with my sweater for a pillow and wake in the morning as if I'd only blinked my eyes.

Most of the customers trickled in later, but Nils sat at the coffee table first thing each morning and drank a glass bottle of Coca-Cola. He was young, thirty-five, with a buzz cut and a cheerful red face, and he'd lean back in his orange jumpsuit and cross his arms and grin and stare at my breasts. Nils was going to Thailand soon. When Arild saw him, he congratulated Nils's upcoming marriage. "No," Nils objected, blushing. "No . . . No. That's not why I'm going. No."

"It's not the worst thing, a Thai girl," observed a man I didn't recognize. He wore a shirt with the logo for Kvitebjørn, the White Bear oil rig.

"You see that shirt?" Nils said. "He wears it so people will think he makes good money."

Arild turned to me. "You know how much money Nils made in six months?"

I didn't.

"Five hundred thousand kroner," said Arild. "In six months."

"But then I was driving trucks twenty-nine hours in a row. That's not legal," said Nils. He was always grinning. He seemed happy that Arild had said it.

As Nils told it, his best friend had gone to Thailand a few years ago and come back with his very own Thai boy. The couple had lived in Tromsø for a while, traveled back and forth to Thailand, but then the boy started sleeping around. He even went to Oslo for sex—he didn't want to be held back, even after all his boyfriend had done for him. So now they were breaking up, and Nils's friend had to get some belongings from the boy's family in Thailand. Nils had said he'd go along, that maybe the sunlight would help his skin, which, like that of many of the villagers, broke out in open sores that were exacerbated by lack of light. He wasn't out for a girl, he promised, when everyone at work and at the coffee table teased him. He wasn't looking for a girl to bring back.

But the truth was, he wasn't not looking for a girl, either. He made decent money and owned his own farm but had no one to share it with. He could have met someone online, but he didn't speak English, and besides, he was too dyslexic to write letters. And although he'd had girlfriends before, and brought them to Malangen, the girls went on to leave him for neighbors. Nils was nice, people agreed, almost too nice—the guy who'd stay sober at a bonfire and drive everyone home after, pull over on turns so that seventy-year-olds could puke out the window, drop them off with a smile and call them the next morning.

Everyone was hoping that Nils would come back with a girl, just so they could say they told him so. But if he wanted a Thai girl, he wouldn't need to go far. The Thai girls around Malangen were all related anyway. No one remembered where it started, but one man got a girl and the next thing he knew she had set up her sisters and friends with other bachelors. Then *they* brought their sisters and friends—a whole community of Thai girls, imported one by one, and it was the girls already here who did the recruiting. An enlistment campaign, Arild called it; he had received some offers himself, after his first wife left him. He was, he liked to say, still considering.

For their part, most of the Norwegian women on the peninsula viewed the whole process with disdain. They thought men who went for foreign girls couldn't handle a woman with opinions. The men responded that local women, with their short hair and broad faces, looked like men themselves.

But as the men explained, there were dangers with Thai girls, too—dangers with any foreign girls, and maybe the Eastern Europeans were the worst. They only needed to stay married for five years to get residency, and then they could keep it after a divorce if their husband had abused them. So there were all these marriages, and then five years in—boom!—suddenly the girl was calling abuse. And what could the man do? Well, if he was the type to be inclined, he could get himself a new one.

"So that's what I can do," I said. The men had talked earlier about getting me citizenship, and with some trepidation I'd joined in the jokes. "Nils, will you marry me and then hit me once after five years?"

Nils was still staring at my breasts. "Yeah," he said. Then he laughed a lot. He spread his arms wide. "My heart is open to you."

"Oh, good." Now I felt shitty.

"Seriously," said Nils. "Everyone likes you. They think you're pleasant."

"I like them, too," I said. But I wanted out of the conversation. There was some spark in it that I didn't trust. Nils was looking at me too hard.

I excused myself from the table and walked outside, past the RVs and around the dock, where sheets of slate extended into the water. I sat down on a stone, which was damp enough to be cool without wetting my clothes. Below me, something small trailed rings at the edge of the water, an invisible rock skipping itself. The rest of the fjord was smooth.

I HAD HOPED, IN LILLEHAMMER, that I was more pleasant than Far made me out to be. In his house I was edgy, petty, inclined to disagree with everything he said. I could find no warmth to offer. It might have been a phase, hormones. It might have been homesickness. And maybe it was, to some degree. But I felt trapped in my own bristles.

Early in the school year I had befriended a girl named Sissel, who lived with her mother on the other side of the lake. Sissel was dark haired and authoritative, the kind of passionate explainer I've often been drawn to in new situations; she coached my accent tirelessly, and clarified at length any cultural reference that I didn't immediately understand. She even dubbed me with a Norwegian name—the impenetrably dorky Målfrid—so that I needn't disclose myself as American when meeting someone. While most of our classmates spent weekends getting drunk and hooking up in barns, Sissel organized small-scale costume parties that involved nonalcoholic punch, treasure hunts, and cake decorating. Of course I adored her.

When I confided in Sissel about my discomforts at home, she told her mom, who insisted that I come stay with them for a night or two. That afternoon I missed the bus, and had to ask my host parents for a ride to Sissel's house. Mor seemed pleased that I had made a friend, but Far hardly spoke to me on the drive over. He seemed to view the sleepover as a sort of betrayal.

That night Sissel and her mom and I ate lasagna together, and afterward we watched a horror film on a basement projector. In the movie, a group of teenagers was trapped in a cabin in the woods, getting murdered one by one. When it was over we sprinted up the stairs to Sissel's attic bedroom, squealing, and Sissel's mom came up and tucked us in. She kissed Sissel and then came over to me, on the trundle bed, and pulled the duvet to my chin. She sat on the mattress beside me.

She opened her mouth and shut it again, and then, after a long moment, she reached out and laid a hand on my cheek. "You're such a long way from home," she said, then hesitated. "You can stay here whenever you want to." Her fingers were cool, like my own mother's, and suddenly I felt so cared for—it was an unexpected feeling. I fell in love a little bit. Then she sighed and stood up. Her hand was on the lamp when she froze.

The sound of a car pulling into the driveway outside. Now, silence. Sissel's mom switched off the lamp and, in the darkness, walked to the window. Sissel and I got out of bed and peered from behind her.

In the dim moonlight it was possible to make out the shape of a vehicle in the driveway. The driver's door opened and a figure stepped out. It shut the door carefully, making only a muffled thump, and stood looking up at the dark windows. Then it turned and walked around the side of the house. Everything was very still.

Sissel's mom spoke quietly. "Girls, I'm going to get the phone. Stay right here." Sissel squeezed my hand. Her mom came back up the stairs, holding the phone low so its glow couldn't be seen through the window.

The figure appeared around the other side of the house, making its way to the car. It stopped and looked up again, right at us, and for an instant Far's face caught the moonlight. Then he got in his car—no longer bothering to be quiet—and drove away. Sissel's mom turned on the lamp again.

Outside, the street was still and shining, moonlight on frost.

The next morning, as we left to catch the school bus, Sissel's mom gave me a hug. She repeated her words from the night before: "You can stay here whenever you need to." I thanked her, but I had already decided not to come back. It didn't feel right to involve her and Sissel in my problem, whatever that problem was.

But the problem had already found them. Far returned in daylight hours with a bouquet of flowers—to apologize, he said, for his behavior. Sissel's mom, afraid to let him inside, accepted the flowers on the front step.

I wrote to the exchange organization, asking to be switched to a different family. The student liaison replied that Norwegians were notoriously unwelcoming, and thus host families in Norway were in short supply. She reminded me that families weren't paid, that my family was hosting me out of pure kindness, that their feelings would be hurt if they learned that I wanted to leave them. She suggested that if I let go of my cultural preconceptions, there was no reason I couldn't stay and work it out.

Far often reminded me, though I never mentioned to him my thoughts of leaving, that it was unlikely that any other host family would put up with me. He accused me of going cold, of refusing to participate in family activities, of failing to appreciate his generosity. These critiques I tried to ignore; anyway, they were mostly true. It was only when he criticized my parents, whom he had never met, that my body tensed with fury. How dare he suggest that they were abusive, or neglectful, or ignorant—judgments he based, he said, on my own ungrateful behavior? I'd stay calm until I was out of sight, then sit on my bed with my hands in fists. My parents were wonderful, and Far had no right to critique them—particularly since, when I tested the waters by griping about him in letters, my parents' responses struck me as remarkably forgiving. How good they were, even to Far himself! They were beyond indebted to this stranger who had opened his home to their prickly teenage daughter.

Finally, one day, after gathering my courage, I wrote to my mother, explaining that I simply could not make peace with this family. I referred to Far as an asshole. I was not confident enough to articulate what, exactly, felt wrong, but I willed my mother to recognize that her "sheltered" daughter would not use such words lightly. As soon as I sent the e-mail, I felt an intense relief: the problem was no longer mine alone. I spent the next few hours in an impervious, if antsy, state, awaiting a response. When the answer came, I opened it immediately, though my hands were shaking.

I have to say that I am disappointed in you, my mother wrote. After all my host family had done for me, after how generous they'd been, she could not believe that I would describe them so rudely. My e-mail, she wrote, had been childish—even embarrassing. Her letter ended: *I hope you are able to shape up.*

It had never occurred to me that when I finally gathered the will to ask for help, help might not come; and I felt too shattered to try again, to explain more clearly something I couldn't even define. My options, as I saw them, were to stay put and stop complaining, or come home and prove that I hadn't been ready in the first place. There was a third option—changing host families, which my parents would have supported—but between the student liaison's prior discouragement, my misgivings about moving into a new community and unknown family in the middle of the year, and a sudden fiery desire to prove myself, I hardly considered it. What if my new family was even worse—or what if Far was right, and they wouldn't want to put up with me? At least in Lillehammer I had friends, a few souls watching out for me. My hurt galvanized into stubbornness: I would stay. That evening I took down my father's bulldog picture and tore it into strips, wallowing in a self-righteous anger that felt, for the moment, a great deal more satisfying than my usual self-doubt and fear. Fuck them. From now on, I would keep my mouth shut. I didn't need anybody's help.

I found other ways to leave the house. I hung out with Sissel after school, and arranged to stay with a local "support family," as administered by the exchange program, for one blissful night a week. On weekends I took the train to Oslo to visit my old friend Natasha, who had grown into a passionate, bitter fifteen-year-old. If I'd seen her on the street, I would never have connected this beautiful girl, with her designer jeans and city dialect, to the fiery child I'd once explored the streets with. Now she could walk into any bar, smile sedately, and leave with promises and business cards from the handsome men who gathered around her. And yet she disdained all of it. "These Norwegians," she would say, lazily burning a business card with her cigarette, "they're real assholes. Norwegians are such fucking assholes." One time she came to my host family's house, but the vitriol between her and Far was so instant and powerful that future visits were clearly out of the question. She never articulated what, exactly, precipitated her dislike, referring to Far only as "a terrible man with a peanut penis." I envied her certainty.

It was with Natasha, in Oslo, that I first tasted vodka, swallowing the heat in my throat, and when she cheered I took another swig. She wanted to go dancing, and I wanted to do anything that would make me feel like I was in charge of my own risks. So I borrowed a miniskirt and a fake ID and together we snuck into the hottest clubs downtown, or at least the hottest clubs on side streets that weren't frequented by cops. Natasha owned her body in a way I couldn't imagine imitating, flirting with bouncers and gulping from bottles that strangers offered on the street. I followed her, trying to look confident, and kept my hand on the door handles of the illegal taxis we took home.

Back at Far's house, I had stopped sleeping soundly; I startled at the smallest sound. I lay in bed and imagined the door cracking open, a line of light growing and shrinking against the far wall, the weight of footsteps. The sink of the mattress when he sat beside me. I didn't imagine any further: Far's presence in the darkness was enough. It was all I wanted. For a few minutes, with the ghost of his body beside me, I could know that he was wrong. I could know that the particular crazy I'd felt all year was justified, was not my fault. At some point my fear had exhausted itself, replaced with an underlying confusion that was somehow much worse. Now I wanted certainty more than safety. I wanted to know.

And then, for one moment of the year, I knew.

We were eating dinner, everybody around the kitchen table. I got up to get more water. As I crossed the room, Far stood and—in the context of some playful remark, which I failed to process, even at the time—he hooked my ankle with his foot, grabbed my arms, and knocked me to the floor. The length of his body rested on the length of mine. He twisted my arm, his elbow pressed into my chest. I caught my breath from the pain.

My dad and I had often wrestled over the years, trying to pin each other down on the living room carpet while my mom muttered about breaking things. We'd try to knock each other off balance, and I had no qualms about head-butting him in the stomach with all my lesser might. But in the thick of the game, the second I expressed hesitation—"ouch" or "stop" or "hey!"— he let go and backed up instantly. I was usually just bantering, and jarred by the sudden change; I never really meant for the fun to end. My father's caution seemed like an endearing personality quirk, another way he worried too much about his only daughter, like when he wouldn't let me wear nail polish—too toxic—or stand by the microwave while it was running. But on the occasion that I did want a break from wrestling, I took for granted that my father's response would be immediate. It did not occur to me that someone wouldn't stop if I asked him to. Surely Far didn't realize that he was hurting me.

"Stop it," I said. "That hurts."

Far pressed down harder.

Never before had I felt that an adult was trying to physically injure me—and yet, even now, the rest of the family sat at the table, watching. I tried to roll away, to pull out of his grasp. But he was too strong, or I was too weak; I felt I was fighting a wall. Finally I went limp, my wrists still caught in his fist.

He started to laugh. And in that moment, I gave up. Far was too strong. I was too weak. It seemed clear that this was what he'd wanted me to know: that if he wanted, I wouldn't be able to get away from him. If he hurt me, if he touched me, it would be his choice. And if he didn't, that would be his choice, too.

My head was twisted, my left cheek pressed hard into the kitchen floor.

The floor was cold against my cheek.

Somehow, in the moment, that single fact crystallized into a clarity that had eluded me for the past half year. My cheek, I thought, should not be on the floor. And like a rising shout, the sentence repeated in my mind: My cheek should not be on the floor. My cheek should not be on the floor.

My cheek *should not be on the floor.*

I lay there, trapped beneath Far, but everything was different now. He was wrong. *This* was wrong, and I was right. All my confusion—it hadn't been my fault. I was not paranoid, malicious, incapable of adjustment—all the qualities that I had, at times, attributed for my unhappiness. No. Far was wrong. Far's behavior was wrong. I knew. I knew.

I wanted to laugh. I felt a burst of energy, almost joy. Far was wrong. My cheek should not be on the floor. *I knew.* When Far finally climbed off me, I rose to my feet weightless, as if lifted, and returned to my place at the table.

But the certainty didn't last. Even that night, lying in bed, I struggled to recall the exact sensation, the conviction I had felt. The feeling of the cold floor on my cheek—that was as real as anything. But was Far wrong? He had been playing, after all, though I couldn't remember how it had started. Maybe he was just bad at fun. Maybe pinning me down was an awkward attempt to make amends for our past tensions. Far might have meant nothing by it. He might have treated his own daughter the same way. Sometimes family members wrestled, and that was okay. How could I base my whole judgment of a person on— what? A few square inches of cold floor?

I raised my hand to my left cheek. It was smooth.

I hated Far in a soul-deep way, less for anything he'd done than for turning me against myself. Although his interactions with me, his suggestive comments and stolen touches, had escalated over my first months in the household, at some point everything stalled; we settled into barely civil cohabitation. I watched him, poised for anything that would give me an excuse to leave, to know that I had not imagined it all. He took any opportunity to condemn my character, to imply that the problems had been mine all along.

He must have felt my hatred. He must have sensed that he had come close to an edge. And through his easing of intimidation, and his endless criticisms, Far made me my own victim. I doubted myself so violently that I split into two: the part that was afraid, and the part that blamed myself for my fear. What more was there for him to do?

The year passed, if not easily then eventually. There were, of course, moments of grace: holidays at Sissel's house, skating at the local ice rink, sleepovers with Natasha when we talked long into the dark. Not least of the grace was, for me, acquiring another language, held less in my mind than in my mouth. I became fluent in Norwegian so quickly that it felt more like remembering than learning, so that every sentence I spoke was a tiny thrill, proof that my connection to Norway—whatever it was, whatever I'd sensed—was real. But still, when the year ended, I was too tired to feel triumphant. I celebrated by promising myself that I'd never have to go back to Lillehammer again. I was well aware of the privilege I'd been given, and yet something had failed, and I suspected it was me.

A WIND HAD COME UP while I sat by the fjord, and the water had grown rough. I shivered. It was too cold to stay put, but I didn't want to go back to Nils and the other men, not yet. So I climbed under the dock and followed the beach toward Sand. The stones beneath me glittered in the light.

As I crossed the bridge over the Sand River, which divided the villages of Sand and Mortenhals, I stopped, as I always did, and gazed to my left. Across an overgrown pasture stood a red building with a peaked glass roof, a barn, a cone-shaped silo. There was nobody there now, and even if there had been, I might not have seen them around; the lives of the folk school students hardly overlapped with the lives of those who lived around them. As I stood there, a single dog howled, and the howl broke off into a series of short yips, then faded altogether.

It was this building, this school, that had brought me to Malangen in the first place. But I felt almost no connection to it anymore.

I turned and followed the driveway that ran beside the river to the front of the school. I passed little red cabins, and then, surrounded by a chain-link fence, the dog yard, which was lined with doghouses and smaller pens. It smelled of dust and urine and the particular faint scent of long-rotten scraps of meat. Through the fence I could see movement, rustling, furred bodies shifting in the cool air, biting halfheartedly at flies. I touched the tall gate, with its ironic yellow signs: Forbidden for Dogs and Contagious Animal Disease. But the dogs started to bark, excited at a stranger, so I stepped back and looked around.

No one was responding. No one had shoved a head out a window to yell *Ti stille! Quiet!* So I lifted the latch on the gate and walked into the center of the dirt enclosure.

For a split second, there was only the heavy scraping of metal on wood as each dog lifted its head or stood. Then, all at once, came an explosion of barking and screeching that seemed to vibrate through my skin, the dogs leaping at me from all sides before being jerked back by their chains. The noise was so loud that I could not differentiate between its elements. But I was used to it. I held out my arms so that some of the dogs struck me with their wet noses when they leaped. There were maybe fifteen dogs, big dogs, their coats coarse and thick with dust. Two white dogs, a gray dog, another gray dog—they were different, their faces too long, too much red in their fur. Except there, in the corner, one black husky.

The black husky was less excited than the others, older. I walked over, placed one hand under his chin, stroked the other across his hard face. He rose to his back legs, as if in slow motion, and pressed his head against my chest.

"Hey, Saddam," I said.

CHAPTER THREE

A FEW YEARS AFTER LEAVING LILLEHAMMER, I received a letter from a classmate with whom I'd seldom spoken, an avowed Communist who was active in a national youth movement. The Communist wrote that he and his friends had been talking about "tough girls," and that throughout the conversation, he kept thinking of me. He wondered if life had been kind to me.

That someone who had only known me during that year might ever consider me tough—and pick me out of a crowd as such—stopped my breath. It seemed at the time unspeakably deep, a recognition so unlikely that the comfort it offered came balanced with an intense anxiety that it wasn't true. I knew I would never be a tough girl. And yet the phrase, with its implied contradiction, articulated everything that I wanted for myself: to be a girl, an inherently vulnerable position, and yet unafraid.

Back in California for my senior year of high school, I volunteered very little about Lillehammer, and moved forward with life as if I had spent nothing but a long weekend away. I'm sure my parents knew that something was wrong. My mom had a sound to her voice, tentative, when she meant to ask a difficult question; but each time I sensed the quiver before it came, and, my skin suddenly electric, I'd interrupt with some inane comment about the weather or the day's plans or the latest news, and my mother would let it drop.

One of her concerns in particular stood out to me. My younger host sister would be studying in the United States that year, staying with a new set of host parents whose photo my mother saw in a correspondence. The photo disturbed her. There was something in the man's expression, my mother said. He gave her a creepy vibe. All that next year my mom worried aloud about my host sister's host father, and all that year, when the topic came up, I rolled my eyes or left the room. Didn't I care? she asked me. The answer was no: I didn't care, not in the slightest, nor could I bring myself to. My mother pressed her lips together. "I'm sure it's fine," she'd assure herself, time after time. "I'm just being a worried mom. I'm sure it's perfectly fine."

But it wasn't fine. *I* wasn't fine. I felt that my time in Norway had been stolen. Worse, it had turned me into a person I didn't recognize, someone who snapped at my mother's concerns and startled awake at small sounds, self-conscious about my body in a way I'd never been before. The solution, I decided, was to go back. Try the whole thing over again. But this time I was going to do it right: I would go to the Arctic. I would go to the place I had yearned for, where I could prove I was the person I had once known myself to be. I just needed a way in.

That year, while my friends applied to jobs and colleges, I considered strategies for going north. If only I could join the crew of an expedition! How easy it seemed, a hundred years ago— stow away on a ship, or cut my hair and tape my breasts and volunteer as a cabin boy. Now every expedition I found, every job, seemed to want someone *qualified*—a scientist or a mechanic.

Nobody wanted a stubborn and dreamy eighteen-year-old from suburban California.

It was Far, in fact, who had first told me about folk schools. They were distinctly Scandinavian—yearlong public boarding schools in which students studied something they loved, no matter how offbeat. "You can even study dogsledding," he'd said. Maybe I sensed the derision in his voice, or maybe I added it later, in retrospect, so that my dream would not be his suggestion. Dogsledding, like I'd dreamed of. Dogsledding, like in all my favorite books.

There it was. My ticket.

I found 69°North online. With around forty students, it was the smallest folk school in Norway, and offered training in dogsledding and winter survival. It was Arctic, all right—closer to the pole than all of Sweden, Iceland, and most of Alaska. Photos on its website showed rosy-cheeked students crossing glaciers, dogsledding over frozen rivers, sitting around campfires under the northern lights, and cuddling puppies. Better yet, tuition was free, and students could do extra chores to offset the cost of room and board. I sent in my application and transcript, hoping beyond hope that my straight As would be enough to place me in the top of the applicant pool; in fact, as I later learned, the school only used transcripts to make sure that applicants hadn't failed gym. Anyway, two weeks later, I was accepted. And just like that, the Arctic was waiting for me.

Like most folk schools, 69°North advertised itself as idyllic: *a school about life, with nature as the teacher.* In reality, it was forty teenagers stranded on an isolated peninsula and thrown into a yearlong series of emotional challenges and hazardous situations, a cross between hippie commune and survivalist camp. The school was part of a dwindling, 150-year-old educational system based on the Scandinavian and socialist principles that fresh air was good for self-discovery, and that a society could not be truly democratic unless all its voters knew themselves. These purposes were diligently hidden from the students—none of whom, I came to suspect, had been drawn to the remoteness of 69°North by accident.

The school program opened with a lamb banquet, held around long tables in an upstairs gymnasium that smelled like Pine-Sol and wet wool. I found myself sitting next to Sven, the wilderness teacher, an ebullient and gorgeous Dane who, it was whispered, had come to 69°North after police found him wandering in the forest months after a breakup, with only an elkhound for company. At one point, when someone mentioned camping, Sven climbed onto his chair in excitement.

After dinner, the principal took the podium. He spoke of adventure, of learning the rhythms of the polar night, of learning the howls of dogs and the textures of snow. He spoke of bonding into the kind of community made possible only through isolation and hardship. The principal wore black pants and no shirt. He had binder clips pinched to his nipples, and occasionally, as he talked, he tweaked the clips with his fingers; he was proud of his tolerance for pain. He wore this outfit on the opening night because he wanted to encourage bravery, and how could he tell his students to be brave without demonstrating his own courage first? For the rest of the year, the principal wore tidy jeans and button-down shirts. He only busted out the binder clips for special occasions.

When the principal finished talking, the students cheered. Sven pounded on the table. After a moment, I pounded on the table, too, joining the ovation. I was in the Arctic, and in the Arctic things happened for a reason. I felt that nothing could surprise me. The world seemed strange and bright.

Most of my classes that year were taught by the dogsledding teacher, Tallak, a compact Sami man with the gift of authority. Everything Tallak said, everyone believed. It wasn't that he was forceful, or overwhelming; rather, his voice carried a calm certainty, slow and light, punctuated by little laughs. Listening to him talk about anything—dogs, racism, foster children, Christmas—felt like discovering brilliant thoughts you didn't know you already had. "I have to be careful," he sometimes said, "because people will believe whatever I tell them." This show of responsibility only made the students trust him more.

At first, students were only allowed to go dogsledding with Tallak; after all, as he reminded us, we knew nothing yet. Day by day we waited our turns, waited for him to come into the common room after school, where students sat on long couches to knit and play cards and get to know each other. When Tallak walked in, we'd stop talking and will ourselves to look competent. He'd scan our faces, indicating his selection with a nod at the chosen student. I was lucky. I was picked on the second day.

September was chilly but snowless; instead of sleds, the dogs pulled welded-steel carts with room for one passenger and one driver. By the time I'd put on my coat and laced my boots, Tallak had assembled a team before one of the carts, which was tied off to a heavy post. It shuddered as the dogs reared up against their ropes. I settled into the lurching passenger seat with my hands in my lap, as Tallak had instructed, so that my arms wouldn't break if the cart flipped over. There were eight dogs in the team, and they were all barking and leaping, the sound and chaos overwhelming. I'd learned the names of their positions: lead dogs in front, then swing dogs, then team dogs, and finally the wheel dogs closest to the cart. The wheel dogs were the biggest.

"Ready?" said Tallak, his voice stern. The cart sank as he climbed on behind me. I started to answer, "I think so—" before I realized he wasn't talking to me. His gaze was only on the dogs, who tensed at the word. Then—

"Ålright!"

Tallak pulled a quick-release and the cart jerked forward, the dogs instantly at a run—*fast,* it felt; I later learned they maxed out at around twenty-five miles per hour—and stones were flying up from those hind legs and stinging my face, a gob of cold mud on my forehead, so that by the time I opened my eyes again we were at the end of the driveway, headed toward a bridge. The bridge had a cowcatcher on it, a yard across, metal bars with open spaces exactly the right size for a dog's leg to slip through. We were going too fast to stop. "Will they be okay?" I tried to shout, but we were already there; and row by row the dogs leaped over the grate, rising and falling, lead then swing then team then wheel, in a perfect wave that rolled the length of the team and culminated in the cart's own rattly pass across the bars. A hard turn onto the road—the cart slid on gravel, I clutched my seat—and we were home free, galloping down the wide paved road of the village of Sand.

The dogs flowed, a perfect thrilling engine. Their legs stretched out like pistons; their ears and tongues bounced in unison. Their running had nothing to do with me. They wouldn't have stopped if I'd asked them to.

They were beautiful. They were so beautiful.

I have never loved anything as hard and as fast as I loved those dogs, as I loved dogsledding itself. I could have watched them for hours. I could have watched them forever. They ran like water, and I was part of it, and I was struck with the instant and undeniable thought that I had finally come to the place that I had spent my life trying to find. Right *here,* of course it was here, in the Arctic, in Norway, between the gray mass of the fjord and the sharp snowy mountains, at the top of the turning world. It was almost too much to acknowledge. It was hard to trust the fact of my body in this place. But here were the dogs, pulling me, proving it.

"Fucking hell," said Tallak. He slammed the hand brakes and shouted to the team. The wheels froze, but the dogs kept pulling, the cart skidding after them, painting black stripes on the road. Finally we bounced to a stop. The dogs were still trying to go.

Now I saw the problem: sheep, sprawled just around a bend. "All we need is another fight with a sheep farmer," said Tallak.

"The dogs would hurt them?"

"Blair," said Tallak. "These are wolves you're working with."

They weren't, of course, but it was Tallak's belief that every dog, down to every last Chihuahua, thought itself a wolf.

He had me stand on the cart while he ran up and heaved the lead dogs around to face the way we'd come. The rest of the team followed in a clump, and on his way back to the cart, Tallak untangled a few that had caught their ankles in the gangline. "Do you want to drive?" he asked me, and before I answered he said, "Better not," and off we went toward home.

The next week, to demonstrate efficient dog training, Tallak brought a four-week-old puppy into the classroom. The puppy had never been inside a building before, or even away from his siblings, none of whom was named yet. Tallak was still considering options. He could name the pups after a theme, like his last litter, the board-game dogs: Risk, Ludo, Chess. He could name them out of spite, like the dog She Bergeton, christened after a nearby farmer following a dispute over a dead sheep. Ultimately, he would ignore all advice and name them after "terrorists": Bin Laden, Saddam, and George Bush for the boys. Condoleeza for the girl—Condy for short. He would name the puppy in question Saddam.

Saddam was black and velvety and round, small enough to be scooped up in one hand, with a white tuft on the end of his tail and the thinnest white line down the bridge of his snout.

As soon as Tallak set him down in the classroom doorway, Saddam tensed. Then he launched into a series of leaps that brought him to the center of the room, wagging his short tail as much for balance as excitement. He shook his head with his jaw open, as if hoping his mouth might encounter something in midair. He keened a wailing, high-pitched squeal and wagged his body against the students' legs, crashing into tables and chairs as we all reached down and tried to touch him. Yes, I thought. This was a good school.

Tallak glanced at the clock. It was 10:35. In twenty minutes, he said, he could train Saddam to stay. He lifted the puppy by the scruff and put him in a corner, by the chalkboard. With a tap, he knocked the dog onto its stomach. "Stay," he said.

In an instant, Saddam had scooted halfway across the floor. Tallak carried him back to the corner. "Stay."

Saddam rolled away.

Again and again they repeated the process—the man stern, the dog largely oblivious. But gradually something changed. Saddam grew cautious; his tail drooped; he didn't leave the corner as quickly. Finally, when Tallak said, "Stay," Saddam laid his head on the ground. It was 10:51.

"He's given up," Tallak explained. He left the room and came back with a slice of raw reindeer on a plate, which he set down a foot or so from the puppy. Saddam's eyes flicked over the meat, but he didn't lift his head.

The lesson was complete. We were supposed to be inspired, but the students were mostly quiet. A girl to my left had tears in her eyes. But I couldn't put my finger on what, exactly, was upsetting. The puppy had been trained. Tallak had proven himself right, and he would continue to do so.

Nowhere were his lessons more urgent than in the kennel. Tallak's dogs were fighters. Almost daily they broke into terrible screaming brawls and we had to come running from the school or the cabins and pull tight fists of fur from their backs and kick their ribs with our boots. I was always scared to enter the mass of flying heads and teeth and blood and would hold back, hoping for someone else to break up the fight first; but then Tallak called me out—"They're hurting each other, and you just stand there?"— and I was ashamed. His dogs were valuable. Ten thousand kroner each, maybe more. We should have no reluctance, he told us, to be rough with them, and as with everything he told us, we were embarrassed to have ever not believed it. Manhandling dogs was simply learning to speak their language rather than expecting them to learn ours. To grab a dog by its scruff and whip it onto its back, then kneel on its chest until its muscles finally relaxed— that was being the boss. Tallak showed us how to grip our hands around the dogs' snouts, to growl deep in our throats and bite their noses and ears. He liked to tell a story about being stuck in a kennel with a strange dog, who was snarling, bent on attacking him. He grabbed a shovel, raised it to the sky, and brought it down on the dog's head. The dog fell to the ground. And then— and then, Tallak said, he unzipped his pants and peed on it. If that wasn't dog language, he didn't know what was.

We didn't, either. None of the students was inclined toward roughness, but neither were we inclined to question Tallak's wisdom.

Once, after a fight, I found part of an ear on the ground, a velvet triangle with one red edge. I folded it between my fingers, distracted from the horror, for a moment, by the softness. Then I remembered, and threw it away from me. That dog would be fine, Tallak said; ears healed themselves. He was more worried about the other guy, who'd suffered a long cut on his chest. Tallak washed the wound with saline and stitched it up on the mudroom floor, while I stared at the slime of muscle just under the fur.

We spent time cleaning the kennel and scooping poop and repairing doghouses and chopping frozen intestines with an ax into meal-size chunks, but also we were learning to mush, first with carts and then, when the first snows came in October, on wooden sleds. As soon as anyone walked into the kennel with a harness, the dogs erupted. Thirty, forty dogs depending on the day, all jumping and yowling as hard as they could, and the trick was to pick out five or six or eight and wrestle their muscular bodies into harnesses and clip them to the gangline that pulled the sled. Finally, when the team had settled down out of boredom or indignation, we could pull the quick-release that held back the sled and it would jolt forward with such force that the insides of my arms felt bruised from holding on. In that moment of stillness to speed, all the noise and screams and howls would stop dead; everything in the world shifted in that one instant when we pulled the rope.

"You are stronger than one dog," Tallak told us. "One dog, you can pin him down, you can make him do what you want. Two dogs, maybe. Four dogs can pull a truck from a ditch. The sled's brake is a joke. It is a suggestion. When the dogs are together, you have no chance of controlling them, unless they choose to please you."

He was right. It wouldn't be long before I saw a six-dog team uproot a birch tree that they were tied to and take off down the trail, tree and roots bouncing behind them.

Tallak taught us the rules: Never step over the gangline. Never trust a snow anchor. Always keep your knife on your belt. Most important, never let go of the sled. If the sled tips over, if it crashes, hold on. Get up if you can. It's nothing to be dragged on your stomach a half mile through the snow. As long as you hold on. If you let go, Tallak said, the dogs and the sled will leave you, and alone in the mountains, on the tundra, you can die. I stuffed my pockets with matches, chocolate, extra mittens, and two headlamps, in case I ever got left behind.

The first time I drove a sled on snow, through a winding trail near the school, I tipped over seven times. Each time, I got dragged, my hands gripping the side stanchions, my arms aching, my mittens slipping loose, my pants filling with snow. I could think quite clearly, being dragged. I gazed forward between my outstretched arms, between the runners of the sled, at the quick back feet of the wheel dogs. The team careened around corners. *Don't let go.* And each time, somehow, the dogs slowed enough that I could clamber back onto the runners. There was something thrilling about the transition, about climbing to my feet on the moving vehicle, the vehicle with six bodies and minds, the vehicle that moved whether or not I was on it, and gliding once more over the smooth terrain.

The trails wound around mountains, across fields, alongside frozen rivers, and the runners made a whispering sound over the snow. The dogs ducked their heads and leaned into their harnesses and bounded through drifts as if they would never want to stop, as if there would never be any reason to. While they ran, while we ran, I practiced reading their movement, noticing the subtle glances and postures with which the dogs communicated. When we took breaks, they bit snow and rolled over and licked my face. There were moments when I felt I would never learn enough, never be good or tough or confident enough to drive the dogs well. And there were many more moments, standing on the runners or sitting in the snow with huskies piling onto my lap, when I was gripped with an astonished joy, and could scarcely remember being happier.

Together with the other students I learned to tunnel into the snow, to sleep sheltered against the wind, to curl up in the dogsled in case of a storm. To build a fire from wet wood in a blizzard. To force movement when my limbs were numb. We went to the Sand River in our long underwear and, one by one, walked into the frigid current and swept downstream until a classmate threw us a rope. The worst thing about cold water was the shock, Tallak told us; the best thing was that it prepared us for future cold. If we practiced submerging, we'd be better equipped if we fell through ice in an emergency.

The temperature dropped to twenty, thirty below. We slept outside two nights a week, then four, then seven.

I learned to grab the dogs by the ruff and yank their strong bodies toward me, pin their hips between my knees so they couldn't get away. If my hands were numb from touching the frozen metal clasps on the gangline, I could slip my bare hands into the soft pockets of the dogs' armpits, until the feeling seeped back into my fingers. I could kiss their bucking heads through my balaclava.

December came, and with it the last sunset of the year— the Time of Darkness, when the sun did not cross the horizon for fifty-seven days. The outside world was lit only by campfires, headlamps, and the pulsing, snaking aurora, which at its brightest cast the mountains a marbled green. Time passed without measure, an endless dusk punctuated by sleep, so that even I forgot what we were waiting for.

It seems almost too obvious to emphasize how much I was scared. In the morning, during the day, at night. I was often acutely frightened—of a sharp turn in the trail, of a tricky river crossing, during storms—and I lived, too, with a deeper fear: that the winter was only starting, that I had so many minutes and hours and days of cold and risk and potential injury. But it was refreshing to be afraid of something concrete. I was no longer scared of some unknown force, of confusion; no, I was afraid of hypothermia. I was afraid of being stranded in the wilderness. I was afraid of crashing the sled. I was as afraid as I'd been in Far's house, maybe even more, but suddenly that fear didn't make me crazy: it made me brave.

In midwinter, Tallak decided that we were ready for longer trips. He called them expeditions, and announced the plans with just a few days' notice. One day he declared that we were going to dogsled to Finland. After consulting some maps, he changed his mind: we would drive the school bus through Finland into northern Sweden, bringing the dogs along, and, upon arrival, we'd build a base camp for day trips. Northern Sweden had cooler temperatures than coastal Norway, as it was farther from the Gulf Stream, but until we stepped off the bus, it was hard to understand what this really meant.

This was not the damp cold by the fjord, the—yes!—*perfect ten below* that had come to feel comfortable enough that students walked between buildings in T-shirts. No, this was a new cold, a cold that assaulted all the senses: burning the nose and throat, glazing the vision, turning each step into a cacophony of squeaking snow and crackling fabric. Whenever I blinked, my eyelids stuck together. Someone said forty below, someone said fifty; the exact temperature was irrelevant. How cold was it? Fucking cold. Too cold for mistakes. Our breath trailed behind us like footprints.

We set up camp in the forest near Jukkasjärvi, Sweden. A day's walk away, travelers wrapped themselves in furs at this year's incarnation of the Ice Hotel, a palace made of ice blocks from the nearby Torne River. They drank at an ice bar under ice chandeliers, prayed in the ice chapel, slept in artist-designed rooms on ice beds covered with reindeer fur. Inside, the Ice Hotel was heated to 23°F. It seemed downright tropical.

We put out piles of hay for the dogs' bedding and set up a *lavvo*, a cone-shaped tent, in a clearing. It was my job to mix food for the dogs, but as I worked, I couldn't help but glance back at the bus. It seemed so solid, clean—as if, by entering it, I could take myself back somewhere warm. The truth was, we were stuck. The bus wouldn't even start in weather like this. The cold seemed to demand something, and I wasn't sure what to offer.

Some of the boys built a fire in the *lavvo*, and smoke streamed from the tent. Earlier the sky had been appealingly pink, but by now, early afternoon, the midday twilight had passed; snow fell from a mass of gray, and a wind was rising. The smoke was a comfort, but a flimsy one. Some of the others had finished their jobs and were warming their hands by the fire, and here I was, stiff with cold, still trying to break apart the dog bowls that had frozen together. Finally I managed to kick them apart, not caring where I dented the metal. What did it matter? They would just stick together again. I scooped hot tripe gruel from a cooker into the bowls, where it immediately began to freeze.

I was feeling sorry for myself. I could hardly see in the blowing snow. My nostrils burned; my joints ached; I hadn't felt my feet in over a day. I was thirsty, but drinking would make me have to pee, a process I didn't want to deal with. Why was I here? How long had I wanted it? It was too cold to remember. The dogs were glad for their food. They ate it in a few bites, then curled up as tight as knots. One dog ignored her bowl. A bad eater—one of the worst traits for a long-distance sled dog. I set her food in front of another dog, who scarfed it.

"That's what you get," I said. I tried to put my hands in the dog's armpits, but she growled and rolled over.

Why was I here?

This was all Far's fault. His fault that I'd been scared. His fault that I'd wanted to prove myself.

His fault that it was so cold.

His fault that I didn't have a nicer snowsuit.

His fault that the dog bowls were stuck together.

His fault that we weren't cozied up in the Ice Hotel.

I started to laugh. "It's not *my* fault," I told the dog, whose ears perked up. The hairs on her head had frosted white like an old man's, and I brushed them clean with my mitten. "It's not *your* fault."

Behind me, through the blowing snow, came a commotion—the rising grumble of a snowmobile, which stopped in the center of the clearing. A very short man in an enormous parka climbed off and removed his helmet. A few students stood to greet him, but Tallak called them off and approached the man himself. Before long the two were yelling at each other in Sami, gesturing wildly with their arms. In a huff, the short man turned to address the watching students in Norwegian: "You shit-cursed Nazis! I'll have you all arrested." Then he got back on his snow machine and drove away, still shouting over his shoulder. Tallak, watching him go, ran a hand over his hat.

"What happened?" someone asked, but Tallak only shook his head.

A few minutes later, though, a police snowmobile pulled up to our camp. Tallak spoke to the driver at the edge of the clearing. At one point his voice grew sharp, and he gestured at the air around him, but he seemed to contain himself quickly; and when the cop departed, Tallak sent him off with a polite nod. When he turned back to us, though, his face was grim.

The news he reported was brief. The short man had threatened to have us arrested unless we left his land immediately—and his family owned much of northern Sweden. It was one thing to camp on the land, he claimed, but that we had the audacity, along the way, to defecate on it—well, the Nazis were the last ones to pull that trick, and look what happened to them. "We have to leave," said Tallak, looking around at the sleeping dogs and the taut, smoky *lavvo*, which was already coated in a layer of soft snow. "We really don't want to mess with the police here."

I could think of nothing less appealing than setting out into the rising storm, and the other students grumbled as they dismantled the *lavvo*. But under the grumbling was a real tension—leave camp, in this weather? There was no question of how we would travel—we could come back for the bus later. But for once even the dogs were reluctant. Some of them refused to uncurl from their knots, crouching even in their harnesses. We had six sleds between us and decided to drive two and two with six-dog teams. I'd travel with my friend Oda, an unwaveringly cheerful lesbian who liked to walk around the school showing off her favorite boob shots from porn magazines. We took off to the west.

Within minutes Oda and I had lost the others. We rode through a treadmill of darkness, our only view that of the trotting wheel dogs, which was as far as a headlamp could illuminate in the blowing snow. We let the lead dogs find the way, trusted their sense of the trail. I was grateful for the darkness that pressed in around us. It was better that way, better than thinking about the vast space we were passing through. For a while I drove, scootering between the sled runners with one foot, while Oda sat in the sled basket with her sleeping bag zipped to her neck. Then we switched places. Sitting in the sled, bundled and passive, was warmer than standing. But it was also dispiriting. The dogs trudged, leaning into the wind, glancing back over their shoulders as if to ask what the hell was going on. All we could see, for a half hour, an hour, was the same lit beam of snow and steam from the dogs' breathing. There were no more trees; at some point, in the darkness, we passed onto the tundra. Gradually the snow fell harder, and our path—a single trail through drifts—began to fill up. The dogs went more and more slowly, sinking to their ankles and then their elbows in the snow. Finally they sank to their armpits, and the sled gathered a mound before it like a snowplow. The team stopped.

I climbed from the sled and waded toward the front, falling to my knees twice before taking my place in front of the lead dogs. There, I trudged one step at a time through the deep snow. Each step I gained, the dogs followed. I walked until I couldn't, sweat running down my back, and then Oda took her turn in front and I pushed the sled from behind. A glow rose behind us; another sled appeared briefly in the dark, then sank away, and we were alone again. So we were all still moving forward.

It was not even worth thinking about the cold.

I halfheartedly suggested hunkering down, digging a hole to stay the night. But somehow, somewhere, there were other people moving with us. If we stopped, we'd be alone. We'd wake up alone. We'd be somewhere on the Swedish tundra, alone.

Hours passed. The snow stopped falling. The wind stilled. Oda and I drove the sled together, each balanced on a single runner, kicking our feet in unison. The sled was narrow; the sides of our bodies pressed together. It was warmer where we touched.

After a while we tossed chunks of meat to the dogs, calling out praise. A few tails wagged. We pulled food from the sled bag—homemade "bombs," nuggets of oatmeal and seeds, designed to deliver the most calories in the least offensive package—and swallowed bites as we pushed the sled. The bombs were frozen, but it didn't make much difference.

"Where do you think we're going?" Oda asked.

"Probably to a hotel," I said. "It'll have real walls. We can take off our snowsuits."

"They'll have hot showers."

"And beds."

"And dinner."

"Oh my god," I said. "Dinner. What do they serve for dinner?"

"Cake," said Oda, popping another bomb in her mouth.

She chewed for a long time before swallowing. "Marzipan cake. Fresh apple cake, with whipped cream. Maybe brownies."

"And a big salad."

Oda hesitated. "You can have the salad."

"Okay."

We pushed on. There were no stars.

"What about the beds?" said Oda.

"They're huge," I said. "Big soft mattresses with down blankets. Enormous pillows."

"Clean white sheets."

"Whiter than snow."

We laughed.

"They're waiting for us right now," she said. "We're close. They're already heating the dog food and laying out the hay."

"Hey, dogs, you smell that?"

"They can smell it."

Oda switched off her headlamp. The sled kept moving through the dark. I closed my eyes.

"Are you scared?" I said.

"I don't know," said Oda.

"I don't know, either," I lied.

"Yeah."

"Hey, remember warm feet?"

"Don't remind me."

We traded runners and drove for a while. Then we switched runners again.

"Blair," she said, "there's a star."

But it wasn't a star. It was a light.

The dogs saw it, too, and trotted faster. It was a small change, but after so many hours of the same pace, it knocked us both off balance and we scrambled to regain our footing on the runners. The light twinkled on the horizon, ahead and to the right. Gradually we came closer, making out the shape of buildings, the sound of howling. By now the dogs were running. The light was attached to a house. There was no road.

Most of the other students had already arrived, and had stretched out chains for the dogs. A few tended a roaring fire, heating dog food. It was morning, they said—we had run all night. It turned out that the property belonged to a Sami family, friends of Tallak's, who had agreed to let us crash in their *gamme*. The *gamme* was a round building made of sod, half-submerged, its roof domed with snow. Oda and I pushed open the wooden door and found a smoky round room, illuminated by a central fire pit. Around the edges was a sleeping platform, piled high with furs. Someone held out a plate of dried meat.

Oda pressed a piece into my hand. "Cake," she said.

We fed the dogs hot gruel and put them to bed on the piles of straw, where their bodies steamed, tendrils rising through the beam of my headlamp. They curled with their tails over their noses, yawning. No worse for the wear. And neither, I realized, was I. After a few hours of dead sleep, I ventured back outside into the pink twilit hours of midday to find the dogs all howling at once, a sonorous and overwhelming howl that rose as a single voice. In the distance slid the black dot of a snowmobile, and above the horizon shone the dim sparks of military rocket tests. Along the opposite horizon, a brown line grew into a shifting wall—a thousand reindeer, like the pictures in my mother's books, covering the land we had just crossed.

A few weeks later, I stood in the dog yard shoveling. It was almost noon, the day after a heavy snow, and the huskies had been trapped in their houses by the drifts; their heads emerged like so many clams on a tide flat. As usual they were barking, a sound so steady and cacophonous that I no longer heard it. It was fun to dig them out, moving the snow until the dogs burst out one by one, shaking powder from their fur and wagging their tails.

I felt the sun before I saw it. I was dislodging a stubborn ice clump when suddenly my vision snapped off and a sizzling feeling filled my skin. In another instant I could see again, and the landscape—the frozen fjord, the mountains behind the school— caught like a candlewick and exploded around me in a blaze of white fire. The dogs fell still and my throat choked shut, and then they were howling and I was laughing, and in another minute the day was over and the sun sank back down as if it had never been. My ecstasy was illogical, uncontrollable; I felt as if I'd been slipped a drug, and could no more control its chemical effects than I could force the sun to resurface. I sank into a snowbank, stunned, and did not move for another hour, until the last blush faded from the southern horizon.

Each day that week the sun stayed up for a few minutes longer, and each day I was shocked and elated, wiped out by the force of my own body's reactions to the light. I was unable to separate the chemical emotions caused by sunlight from my own mind. I wrote in my diary, "It is no longer physically possible for me to be unhappy while the sun is up," and I earnestly believed that this would be true for the rest of my life.

That spring, during weekends and on school vacations, I started working at a tour kennel a few hours away. There, I helped care for seventy dogs while their musher, Eirik, was off training for races, and I was surprised to learn that the violence I'd taken for granted in Tallak's kennel—the dogfights, and the force with which he broke them up—was not universal. If at the tour kennel a team got tangled in its gangline, and it took me a few minutes to pull the dogs apart, nobody would lose an ear; when I walked an individual dog through the yard, the other dogs wagged their tails rather than tried to attack it. The gentleness was a relief; I had not liked being hard. And although it felt odd to be in a kennel alone, without the company of other students,

I found that I appreciated the intimacy with the dogs. I could hang out in the dog yard all afternoon, petting the huskies and enjoying the sunlight. Whenever I wanted I could hook up a team and drive by myself down a nearby frozen river, moving silently through crystalline, snow-draped forests lit rose by the ever-low sun.

For all its occasional monotony, driving a dogsled never let my mind wander. It was an overwhelmingly physical experience: the cold, the shifting runners, the wandering trail. It made my mind shallower. There was the brushing sound of snow under the sled. There were the dogs, the beautiful dogs, running, and I could spend hours watching the changing, hypnotic rhythms of their back legs punching up and down. Occasionally I talked to them, and then I'd drift off in midsentence and recall the rest of my thoughts minutes later. Or else I'd run up a hill, or fix a tangle, or scooter my feet to keep warm. It didn't matter. I was still just driving dogs.

Sometimes tour groups came by the kennel, and I was responsible for distributing snowsuits and boots, maintaining a fire in the *lavvo*, and giving short demonstrations on how to drive a sled. I felt self-conscious, certain that the tourists—especially other Americans—would be able to read me as an interloper. But, astonishingly, they took me seriously. When they asked questions about my life, my childhood in the north, I lied without thinking, telling breezy stories about blizzards and living in igloos and dogsledding to school. What about the darkness? they asked. The cold? Being alone in the wilderness? And, although I'd lost sleep over these very things, I shrugged off the concerns as juvenile. "I guess it's all what you're used to," I'd say, pocketing their tip money. The tourists' respect was addictive. After all, wasn't this the person I had always known myself to be? It was easy to believe my own act.

I loved being alone, and working with tourists, but I envied Eirik, too, for his racing. I watched him prepare for Finn-marksløpet, the longest race in Europe, packing sleeping bags and pots and frozen meat into the belly of his sled, waxing new runners and selecting his team carefully. On the morning of the race, downtown Alta was packed with dozens of trucks, hun-dreds of dogs waiting or leaping on chains, mushers making last-minute adjustments, their handlers checking and rechecking the required gear. Despite the commotion, Eirik was calm. He had raced before, he had won before; chaos slid right off him. He had the particular tranquil bearing that I was coming to recognize as characteristic of those who had spent years of their lives sur-rounded by overexcitable huskies, a composure that increased in proportion to the drama of any situation. At the starting line, under an archway made of ice, it took eighteen volunteers to hold back his ten-dog team; and when the countdown ended and they all let go at once, he surged forward into instant, high-speed si-lence. His dogs ran the length of the main street and then they crossed into tundra, where they would spend the next five hun-dred kilometers in solitude—a journey known only to the other mushers and their dogs—only to appear from the wilderness days later and pass under the very same arch. A sport in which the bulk of the action played out in secret.

Back at the kennel, the house and the dog yard were still. I moved through the hours carefully, alone, tending to the re-maining huskies, who were quieter than I had ever seen them. The next morning a moose wandered into the yard, and the dogs hardly even freaked out as I chased it away, weaving between the doghouses, hollering and waving branches to make my arms look longer. At night I drank tea and watched the northern lights and wondered if Eirik was running or resting. I told myself that someday I would race, too; I would be part of a team, out on the trail, on the inside of this strange and mysterious process while folks at home gazed into the dark mirror of nighttime windows.

They would know nothing. But I would know. I would be at the heart of all of it.

Two days later, Eirik finished the race in fourteenth place. He gave me his race bib, a reflective vest with sponsors' logos and the number 98, stained down the front with dirt and meat. Back at the folk school, I hung the bib on the wall above my bed. I thought about framing it.

As a culmination of our winter training, Tallak arranged a trip to Svalbard, the barren archipelago halfway between mainland Norway and the pole, where he knew of some sled dogs we could borrow. I could hardly believe my own life. Svalbard was legendary, sharp and ethereal, that particularly arctic combination of spectacular and austere; short of an expedition to the pole, I could go no farther north, no closer to the top of the world. It was March. The sun there had not yet risen. For a few days we hung around the primary settlement, Longyearbyen, where fat reindeer shuffled down the main street. Then we rented some dogs and an armed guide, in case of polar bears, and set off into the interior. That night, atop a glacier, we made an unusual camp: a cluster of tents, with the dogs staked in a ring around us. The dogs were not in a circle so they could fight off a bear. They were in a circle so that the bear, when it reached us, would already have a full stomach. I volunteered for the first watch shift, from ten to twelve, to get it over with. My headlamp was dim. It didn't illuminate past the first row of dogs.

"How will I know if there's a bear?" I asked the guide.

"The dogs will know."

"And then?"

"Wake me up. I'll sleep with the gun."

He stepped into the nearest tent, zipped it shut after him. All around, students in the other tents were closing down: flies zipping, lights switching off, the first snores filtering out into the night. I stomped my boots, kicked at the wind-packed snow, shook my hands to keep warm. Somewhere across camp was the other watch, but I couldn't see her.

My headlamp flickered. It was too cold for the batteries. I switched it off and waited for my eyes to adjust. There were no stars, no northern lights, but the land was too white to ever be pitch black, no matter how dark it got. Instead, the snow, the mountains, the sky—everything was gray. I stood suspended in it. Gradually I could make out the tents. The dogs were small mounds, curled in nests of snow.

Somewhere nearby, I thought, is a polar bear. Polar bears eat people. *Eat* them. Just when I thought I'd been getting used to things.

Should we worry? My mother had asked me, after I first arrived at the school. I'd assured her that she shouldn't. I loved her dearly, but her worry felt intrusive. *Now* she would worry about me. Now that I was facing challenges I wanted.

But I hadn't said that. Instead, I'd made an appeal more hopeful than logical, pointing out the threats that were lessened here: Car crashes. Terrorism. The flu. The dangers here were different, I argued, but no worse than the dangers at home. It was simply an adjustment. I promised not to be stupid.

The truth was that when it came down to it, the land here seemed kind, and that kindness seemed to be the great secret of the Arctic, at least on the mainland. All its dangers distilled into one crisp feature: cold. And what was cold but a call to the moment? Cold couldn't creep or consume, stalk or drown. It necessitated only insulation. The things that survival demanded—covering our bodies, keeping them separate from other bodies—were things that I already wanted to do. In extreme cold, nobody thought of any body but their own. Nobody would think about mine, wrapped in its layers upon layers.

Of course, there was the matter of keeping warm. But after

months of winter, even cold was easily solved. To live in cold, I had only to internalize its counterintuitive rules: When my body wanted to clench, I had to force it open. Swing my arms when I wanted to pull them in. Jump when I wanted to sit. Pee when I would rather stay clothed. Change into dry long underwear even when the air bit my bare limbs. Cold was the mind's distraction and the body's one demand.

Of course I was scared. But at least I was scared of dangers of my own choosing. At least there was joy that came with it.

I walked to the edge of the ring of dogs and stared into the gray, searching for movement. I squinted into the dark.

Are you safe?

I'm as safe as I'll ever be.

And the dogs exploded.

It happened all at once. The dogs were lying curled in their mounds and then they were shrieking, growling, *screaming* with an energy I had never heard before. I hit the side of my headlamp and shone the beam around the circle but all I could see was the dogs' tense bodies and the snow that swirled around them. The guide, I thought. The *gun*. But my limbs felt weak. I kept sweeping my light around me. Dogs, dogs. And now the guide was beside me with his rifle high, shouting something I could barely make out—Where were the dogs looking? And I realized, with horror, that they weren't facing an approaching danger, something they'd scented on the wind. Whatever the dogs were barking at, it was already inside the circle.

I turned around and swept my light: snow, dogs, tents. Nothing. They were barking at nothing.

But their hackles were straight in the air.

The guide saw it first. It was a dog, one of the closest dogs, a little black one named Lucifer. He was on his side, convulsing. The guide ran to him, and I and the others—scrambling from their tents—ran to him, too, and held his legs as the guide instructed us. Lucifer was twitching, his mouth foaming, his body shaking in a way no dog's body should. But I kept looking over my shoulder. What about the bear?

The dogs didn't quiet until Lucifer lay still.

"Epilepsy," said the guide, breathing hard. "We've tried everything for it." He stroked Lucifer's side with one hand. He was limp.

A ring had gathered, students blinking in their yanked-on boots, shaky with adrenaline and sleepiness. Slowly they traipsed back to their tents. I still had forty minutes left in my shift.

And then I was alone again. The night had a different quality now, the ringing of silence after noise. I was tired but dreaded climbing into my tent to sleep, where I'd lie pressed among three classmates. Even after months of practice, I couldn't sleep well with other bodies close around me. I was too conscious of their breathing. I woke at small movements. And since I was restless, anyway, and revved up, I decided to make myself a snow cave and sleep alone, where at least I'd get some solid rest. Besides, the digging would keep me warm.

I chose a spot and started to dig with an avalanche-rescue shovel. A sharp, low wind was picking up; it blew straight across the snowfield, blurring the ground with blown snow. It felt like standing in a cloud.

The cave was nothing fancy. I had made a dozen like it before. First I dug a hole straight down, chest deep. Then I hopped into the hole and began to carve a tunnel sideways from the bottom, extending out in an L shape. This was the chamber I would sleep in, a cocoon just long and wide enough for my sleeping bag, just tall enough that if I lifted my head, my nose scraped the ceiling. I finished around the time that the next watch, my friend Iselin, stumbled from her tent. I wished her luck, then started the long process of maneuvering into the hole.

First, standing in the vertical entryway, I put on all the

clothing I had and zipped the sleeping bag around me. It strained to close over my parka. For a moment I stood like that, bundled and warm in the polar night. Then I crouched, threaded the foot of my sleeping bag into the bottom of the L, and wiggled the rest of my body in inch by inch. Finally horizontal, I propped my backpack behind my head, to trap the warm air. The wind moaned across the mouth of the hole.

For a split second, I felt a flash of panic: I was lying in a coffin. No. No, I wasn't. I took a deep breath and turned off my headlamp. The snow hugged me from all sides. I wrenched my arm from my sleeping bag and touched, in the darkness, the ceiling a few inches above my face. It was slick, like ice. Already my breath had smoothed it.

I was warm. I was comfortable. I was, I hoped, polar bear proof. I was in a shelter I had made myself, to take care of myself. I was at the top of the world. I was—wasn't I?—tough.

The thoughts relaxed my still-racing heart, and before I could think much more, I fell asleep.

I woke to voices and footsteps far above me.

"Where is she?"

"She never came in the tent last night."

It was pitch black and I couldn't move. My sleeping bag cinched tight around my face, so that only my nose poked out, but I couldn't reach up to untie it. No room to bend my arm. And something was blocking my hand. Oh: a baffle cinched around my neck. I fumbled to release the bow that tied the baffle, then reached my face, untied that, too. Cool air stroked my forehead. Where was my light?

More voices now. "Did *you* see her?"

My light was on my chest. I switched it on. Two flickers, and then a dim circle appeared on the snow just above me. Much too cramped in here. Got to roll over. I shimmied against the ground, landed facedown, and arched my back to lift my head. The snow was lumpy under me, hardened to the shape of my body. I wiped off my face. There was my backpack, empty. I reached out one hand to shove it away so I could climb out. But the bag didn't move.

I snaked my hand past it and felt packed snow.

Fully awake in an instant, I understood. I saw, in a series of flashes, last night's wind sweeping snow across the plain. The snow packed, layer upon layer, into the entrance to my hole. The entrance smoothed over, as if it was never there. And then, flashing forward, I saw myself trying to dig into the tunnel with my hands, burrowing my way out, and the packed snow expanding as I scraped it from the wall, filling my airspace, smothering me before I could reach the surface.

My light was flickering again. I switched it off, lay still in the darkness. Then I pulled my arm back into my sleeping bag and reknotted the neck baffle. I couldn't move. Shouldn't lose warmth.

One, two, three. As loud as I could: "HELP!"

Nothing.

Now the footsteps were coming back. I recognized the voices. "She goes for walks alone," someone said.

"Not here." Oda's voice was high. "She's not crazy."

"Down here!" I shouted.

"Who saw her last?"

They couldn't hear me.

I closed my eyes—not that it made a difference—and counted my breaths. I wondered about oxygen.

Snow held plenty of oxygen. That's what everyone said.

One.

Two.

Three.

Four.

Five.

"Iselin saw her."

"Iselin saw her?"

Six.

Seven.

But Iselin *had* seen me. And now her voice joined the choir.

"Guys, she was digging."

"Where?"

Eight.

Nine.

"Over here."

Ten.

Eleven.

Twelve.

The sound of scraping, coming closer.

Thirteen.

A lump of snow fell from the ceiling and landed on my legs.

"RIGHT HERE!" I bellowed.

"Blair? Are you okay? Answer me!"

"Iselin?"

She said something quietly. Then—"Oh my God. We'll get you out."

More digging, more snow falling onto my bag. And then, with a burst of frigid air, the ceiling opened above me and I found myself staring into a circle of headlamps. Arms reached down and lifted me out.

The rest of spring passed quickly, rolling downhill toward May. Suddenly I was faced with the prospect of leaving, or maybe returning; I wasn't sure what was home, what was away. I had found something here, some surprising strength, but that strength was utterly dependent on this place, with its howling dogs, its dark days and white nights. When I left, I feared that that part of myself would be peeled away, too. I stood in the dog yard and tried to look forward: I saw college orientation, lectures, dorm room parties. What did people do in college? Hook up? There would be no dogs, no snow caves, no space, nothing to force my body through and come out triumphant. Some of the other students had found ways to stay with dogs, taking jobs at kennels around Norway, but my visa was running out, and besides, I had promised my parents I'd come back to the States. It all spread out before me: I saw this year—this year!—as having been one brief phase in a life that would soon return to its predictable trajectory. But it felt more like a beginning, the start of something that could easily be lost. So, one insomniac night, I sat up looking for jobs on SledDogCentral.com.

One in particular stood out. Iditarod finalist Noah Daron was looking for experienced mushers for his summer tour company. The mushers would live with their dogs on a glacier in southeast Alaska, at a camp only accessible by helicopter. I pictured myself atop an icefield, surrounded by huskies, impressing tourists day after day until their idea of me eclipsed who I actually was. Playing a role that would be my life. I filled out an application immediately, trying to put the best possible spin on what felt like my rather limited experience.

Noah called me on the school pay phone. His voice was friendly but firm. Though I hadn't had many job interviews before, this one struck me as unconventional. What one thing would I want if stranded on a desert island? A notebook and pen, I answered. If the staff was trapped on the glacier for an extended period of time, what would I do to increase morale? Um—organize a snow-sculpture competition. "We've never lost an employee," Noah told me, "yet." On the glacier, I would live in a tent city with nine other mushers, each of us responsible for twenty dogs. I'd give eight hour-long tours each day for the appealing salary of $11 an hour, plus plenty of overtime. My regular shifts would run six days on, three days off, but it was possible that I'd be stuck on the ice for up to a month at a time: in foggy southeast Alaska, the helicopters couldn't always fly. Though the glacier was covered in snow, the snowcover thinned over the course of the season, and there was a real chance of falling into an unseen crevasse at any time. In an emergency, there would be no guarantee of help arriving. Was I still interested?

Obviously.

"Then welcome to Dog World."

CHAPTER FOUR

MORTENHALS. MY PHONE RANG AT NIGHT as I lay curled in my orange bed above the shop. "I know you," said an unfamiliar man's voice on the line. "You're the girl who likes stories."

"I think so," I said.

"Listen," said the voice. "I'm inviting you and fifteen young people to sail for five days in my wooden boat. There will be acoustic guitars in the evenings. We leave next Friday."

"Who are you?"

"I've heard people talking about you."

"I can't go," I said. "I have to work in the Old Store. Who are you?"

"Think about it," said the voice. "You don't know me, but you've probably heard of my former boat *Vulcana*."

"I'm afraid I haven't heard of a lot of boats."

The voice paused. "Oh. Well, people have been talking about you. They say you're fair, a fair person. That makes me interested." Another pause. I wasn't sure when to answer. "You'll hear from me again."

Dial tone.

I went into the living room, where Arild had come back from the barn and was watching the news. There was a close-up of a runner panting with his hands on his knees. Arild leaned forward, watching. The runner, explained a disappointed female voice-over, had been caught doping.

"Look at this," Arild said, without turning from the screen. "Caught doping. And where do you think he's from?"

"I don't know," I said, though I knew.

" . . . *the American runner* . . ."

"Oh ho!" said Arild. "A*mer*ica!"

"Arild," I said, "I just got a phone call from a man who owned a boat called *Vulcana*."

"What?" He reached for the remote and turned off the TV. "Helge Jensen called you? How did he get your number?"

"I don't know. He invited me on a trip but I said no."

"You know, if you fly Norwegian Air, you can look in the magazine on the flight and there's an article about that boat. It's——" He stopped. Helge Jensen, he said, was the closest thing to an old-fashioned cowboy that Malangen had ever had.

"You mean like a Viking?"

"No, like a cowboy. Once, his ship sank far out at sea, far past the islands, and he lay there alone in his lifeboat floating out to sea for hours and hours, all alone, shivering, and when finally he was rescued the reporters all asked him how it was, you know, and he said it was hell. Yes, they said, tell us more, how was it hell? And his lighter had got wet, you know, when the ship sank, so he couldn't light his cigarette."

I waited.

"That's all," said Arild. "That was his hell. Not that he was floating into the sea! But that he couldn't even light a cigarette. Another thing about Helge Jensen is he has that hair." Then Arild abruptly got bored with the subject and turned the TV back on. But the next morning he told every person who sat at the coffee table that Helge Jensen had called she Blair. Everyone had their own story, or a different version of someone else's story, and all of the stories, it seemed, were secondhand. "Helge *Jensen*," said Odd Jonny, a regular. "With the hair! You, that ship he has, it sank three times last year alone. Like the *Titanic*. It just doesn't float. Once he was out to sea and had only this tiny little raft where his feet hung off the edge, and his boat was entirely gone, and he just lay there drifting with his feet in the water. They picked him up hours later and he said it was like hell—his lighter had gotten wet and he couldn't light a smoke."

"I heard that," I said. "Arild told me."

Odd Jonny didn't slow down. "So the next time his ship sank, he swam to shore with his lighter taped on top of his head."

"On his head," repeated Rune.

"Uh-huh," said Odd Jonny. "And another time in the middle of winter he sank in a fjord with three men and a dog. But the dog got stuck on a rock and couldn't swim, so Helge Jensen swam all the way back out so the dog could ride on his back. The men on the shore said it looked like the dog was standing on top of the water."

Arild was impressed. That was a new story for him.

Anne Lill was the only one who didn't seem excited. "I'm glad you're not going with him," she said. "Those people use drugs."

That afternoon, a storm like a black curtain slid up the fjord, and talk in the shop was of rivals: the shop in Sand was faltering. No one was vulgar enough to celebrate the competing shop's struggles, but it was understood that those struggles would certainly not *harm* the business of Johannes Kristoffersen's Descendants.

The Sand Shop was nearly identical to Arild's in size, wares, and even shopkeepers, who were only months apart in age, and grew up together. In fact, Egil and Arild had been good friends as boys, bonded as shopkeepers' sons, before their family businesses pulled them onto parallel paths on either side of the small river. They had not laid eyes on each other in years. Their clientele, with loyalties passed down through generations, did not intermingle. With the exception of a few known drunks who bought beer at both shops to seem like they were buying less, anyone entering the "wrong" shop without an obvious reason was grounds for weeks of gossip. This peninsula-wide division struck me as a brilliant strategy for keeping alive two businesses that should not, in fact, exist so close to each other, but when I floated this theory by the men at the coffee table, they scoffed. Strategy? They stuck by their shop because it was better. Arild's shop had the coffee table; Egil's response had been to add some cafe tables and a coffee dispenser in the back of his own shop, but the beverages were more for caffeine than community, and the tables were usually empty. There were rumors that Egil ran a speakeasy out of his basement called the Nice Boys' Club, but of these, none at the coffee corner would speak. "*I* wouldn't know," said He the Rich One sadly when I asked, but then he brightened—"Darling, does that mean you're asking me on a date?"—and it took groans from around the table and a whack from Anne Lill's flyswatter to dishearten him again.

Lately, there had been murmurs of change in Sand. Egil's supplier was considering cutting off its northern stores, and it seemed unlikely that Arild's supplier would cater to two competing shops in such proximity. Besides, Egil struggled with his health, and was perhaps already slipping. In fact, just last week, a number of strangers had come to Arild's shop and purchased only bananas. "Aha," said Arild, regarding with pleasure his full banana shelf, "he Egil has run out of bananas." But his pride was too hasty. Soon the increased demand exhausted his own fruit, and he had to make an emergency trip to Tromsø to save face. If

WELCOME TO THE GODDAMN ICE CUBE / 91

only one shop was to survive, fate would decide the outcome, but Arild wasn't about to leave fate to chance.

There were murmurs of other change in Sand, too. Martin's house had sat empty since his death, but no longer—his sister Martha had moved in, and she was American. Though she was born on the peninsula, she'd moved to Florida ages ago, fallen in love with a Mexican man, and raised three children on Cuban food. Now she was back, though no one had seen her yet; they gathered her presence through glimpses of a brown-haired boy on a bicycle and a little dog—"One of those carpet pissers," Rune reported. Most recently, someone had hung a Norwegian flag in front of the house. The flag seemed like a message, and the men were suspicious. Why would the American hang a Norwegian flag? What did she want? What did it mean?

A boom of thunder jolted everyone out of speculating. The rain came hard and suddenly, pounding the street in a heavy wall, splattering through the open door. A moment later, a flash, and the lights went out; the buzzing freezers fell silent. The stunned quiet around the table only highlighted the noise of the storm—pouring water and a long groan of thunder that ended in a sharp crack. I peered out the dark window but could not see the fjord through the rain.

"The last such storm," announced He the Rich One, "the water sucked all the way back off the beach. I ran down with a bucket and picked the fish off the sand. They were *jo* just flopping there. Fish for days."

"Nah," said Nils.

"You weren't alive," said He the Rich One. Another clap of thunder sounded, and he looked out the dark window and sighed. "What I don't understand," he said, "is why we all don't live in Mallorca."

Arild opened the ice-cream freezer and stuck his hand in, testing. The cold would hold, but what if it didn't? He pulled out a handful of bars and passed them around the table. Ice cream for everyone. The Sailor preferred coffee, himself, and took the opportunity to pour the last drops from the thermos before anyone else could get to them. He handed his ice-cream bar to a little boy who sat at the end of the table, on his father's lap. This was a tiny solemn child who did everything with great deliberation, and had the kind of pointy upper lip peculiar to small boys and certain reptiles. Now he had two ice creams. He held one in each hand and gazed up at the Sailor, paralyzed by choice.

"Wasn't long ago," said the Sailor, "that that trailer blew from Senja and landed in Roald's yard."

The island of Senja was just south of Malangen, closer to the open sea and weatherhard. The houses there were packed close together, their seaward walls protected with sheets of metal, their roofs tied with thick ropes to boulders to keep from blowing away. Tides churned through narrow passages, swirling into maelstroms. That a trailer should blow from a field in Senja and float away astonished no one, except for the man who found it in his yard.

When the rain slowed, the customers got up to run for their cars, calling after them—"Thanks for the ice cream!" and "I'll pay for my groceries later." Rune watched them go. He tried to pour some coffee and was disappointed to find the thermos empty. The boy had left his second ice cream behind. It was vanilla, in a sideways cone shaped like a boat—Arild's favorite. Rune unwrapped it and took a bite. No sooner had the cars driven away than the skies opened again and the rain poured back down.

Now we were three. We sat and gazed out the window.

"He's raining," I said. I was practicing my dialect.

Rune beamed at me and stood up. "Yes," he said. "That's what he's doing."

A minute later, a flash and a boom, so loud that I screamed. The air seemed to ring with echo. A bolt of lightning—no, a web—had lit the sky, extending to the earth. Though its branches seemed to arc over the whole village, it did not strike the folk school, with its peaked roof, or the church on the hill, with its steeple, or even Rune, who had stepped outside and stood alone on the rain-splashed concrete, his first shower in weeks. No. With the precision of a curse, the lightning had touched its sizzling finger to the Sand Shop.

After the storm ended, I cleaned. There were branches strewn over the road, knots of seaweed on the front steps of the shop. Some sheep had come down from the mountains and crowded into the barn, and I chased them up the hill past the church, hoping they'd walk the rest of the way themselves. "Next time they come down," Arild swore, "I'll write down their numbers and send them for meat." But he'd said that the last time, too. He had enough difficulty sending the lambs to slaughter as it was.

One morning, while browsing a history book, Arild found a picture of a millstone stand—a little table with a spout—and enlisted Rune to build a replica for the Old Store. But the picture was a line drawing, imprecise, and Rune built the spout without any downward tilt. When Arild suggested to Rune that perhaps the spout should angle downward to enable the flow of grain, Rune threw his hammer onto the grass and stormed away. This was typical of Rune, to abandon a project right before completion. Rune stayed away for three days, the longest he'd been gone in months, until I went to his house to talk him down. His house was recognizable by the careful heaps of firewood and sticks that adorned his lawn, steps, and—once indoors—his living room. "You have a lot of wood," I told him, and he beamed, pleased that I'd noticed. I assured him that his millstone stand was excellent.

Mollified, Rune returned that afternoon, finding me outside the Old Store, where I was planting flowers by the entrance in a cast-iron pot. He reeked of beer and carried a stone in his arms. He was agitated. "You see the boat?" he said.

A small motorboat drifted in the water not far from shore, with three standing figures in it. The boat was blue and white, part of a fleet that belonged to the Brygger, an ostentatiously minimalist resort and conference center between Mortenhals and Mestervik. The resort was only five years old, and enormous— eighty cabins and hotel rooms, glassy by the shore, built to capitalize on business retreats and fishing tourism from Russia and Eastern Europe. But as it turned out, demand for luxury accommodations on Malangen was less robust than hoped.

"Yeah," I said.

"They're Germans," he said, "watching us."

"How can you tell they're German?"

"Germans stand up to fish," said Rune. "That's why so many of them drown."

There was nothing to do but agree with him. I asked about the stone in his arms.

"It's an antique," Rune said. "For to sharpen knives." It looked like any old stone off the beach. He wouldn't tell me where he'd found it. "No," he explained, "because then they'll take it, the folks from Tromsø. They think they should have all the old things that still exist." His wiped his mouth with the back of his hand.

"I think it'll be okay," I said.

"No," said Rune. "It's from Malangen. What's Malangen's is Malangen's." He liked the way that sounded, so he repeated it, more forcefully: "What's Malangen's is Malangen's!"

"Where should we put it?" I asked.

Rune's face was red. He looked around the Old Store. Then he shook his head: it was too risky to leave the stone. The folks from Tromsø might find it. He walked away, hugging the antique knife sharpener to his chest. He was going to

Martin's grave, he told me, and I promised that next time I'd come along.

Rune wasn't the only one with an artifact to share. One neighbor donated a yarn winder, another brought a box of carpentry tools. Later that week a car pulled up and a figure stepped into the doorway and regarded me. I recognized him from the shop—he was the customer I called the Sailor.

The Sailor was a thin man with a small, puffy face, who wore white T-shirts and clogs that were always at risk of slipping off. He sat quietly at the table for hours, exuding an air of exhausted relief, as if he had just received bad news that nonetheless lifted a great uncertainty. For thirty years he had traveled, an able-bodied seaman, through all the world's seas and lands: dancing in nightclubs in Hong Kong, trapping seals on bergs in the Arctic Ocean, exploring the endless streets of New York City. Then seven years ago, in his fifties, he'd gotten epilepsy, and just like that, his sailing days were over. Now he lived alone near his childhood farm, stopped by the shop in the mornings, rode his motorcycle to the city if the weather was nice. I'd asked him, once, if he missed the ocean. He had turned and stared at me long enough for me to understand that the question had been a mistake. "Can you even imagine," he said. I had to look away.

Now the Sailor smelled like beer, too. "I have something to donate," he said. "I found it. To hang from the ceiling."

I was experimenting with a new arrangement of stockings, and I put down the garter belt I'd been folding. "What is it?"

"A nail," said the Sailor.

I was supposed to say something, but I couldn't tell what, so I just waited.

"Nobody's going to believe it's a nail," the Sailor said. He went to his car and came back with a rusty spike as long as his forearm. I climbed on a chair and hung it near the door with a piece of string. The Sailor watched approvingly. "Nobody will believe it's a nail," he said again, in case I hadn't gotten the joke, and then he stood in the doorway for a while and watched me fold stockings. "You!" he said, after a long time, and when I looked at him he turned his gaze out the window, and opened his mouth, and left without saying a word.

My final task in the Old Store was to sort through the back room, which had been the shop's storage room. I stacked children's clothes with American-inspired labels—Cowboy Pants, Alaska Parka—on a shelf made of dynamite boxes. I hung sealskin-covered skis over a cracked window that overlooked the pasture. On the back wall I arranged a jigsaw puzzle of tools: scythes, nets, herring flashers, shoulder yokes. As a final touch I balanced some plywood on herring barrels, and on this makeshift surface I spread everything else: a carved butter mold and a sugar cutter, some baskets, a spindle. Then I stepped back.

It looked like a bunch of junk on a table.

It was as if something in my gaze had shifted. This was not a magical time-traveling world. It was a cluttered storage room, the back of someone's closet. I closed my eyes and opened them again, willing the magic back. It was a well-organized garage.

"This is a museum," I said aloud. "These are artifacts."

Briefly, back in the States, I had volunteered at an Arctic museum in Oregon. I missed the north, and it felt good to be surrounded by stuffed polar bears and musk oxen, parkas and knives. I curated an exhibit about Sápmi. But it was disarming to arrange behind glass the very objects I had used for survival, to touch with white gloves the same kind of reindeer-skin boots I had recently used for slogging through the dog yard. In the end, the museum, which I had hoped would connect me to the north, only served to remind me of how very far away I was.

"She likes old things," Arild told people when they asked about my work in the Old Store. And it was true, I guess; I liked the Old Store, liked the way it captured a time that felt close but absent, a sun just slipped behind a mountain. But my passion for the project was less about an inherent fascination with history than it was about creating a place to belong. I wanted to make the Old Store because I wanted to be part of the village.

Every day, Mortenhals felt more like home. When I walked past the barn, and the lambs, bleating, bumped into the backs of my legs. When Rune and Nils and He the Rich One wanted to talk to me. When I went for a hike in the mountain village and came back to find customers wondering where I had been.

And that was what made the magic: that in every decision, every scythe hung on the wall, I was building myself closer to Malangen. I had come and gone before. But now I was the museum director, albeit of a shack behind a barn. Now there was something here that wouldn't exist without me. And if the Old Store was important for Malangen, as I believed it was, then so was I.

STAGE TWO IN MISSION: ARCTIC EXPLORER STARTED, auspiciously enough, with a private helicopter ride to the dogsled camp on the glacier. The world shrank away, the roofs of Juneau tiny between mountains, the tremble of the rotors both violent and thrilling. A line of cruise ships on the waterfront below shone bright as a string of pearls, the turquoise of their on-deck swimming pools garish against the dark marbled water of the Gastineau Channel. The pilot shouted to me about his new kit Lamborghini. Sometimes he borrowed a lead dog, he said, who liked to ride in the passenger seat with her head out the window at ninety, a hundred miles an hour. It was epic.

We flew over stony mountains, dark green and gray, dustings of snow that grew into snowy peaks that in turn stretched down into a great white valley. The icefield was like water, pressed around the islands of mountaintops. Monochromatic and

bare. A desert, a moonscape—I found myself groping for a meta-
phor, trying to make sense of the alien world that extended to
the far horizon. I didn't notice the camp until we were almost
directly overhead. The tour trails made five concentric rings just
slightly darker than the snow around them. These were the con-
fines of Dog World, a speck of dirt on a vast sea.

As the helicopter descended, I could make out more of the
camp: a cluster of white wall tents alongside a grid of white doghouses, which were arranged into ten kennels. Figures walked
between the kennels, dogs paced and rolled, a snowmobile drove
along one side. In a moment we landed, a bump on snow, an
American flag nearby whipping in the rotor wash. Before the
rotors had stopped moving, a bearded man pulled open the helicopter door and waved to me furiously. He took my hand to help
me out.

The man wore bulging reflective sunglasses with leather
sides and a black nose flap. He looked like a serial killer. Glacier
goggles, to prevent snow blindness—they'd been on Noah's list
of recommended gear, and I'd bought my own, though at the
time I couldn't imagine needing them. Now, squinting, I pulled
my goggles from my backpack and put them on. I followed the
man past the rows of dogs to the cluster of wall tents at the far
end of the kennel. The snow was coarse and soft, and I tripped
where my feet punched through, though I tried to catch myself
before the man noticed. He stopped at a tent and waited until I
caught up. "Here's yours," he said. "Jimmy'll bring your luggage
on a snow machine." The tent had a plywood floor and three
army cots, two of which had sleeping bags on them. I dumped
my backpack on the third.

Since it was my first day, the man said, he'd give me an hour
or two to get settled. At lunchtime I would meet the other mushers. Then someone would introduce me to my dog team. After
that? "Full speed."

He stepped out onto the snow, then looked back. "One more thing," he said.

"Yeah?"

"Watch out for glacier snakes."

Before I could ask, he was gone.

The afternoon passed in a blur of instructions and deep snow and twenty new dogs—their names, how fast could I learn their names?—and five helicopters like birds growing over the mountains and whipping us with wind, disgorging stunned and immaculate tourists who blinked as much as I did, the birds sinking back into the distant air to reemerge an hour later with a new supply of blinking humans. There were systems for feeding, for harnessing the dogs, for booties, for greeting the tourists, for heating water, for melting snow, for scooping shit, for pounding the shit into barrels, for the barrels to be slung back to Juneau on long dangling ropes. Figures strode through the snow, purposeful and foreign. My tours would start the next morning—eight per day—and then there was dog care and kennel care and people care, a thousand chores for the thousand tasks needed to keep the camp running. Finally—the last helicopters gone, the dogs fed, and the kennel cleaned—I followed the other begoggled figures toward the dining tent for dinner.

The dining tent was a taller wall tent with three picnic tables inside. I sank onto a bench, too tired to do anything except eat the meat loaf and gravy that came from the kitchen tent next door. The tent was full of chatter, mushers comparing tours and tip money, managers laying out plans for the next day. There were fifteen of us—ten mushers, two managers, two assistants, and the cook. Everyone had goggle tans; most everyone wore a mix of faded shirts and zinc-smeared wind pants and high-tech gear from sponsors. After eating, the others scattered for evening chores: grooming trails, washing dishes, cleaning outhouses. I could not even imagine standing up. My mind spun from the landscape; my legs were rubbery from trudging through the snow; my arms ached from hauling buckets. And yet the others had been working since six that morning. As I would, tomorrow. I watched them walk out into the white.

As the tent emptied, one man stood from a nearby table and joined me on my bench. He was strong looking, with a friendly face and a streak of sunscreen down one cheek. He was from British Columbia. His name was Dan. He shook my hand and smiled.

I smiled back.

Dan wanted to know all about me, and I answered readily, relieved to put my mind somewhere more familiar. I told him about the folk school, that I'd just arrived from Norway. "We always got into problems with reindeer," I told him. "They don't know how to get out of the way. They'll just, like, run between the lead dogs. And then they get eaten." Dan was laughing, which gave me confidence. "That's one good thing about the glacier. No reindeer."

"Nope," he said. "Nothing alive here but two hundred crazy dogs and some even crazier people. Then there's the tourists." He pronounced it funny: tur-ist. "And if you stick around long enough, we get two ravens in July." When he saw my face, he leaned close. "Aw. Gary told you about glacier snakes, didn't he?"

I shrugged.

Dan pursed his lips. "People get weird on the ice. You can't take them all seriously." He nodded his head toward the door. "And as you might have gathered, we don't get a lot of girls up here. How old are you, anyway?"

"I just turned nineteen." Already it seemed so long ago— my birthday at the folk school, two weeks before. Had I really just been there?

"Wow," said Dan. "You look older."

There was a rumble outside. The trail groomers were back

from their chore. Some guy came into the dining tent and started smearing peanut butter on a slice of bread. Dan and I both stood. It was late, but I reached for my goggles again; everything was so bright.

"Hey," he said, as we turned toward our respective tents. "The first day is exhausting. You'll catch up fast."

"I hope so."

"If anyone gives you trouble, come to me."

"Yeah?"

"Yeah," said Dan. "I try to help people out."

"EXCUSE ME, SIR," ARILD TOLD RUNE when he walked in. "You passed it. First aisle by the door, second shelf from the bottom. Let me know if you have any questions."

"Huh?" said Rune.

"Yes," said Arild. "We sell soap."

Rune stood frozen, then started to giggle. "*You*," he said, and sat down at the table. It was true: He reeked. He the Rich One scooted his chair back.

It was early still, and the cars outside glistened with frozen dew. I took a sugar cube from the box on the table and tucked it behind my teeth, sucked coffee through it. Sweet.

Nils spoke up. "You know, she Blair and I are getting married."

So he remembered.

"Yeah so?" said He the Rich One.

"Yeah," said Nils. "Then she'll move to Malangen. To the richest country in the world."

Rune glanced at me.

My sugar cube was gone, and I felt with my tongue for any last grains. No. It was gone. "Then I can get citizenship," I said. "But the deal was that after five years, Nils will hit me, right? Since then we can get divorced and I'll get to keep living here.

So we can get married, and then five years later he'll be a real gentleman, just hit me once, maybe not that hard, of course, but maybe he'll leave a bruise—enough that I can complain about it—"

"She *pia*'s getting cheeky," He the Rich One said, pleased.

I felt strange, suddenly antsy. Rune was flipping through yesterday's *Northern Light* and Arild leaned back with his hands on his stomach and Nils was grinning into his coffee, but it seemed they were all looking at me. I stood up and went to the back hallway, where the day's breads were done baking, and I slid each loaf into a plastic bag. The crusts were hot and flaky and felt good to grip. I brought out all five loaves at once, cradled like babies in my arms, and by the time I got back to the table Nils had left and Rune was out having a smoke.

That was better. I sat back down.

That Saturday we opened the Old Store. I hung a poster on the side of the barn: OLD STORE MUSEUM, OPEN TODAY 12–4. WAFFLES INCLUDED WITH TICKET. Arild had put an ad in the paper. Now there was nothing to do but wait.

Arild was nervous all morning, though he wouldn't say why. He was quiet over coffee, and kept glancing out the window at the cars that slowed or pulled into his lot. When he mixed the waffle batter, he added an extra tub of sour cream in his distraction. I cooked the waffles in the storage room with an iron that imprinted the words NEAR-STORE onto each one. "If nobody comes," Arild suggested, "you and I can have a waffle party."

By the time I'd used up the sour batter, it was almost noon, and I carried the platter to the museum, propped open the door, and tried to think inviting thoughts. For a while nothing happened. Then one car pulled up, and another, and by the time I greeted each arrival, three or four more had crowded in. They came from the mountain village, from Tromsø, from Storsteinnes, from farther east. I tried to corral the crowd to give the tour that I'd prepared—a lecture on Mortenhals, on the old ways, including a series of facts and dates that I'd jotted on my wrist—and to show off my favorite artifacts, like the little brass bloodletter, which with the flick of a switch cut eighteen slices in a patient's arm; or the corpse chairs, which were said to creak when a new body was on its way to the church to be buried. But no sooner did I try to raise my voice than it was drowned out by some new exclamation: "I bet this is worth a lot," or "Heavens me, buttons! Look, Solveig! Buttons!" A little boy ran around the edge of the room, reaching into the syrup barrel and the jar of shoe nails, and I winced as he started winding the gramophone with greasy waffle fingers; but the worst touchers, by far, were the old folks, who had clumped into groups of two or three and turned over the shoes and chocolates and hairpins that they remembered from their youth. How could I tell them not to touch? A woman had tears in her eyes. "We had these," she kept saying, and I was struck with the absurdity of the thought that I could ever imagine this museum as more mine than hers.

"We didn't know Arild took care of all this," people kept telling me. "All this history." But the Old Store had never been a secret. He'd opened it once before, sixteen years ago, for the shop's one-hundred-year anniversary. He'd set up a dance floor, hayrides, hot dogs for everyone. Hundreds of people traveled from all over; a wedding party at the church had come down the hill to join the festivities; his youngest daughter, Emma, had dressed up in his aunt Aud Unn's purple dress. Arild had been particularly impressed by the willingness of a certain neighbor to plan and manage the celebration. With his help, the whole community came together.

Not long after, Arild's wife left him for the neighbor. That was the worst part: that the whole community had already known.

After a few hours, the crowd in the Old Store thinned. The

lambs bawled outside the window. I walked along the shelves, straightening, and fitted a board back over the broken window. When I turned around, a new woman had come in. I'd never seen her before. She stood in the middle of the shop with a camera, taking pictures of every wall.

"Hi!" I said. "Welcome to the Old Store. Admission is fifty kroner."

"I don't want to come in," she said. "I was just taking pictures."

She was already in, but I didn't feel like arguing. Now she looked at me strangely. "Who are you? Where are you from?"

I straightened my posture. "I'm the museum director. From America."

"The *museum* director? I see. You're Martha's daughter."

"No." Now I didn't like her.

The woman took one more picture, then slipped her camera into her purse and left.

I didn't think much about the encounter. It was only later, when I recounted the day to Arild and he asked if I'd had any problems, that I remembered the woman. When I told him what had happened, his face grew slack. How old was she? he asked. Did I get her name? What car did she drive? I shook my head. She was maybe in her sixties. I hadn't noticed anything else.

"Really, it's okay," I said. "She didn't bother me. We don't even want her fifty kroner!"

Arild turned away. "The lambs are hungry," he said. "Can you find them on your own? They're medium size, dark faces, say 'baa'?"

It was custom to stop feeding nursing lambs once they were big enough to survive on their own, but Arild's feeding schedule showed no signs of waning, and the job fell mostly to me. "If they die, she dies," I had overheard him telling customers at least twice. I tracked down the fat things behind the barn.

When I got back to the shop, there were two forked sticks on the steps. They were labeled with Post-its: Water Finder (Large) and Water Finder (Small). I had just lifted the small one when Arild came out the side door and picked up the other himself. He seemed brisk, as if intent on distracting himself.

"You know I don't believe in most of that foolishness," he said, "but blood stopping and water finding, I have *jo* trust in those. I haven't done it myself in many years. We'll see if I re-member."

He led me out by the diesel pump and pointed to a crack in the asphalt. The crack had a water pipe underneath it, he said. The stick would find the pipe. It was just a matter of grip-ping the forked ends of the water finder and bending them out-ward, so that the point wobbled in the air. When you passed over water, the point would swing down. Arild backed up a few paces, then walked forward over the crack. Sure enough, his water finder tipped down.

"Now you try," he said. "And in case it's not clear, I didn't do anything. It does that *jo* by itself." He held out his palms to show where the stick's movement had scratched his skin. A pearl of blood had formed on one of the scratches.

I gripped the water finder and crossed the asphalt, stepping over the crack. But the stick didn't move.

"Walk more slowly," Arild suggested.

So I did. I walked as slowly as I could. I walked with my eyes closed. I walked backward. I walked over a puddle by the leaking garden hose, in case my water finder needed a more ob-vious hint. I even tried to cheat, and swing the stick down my-self, and then I traded with Arild and tried his. But the water finders would not find for me.

It was late at night, the sun small, the air still. Somewhere on the fjord the quick gasp of a porpoise carried over the water. Used to be that men sat out on the dock with guns, waiting for a porpoise to breach so they could shoot it for dinner. The trick was to shoot on the second breach, after the porpoise had air in its lungs. Otherwise it would just sink. I knew. Of course I knew. I had heard the stories.

We both turned to look, but the surface was glassy, a trap-door to the sky.

"Arild," I said. "Who was the woman with the camera?"

He held his water finder carefully. "I am afraid," he said, "that it was my sister."

CHAPTER FIVE

I T WAS THE DAY BEFORE MIDSUMMER and the shop was already out of milk, which was almost as bad as being out of butter on Christmas. How would the customers make rice porridge? Arild called Anne Lill to ask for help, but she was away at her second job, mopping floors in Mestervik. "You should have thought of that earlier," she told him, and he sank down at the table in despair. The Sand Shop's refrigerators had been out ever since the lightning strike, so Egil's customers had turned to him. He hadn't anticipated the double demand. How could he have known?

He the Rich One leaned forward. "I'll tell you what," he told Arild. "You stay here, I'll drive *pia* to the dairy and we'll get as many cartons as you want."

Arild gazed out the window. How He the Rich One tested him. He had recently acquired a box of grocery bags from He the Rich One's bankrupt shop, and took great satisfaction in using them when bagging the man's purchases. When He the Rich One objected, Arild feigned innocence—"Surely you've noticed that I use these these days? They're cheaper." Thrift was something that He the Rich One, who grew more careful with money the more of it he had, could begrudge no one.

"It's St. Hans," said He the Rich One. "Your customers need milk. And besides, *pia* and I can get some quality time together." He winked at me.

Over the past few weeks, He the Rich One and I had developed an exaggerated game of flirt and duck. He brought me gifts of cognac-smoked herring. "I missed you, darling. Comfort me?" he'd say, extending a leathery cheek for a kiss, and I'd pat it with my hand and dart away. He the Rich One was gifted with great subtlety of expression, and was particularly adept at looking wounded in such moments. I liked the games, which allowed me to express my lack of interest to the same degree that he expressed his interest. It felt like everything was on the table.

"Okay," I said. "I'll go along to get milk."

Arild started to hum.

"Come on, *Egil*," said He the Rich One, invoking Arild's rival shopkeeper.

"Yeah, Egil," I said. "Come on."

Arild lifted the thermos and shook it, checking for coffee. He glanced at the clock. A car slowed outside, then drove on by. "Blair," said Arild, "it's not that you must, but it would be greatly useful to me if you would watch the shop."

I nodded.

He the Rich One frowned. "You're not going to leave her here alone."

"Why not?" Of course I could handle the shop by myself.

He the Rich One leaned on his elbows. "You know what happens," he said, "is that six Romanians come and ransack the whole store. One of them takes care of *pia* and the rest just steal whatever they want. You'll be helpless to do anything. You just sit there and watch—if you're lucky."

"That doesn't happen," I said.

"Yes," said He the Rich One. "It happens often. I had *jo* a shop myself, remember? I know."

While we argued, Arild stood and walked out. I heard an engine start. In a minute, he passed by the window in his van. Then He the Rich One gathered his potatoes and cheese.

"Hold on," I said. "*You're* not leaving now."

"Of course I am," he said. "I have things to do. Don't worry about me, sweetie. I'll pay later once there's milk in this place."

I didn't *think* He the Rich One was right about the Romanians. That was silly. I'd been here a month and had never heard anything of the sort. I swiped a licorice coil from the candy bin and walked over to the counter, unwinding the coil with my teeth. I sat down in Arild's chair. It smelled like the tobacco that he kept behind the counter, hidden under a black garbage bag. I lifted the garbage bag to take a look. We were low on snus tobacco.

It was Monday, a quiet day in the shop. A few flies buzzed around the window. I flipped through *Northern Light*: Microsoft was building an office in downtown Tromsø. A Sami psychic offered her services at a discount.

The Sailor stopped by for a dozen beers. I wrote his debt in the book.

Some folk school students bought ramen, tobacco, and chocolate milk.

A woman walked in, clicking in high-heeled boots, her sweater unzipped to reveal ample cleavage and a shirt that read I Hope There's Room on the Red Carpet for My Tractor. Jeanette was one of the only young women around, tough and flirtatious. She had moved in with her boyfriend at sixteen, when he was thirty-seven; now, ten years later, the two had settled into each other with an ease that made them one of the most enviable couples on the peninsula. "She's a year older than you," Arild had once helpfully pointed out, "and she's got a man, three kids, two horses, six goats, and her own farm." But Jeanette was having a bad year. The kindergarten had reported her children to child protective services on the claim that she beat them. Jeanette and her boyfriend were fighting to reunite their family, but the going was slow. They split their days between driving from town to town to visit the divided children one by one. She was exhausted, but how could you rest when your children weren't home? Jeanette met my eyes, but she didn't sit down. She bought an energy drink and an ice-cream cone and left to eat them in the car.

The enthusiastic German organist, who had been recruited to the country with her husband as an employee of the church, stopped by for a bag of unsalted almonds. She had recently begun exploring a raw food diet, and she felt fantastic.

Then nobody came in for a while. I glanced at the clock: 12:00. Anne Lill would be back in an hour. I made some fresh coffee and rearranged the shoes on their shelves: high heels on top, work boots on the bottom. Arild sold them all for 200 kroner each, though some of the pairs were worth ten times that. I wrote down some fake prices—1,550, 2,100—and taped them to the soles of the nicer shoes, so they would seem like a better deal. Then I ate a yogurt.

It seemed like Romanians weren't what the shop had to worry about. Arild believed that his sister was out to run him into the ground.

The whole thing had started when he'd been running the shop with his son, Henning, a decade earlier. He and Henning had both been driving trucks on the side, and he supposed they hadn't kept track of the books, because money grew scarcer and scarcer. Finally, desperate, he'd asked his sister Ingeborg for a loan. "But she wanted, instead, that I should write the shop over to her so it couldn't be seized if we went bankrupt. She was my sister, you understand—I didn't know. She kept asking and asking. I wrote the land over but not the shop. Just to quiet her." Now they were embroiled in a years-long lawsuit: Ingeborg wanted to use the shop as her vacation home, and Arild wanted to keep running it. He said he would gladly share the property with her, and the profits, but he found her tactics disturbing; she had once, in a fury, tried to nail the door of the shop closed, and he also believed she had forged legal papers. The whole thing struck him as tragic, and he steeled himself with thoughts of tradition. Ingeborg might have been firstborn, but Arild was the firstborn son. Mortenhals was his land and his life, the only thing he had to defend.

On Midsummer, it rained. There were no bonfires, no late nights, save a few hooded figures using the cover of St. Hans to burn their trash illegally on the beach. But at least the villagers had milk for their rice porridge, a proper festive meal for the longest day of the year.

In Alaska, we'd celebrated Midsummer for a different reason: it meant winter was on its way back. That was one of the rules: dogsledders' lives revolve around winter, and the glacier, for all its snow, was just a stopgap until fall. Of course, we told the tourists that the summer season was vital training for next spring's races. That enough tours could practically prepare a team for the Iditarod. The tourists liked to think that their participation was useful.

This was an excursion for which tourists paid $500 each—plus a fuel surcharge for those who weighed over 240 pounds. Most of the guides' earnings came from tips: twenties, fifties, or the occasional hundred folded tight and slipped into our jacket cuffs as we shook hands at tour's end. Our goal was to provide a luxury experience, a taste of Real Alaska! with absolutely no discomfort, either physical or mental. For instance, we were not supposed to reprimand the dogs when tourists were present.

We were discouraged from acknowledging climate change, even as the glacier melted away beneath us. We cleaned the kennel constantly so that tourists were spared the sight of a single piece of shit, and we raked up dog hair that collected on the snow, piling it in the Woolly Mammoth, an enormous mound hidden behind the tents. Our job was to provide the unspoken reassurance that everything was totally, 100 percent under control at all times.

It didn't take long for me to realize the falsity of the pretense. Those of us who lived on the glacier learned to expect nothing from the landscape, to adjust to its changes without question. We no longer jumped at the gunshot crack of avalanches on a sun-warmed afternoon. Turquoise lakes a half mile wide formed and vanished overnight. As the surface snow melted, the foundation under our camp sank steadily away, and we'd wake to find our tents, which were on skis, perched atop pedestals of hardened snow. The glacier was a closed cycle: if we ate cherries at lunch, we'd be picking their pits from the outhouse pump two days later—and getting a lecture from our manager about not swallowing the pits in the first place. On a bad day we called it the Goddamn Ice Cube. On a good day Summer Camp on the Moon.

One evening a storm came in, fast and hard, thunder booming from black clouds that swept low above our heads. Common knowledge had it that electrical storms rarely hit the icefield—I'd been told that in its ten-year history, the glacier camp had never seen one—but as we rushed for the community tent, a flame of lightning lit the south tongue of the glacier. Crouched on the tent's plywood floor, dripping and steaming, the staff realized, as one, that none of us knew if ice conducted electricity. Here we were, the tallest thing on the icefield, trapped—perhaps—on a conductor the size of Rhode Island. Lightning cracked again, closer, illuminating the tent walls with a flash of brilliant white. We stared at each other. Then—"Dogs," somebody said. The musher nearest the door flap jumped to his feet and ran into the wall of rain, but before anyone else could follow, the manager blocked the way. "No way," he said. "Nobody else is setting foot in that snow." I felt nauseous. Surely the dogs were in their plastic houses. Maybe plastic was better than plywood. We crouched there, eleven of us, listening, as the storm passed overhead. Twenty minutes later the sky opened pale blue.

The icefield, I decided, was hardly real, a snow globe repeatedly shaken so that everything was chaotic and everything was the same. The tours repeated themselves, the days repeated themselves, the weekends off-glacier came and went. My face and hands darkened. I grew muscles I'd never had.

It wasn't long before Dan and I were together. Of course we were. The relationship seemed to happen on its own, as natural a course of events as the avalanches tumbling from the mountains around us. Dan had an easy confidence that suggested he belonged here, on the ice, in a place where no one could truly belong. He had a sardonic humor and a handsome, boyish face, and seemed to me indiscriminately *older*, experienced and wise, though in fact we were only six years apart. Off-glacier, he invited me to restaurants or for walks on foggy beaches. On one of our first dates, he laid out his shirt for me to sit on, then sat beside me on the sand as the tide slipped in and the pearly cruise ships rolled from port and shrank into the gray distance. He was talking about his favorite lead dog; his fingers brushed mine, then lingered, and my skin burned where we touched. His hands were smaller than mine, smooth and compact, which only endeared him to me more. "Sometimes I'm not very good at saying things," he admitted, and took a breath. "Like right now. What I want to say is that you're beautiful, and I feel incredibly lucky to be here with you, and I like you a lot." Later we took a drive down the coastal road. Dan wanted to take some photos for his mother, so we stopped at an overlook with a few other tourists. When they left, I tipped up his cap and kissed him as if I'd been doing it for years, and his arms closed around my back and pulled me in against him.

Alaska! I liked Alaska.

I soon realized another benefit of being with Dan. Though there were a few female mushers, the men on the glacier domi-nated social life; their authority came with an edge of sexism that seemed at once inevitable and disconcerting. In my first weeks, men flicked their gaze down my body, then caught my eye and smiled. Someone walked behind me in the snow, and when I slowed to walk beside him, he urged me forward: "We don't get this kind of view much around here." I overheard muttered jokes about catching me alone on the trail. I shed the comments with a teenager's optimism, and was bothered mostly to the extent that they framed me as different, sug-gesting, with a smirk, that I didn't belong and was therefore unfit for glacier life. But I already loved the glacier—loved the absurdity of it all, the drama of helicopters and mountains and howling dogs, the way the endless bright, bare space made me feel at once strong and important. Standing on the ice, I felt like the beating heart of the whole glacier. And there were comments; so what?

But the murmur of violence that had colored my first weeks on the ice dissolved instantly with Dan's arm around my waist. Suddenly I counted: mushers held tent flaps open for me, laughed at my jokes, took my feedback into account as they discussed problems with their dog teams or tourists. If I felt, privately, that Dan's approval proved I belonged on the ice, that sentiment was only reinforced by the ways in which others seemed to believe it, too. And sure, we had a few off moments,

Dan and I: comments he made that seemed to edge into dis-respect, the language men use to set women apart. But in the moment, I thrilled at the prospect of my first real, grown-up boyfriend. Dan and I wrote each other notes and passed them back and forth in dog booties; during a rare free hour he helped me build a snow bear by the kitchen tent, with bleeding M&M eyes, that lasted until someone drove a snowmobile through it two days later. On days off, Dan drove me to get groceries, took me hiking on rainforest trails, and packed picnics for private beaches. "You're the nicest girl I ever met," he'd tell me, wink-ing at me between tours, mouthing my name over the roar of the helicopter, squeezing my hand as he kissed me good night. "How did I get a girl so nice?"

"I'm not nice," I'd say. I wouldn't have minded; it just didn't seem particularly true, not in this world of ice and dogs and work and men. But Dan would just laugh. He knew all about me, he said. He saw things that even I didn't know.

One weekend Dan bought a cheap tent so we could go camping on our days off, far from the dingy, gender-segregated apartments in Juneau that the company provided. What he meant, I knew, was that we could have sex. I'd never had sex before, and the prospect daunted me: How would I know what to do? What if it hurt? For a while I avoided the outing, main-taining that the last thing I wanted was to spend my days off in another tent. But after a few weeks I figured that I'd exhausted my reasonable waiting period, and so I finally agreed. I was nervous, but sex seemed like a good thing to check off my list, a logical extension of the adult world in which I found myself. I liked that Dan wanted me, and I liked what we *had* done together—making out in hidden corners, his hand trailing shivers up and down my ribs. He had a way of just barely kiss-ing me that sent heat through my whole body. That restraint from—what? Desire was as foreign a world to me as the glacier, and Dan seemed a worthy guide. He had played baseball and hockey, and though his muscles held the memory of training, solid and strong, he was gentle when he held me, brushed the hair from my face.

We left Juneau at 9 P.M.—night, although it wouldn't be dark for another hour—and drove to a campground across a lake from the Mendenhall Glacier. We didn't really talk in the car. At one point we passed a porcupine on the side of the road, and Dan pulled over to take a look. The porcupine was fat and yellowish, its quills like a halo. Dan said a few words about taking off his shirt and tossing it onto the porcupine, a trick that Chad, another musher, had told us about. The idea was that the porcupine would expel a few quills into the shirt, then wander away, leaving both shirt and quills behind. Then you had quills to keep. Chad had five or six, which he'd shown us over dinner one night. They were smooth and striped and I wanted Dan to get some for me, but he waited too long, and the porcupine waddled into a drainage pipe and was gone.

We didn't really talk in the tent, either. "It's not supposed to feel good the first time," Dan explained, though I hadn't expected it to. I lay back and waited. The sex was a strange feeling, like a fist had reached inside my gut and started punching. Dan was sweating, and drops fell on my stomach and arms. After a while his body got stiff, which meant he was done. "Don't worry, it's not supposed to feel good yet," he said again, and then he kissed my forehead and fell asleep beside me.

For being so cheap, the tent was pretty nice. A breeze ruffled the fly but the sides were taut, the dome high. It was darker here than on the glacier. I could see the shape of Dan's face pressed into the pillow we were sharing and I sat up and looked down at him and tried to figure out how I felt post-virginity.

He looked so defenseless, sleeping. It repulsed me slightly.

Mostly I felt blank, or faintly amused. So that was sex, and now I had tried it. I pretended to sleep, lying very still so as not to wake Dan, and opened my eyes after forever, when the shapes around me were a little easier to see. My fleece and pants were bunched at the foot of the tent. They were not the clothes I'd brought to Alaska, but rather men's clothes that I'd gotten at the Salvation Army on my first day off, after realizing that femininity wasn't doing me any favors. I knew how the men watched me. So I had bought men's Carhartts, button-up shirts, vests to cover the shape of my breasts, a sports bra to flatten them. Anything that might help me fit in. Dan said the new clothes made me look like a lesbian, but that he didn't mind.

Now I was grateful for their bagginess. I pulled on my pants an inch at a time. My sneakers were outside. I unzipped the door slowly and stepped out. The campsite, the fire pit and picnic table and Dan's car, everything was moon-bright and dewy. The air felt solid in my throat. The ground was hard; for once I stood without sinking. It was suddenly very nice to be standing there alone.

A trail passed the back of the campsite, and I followed it through the woods. My hips felt loose in their sockets. Mist rose off a marsh and drifted through the trees, and in the mist a white swan floated like a paper cutout. It seemed unreal. I squinted: still a swan. It lifted its neck.

Then the trail opened onto a beach. Across the lake, the Mendenhall Glacier lay like a dropped towel. Even on this side, clumps of ice bobbed in the water and bumped against the shore. Most were small, but there was one about ten feet out that looked big enough to be interesting. I took off my sneakers and stuffed my socks into the heels, dipped my right foot into the water. It burned cold; a chill rose through my body. My hips ached. White mist flowed from behind me and faded as it passed over the water's surface.

I unzipped my pants, stepped out of them, and walked in.

Walked until my sore hips were submerged and began to numb. The worst thing about cold water was the shock. The best thing was that it prepared you for future cold.

On the ice the next day, I felt myself walking funny, and hoped that it wasn't noticeable to my colleagues. But the truth was that my hips were the least of it. The glacier was hard on bodies, both human and canine, and over the weeks it constantly found new ways to wear us down. First was the sun—stronger than I had ever felt it, reflecting off the ice so that it shone equally from above and below. On my second day, I had developed a blistering sunburn on the insides of my nostrils. Dan had assured me that everyone burned their nostrils in the first week. There wasn't much to do about it, he said, except wait until I built up a nostril tan. Besides, it was nothing compared to the armpit burns that resulted from sunlight shining up the sleeves of a T-shirt, or the sunburns that male dogs got on their balls, in anticipation of which I smoothed on a layer of diaper rash cream—lick-proof sunscreen—several times a day. When rain came, it brought its own problems—days of downpour, fast-melting snow, puffy waterlogged skin, mild trench foot. Sometimes a fog rolled in, so thick and fast that one could get lost in the snow between the dog yard and the tents. Out of all the glacier conditions, the fog was perhaps the strangest; it felt like being suspended in a Ping-Pong ball. Objects invisible from ten feet away would loom suddenly from the pale darkness. Then helicopters couldn't fly. We spent the days probing for crevasses with steel poles, working a tight grid through the veiled camp until our palms blistered and our muscles burned.

The skin on my hands, thin and damp, split over each of my knuckles. Then the splits got infected. I took to wrapping my fingers with duct tape each morning, though when I removed the tape in the evenings my soggy skin came off in strips. Although there were no showers on the glacier, I tried, at first, to keep my hair relatively clean, kneeling in the snow by my tent at night, washing my head in a bucket of ice water. I liked being the last one outside on the ice, a lone soul in the wilderness. I tried to feel the whole expanse moving, slipping toward the sea. Sometimes I found myself building in time like that, quiet moments between rushing to prepare teams and appeasing tourists and scooping shit, when I could take a few breaths to be properly stunned by the space around us. But one night, two of the male guides stood and watched me, murmuring about the way my wet shirt stuck to my skin. I felt intimately exposed, humiliated, as I dipped my head once more into the bucket to rinse the last soap from my hair, feeling their eyes on my back, making my body theirs. By the time I stood up, they were gone. I wondered what they would have done if I wasn't Dan's girl. I stopped washing my hair, and wore more hats.

My joy was the dogs. *My* dogs—mine for the moment, to feed and brush and train, to care for, to carry me through the days. They leaped up when I approached, licked my face, buried their heads in my chest. There was Mabel, a ten-year-old leader and veteran of multiple Iditarods, who curled into my lap whenever I sat on her house; Monkey, part hound, with legs nearly as long as mine; Jaxon, a yearling built of solid muscle, who wagged his tail so hard that it bled from the tip. They wanted love and they wanted to run and those were two things I could give them, two things they could give me.

I refused to have sex with Dan on the glacier. For one thing, our bodies were disgusting, unshowered and greasy and covered in a days-old film of dog shit. And although Dan promised that sex would start to feel good to me, I was yet to be convinced; the few other times we'd had sex it had left me just as unmoved as the first. But most important, the glacier lacked privacy. Every thump, every murmur, traveled clearly from one tent to another, and the last thing I needed was for the men to hear *that*, to picture my body in its most vulnerable of states. So when Dan slipped into my tent late one evening, I tensed. "Hey," I said. "I just don't—"

"Don't worry," he said. "I know." He wore a zip-up jacket and now he shrugged it off in one movement and sat down at the edge of my cot. "I can't stop thinking about you. I just want to hold you. Can I do that?" He tucked a hair behind my ear. "You're pretty," he said.

"No sex?" I whispered, quiet as a moth.

"No sex. I promise."

I thought about it, then scooted over and made room for him on the cot. He crawled in beside me and arranged my sleeping bag so that it covered both of us. Our faces were close together. His breath made me giggle. "Hi," I said.

"Hi," said Dan.

Outside, somebody's footprints crunched in the snow.

Dan's face was solid, impenetrable, but his hands were moving. Lightly, decisively. One at my throat. One tracing my hip, hesitating, then slipping into my underwear, sliding down between my legs.

"Doesn't this feel nice?" he said.

It didn't feel nice at all. I reached down to move his hand, but when I tried to push it away, his arm hardened. Our bodies were frozen, my hand on his wrist, his arm unyielding. My back pressed against the tent wall.

"Hey," I said.

Dan wiggled his fingers, just slightly. A pulse. "How many people can say they've had sex on a glacier?"

"Come on," I said. "I told you I don't want to."

Now he smiled and pushed a finger inside me. "Yeah, you want to. I can tell. Look at you, you're so innocent and sexy." He brought his mouth to my ear and purred. *"Rawr!"*

And I thought, *Rawr*? Who says that?

But he was tugging my long underwear off my hips, kissing me even as I pressed my mouth shut. Pulling a condom from his pocket, rolling it on. As soon as I saw it, my heart sank: he had come here for this. I pressed my knees together. He shoved them apart easily. "Please stop—" I whispered, but he put a finger to my lips.

"Shh," he said. "We don't want everyone to hear us."

Everyone meant the men on the other side of the canvas. They couldn't know. I couldn't face them if they knew. I closed my eyes and let my body go slack. It wouldn't occur to me until later that maybe Dan wanted to be heard.

When Dan finished, he got up quickly and slipped through the tent flap. He walked out backward, so that his floating head was the last thing I saw. "Now we can say we've had sex on a glacier," his head said. "Admit it, that's pretty cool."

I grabbed a baby wipe from the box on the floor, rolled over and faced the wall.

After that night, something changed. Whereas before I had regarded sex with Dan as an interesting experiment, it now struck me as grotesque, and incessant, though it probably happened once or twice a week. "I don't want to," I'd tell him. Sometimes that was enough. But usually he'd laugh like he knew better, reach between my clenched legs and rub until he pulled his fingers away damp, then climb onto me. During sex he was a different person, focused and cold. Then, when it was over, he loved me, he traced his fingers on my skin. "Don't worry," he promised every time. "If we keep doing this, it'll start to feel good." The whole thing left me with a jumpy energy in my chest. I wished every day we had never started.

After a few weeks I accepted that Dan would fuck me regardless of what I said, so I turned my focus to getting it over fast. I lay dead still on my back, my eyes tightly closed, my body open and waiting. Sex was only an unpleasant feeling, nothing worse than a bad-tasting food you had to chew before you could swallow. One day, instead of lying still, I tried rocking my hips. It worked: Dan moaned and came, and I was pleased with my ingenuity. But then he sat up between my legs and grinned. "See?" he said. "I told you you'd start to like it." In that moment I hated him.

He was right about one thing, though. A year or two later, in college, an impromptu contest developed around the dinner table: What's the weirdest place you . . . ? On a glacier, I said. Everyone was very impressed. I won the last whoopie pie.

IT WAS AFTERNOON, ON A SLOW DAY. I drifted around the shop and arranged belts on a belt rack that Arild had gotten cheap from a dead store in Finnmark. The belts were garish, metallic pleather with studs and rhinestones. Every now and then I tried one on over my shirt. Nils drank his Coca-Cola and watched me from the table.

A few nights earlier, Nils had invited me to a party in the mountain village, a bonfire by the lake. "The young people will be there," he promised. I was intrigued to meet these new young people. But when I got there, it was the same people I saw every day at the shop, plus a few men who were usually off driving trucks or working oil rigs. They sat around the fire on logs, roasting hot dogs, drinking beer, dancing drunkenly to music from someone's car stereo—Queen, and a Norwegian country group called the Hellbillies. A guy asked me about America, talking too close with his breath in my face, and Nils cut in by tipping my log backward and catching me when I fell. I gasped. His arms were strong around my shoulders, but I squirmed away.

I was comfortable flirting in the shop. Those were careful transactions of attention and flattery, in a space I could enter and leave at will, and with an age difference between myself and the regulars that meant nothing was too real. But the party felt serious. The few women seemed to be pairing up with their chosen men, and the rest of the men were debating how to get some. The conversation centered around Dag Ole, a ruddy young man whose Thai girl was arriving in two days. Dag Ole would fly to Oslo to meet her, so that they could take the last leg of the journey together. He couldn't stop smiling. They'd been video-chatting for weeks; he rose at 2 A.M. to see her off to work, but he didn't want her to think him overzealous, so he pretended that the sun outside his window meant daylight. Dag Ole was twenty-eight and rumored to be a virgin. Everyone was very excited for him.

I sat on a log and accepted sips of Turkish Pepper liqueur that a teenage boy offered me from a soda bottle. It was salty. I was antsy, and wanted to go back to the shop, but I wasn't sure how to leave. Finally I stood up and asked Nils to drive me home. He grinned on the drive, but his smile was stiff, sinking. I liked him. I wanted him to be happy. Nils was the good guy, the one who'd invited me, the one who'd snap Odd Jonny's shoulder back in place when he fell off a picnic table and dislocated it later that night. I was afraid he would try to kiss me. I got out of the car fast and thanked him through the window, pretending not to notice his disappointment.

When I got inside, Arild stood in the kitchen, making an omelet: a stick of margarine, six eggs, heavy cream, chives. He cut the omelet into thick slabs while I set the table and sliced bread. Then he opened the window and called his birds, tossing them the crusts. We ate the omelet while seagulls and crows fought over the pieces. When I finished eating, I thought suddenly of going over to Arild's side of the table, and resting my head on his shoulder. Just to sit there, beside him. But that was an odd thought, too personal even to witness in myself. I was careful not to look at him, and instead threw more bread to the birds.

Now, in the shop, Arild was intent on solving Nils's romance troubles—and making a few sales along the way. "One thing you should do," Arild suggested from the counter, "you should bring good Norwegian belts with you to entice the Thai girls."

"No," said Nils. "No, no." He took a long swig of Coke. The bottle made a breathy squeak as it left his lips.

"Nils doesn't need belts to entice them," I said. Facing away, I draped a fat silver number around my hips. A stupid thing to do, I thought, buckling it, but my body seemed to move on its own: my weight shifting, my hands unbuckling the belt more slowly than was strictly necessary. I knew Nils was watching. When I turned around, he pressed something into my hand: a bottle cap, with words inside it: *I live alone.*

"You need to take this with you," I said. "Get someone to translate it into Thai."

Nils frowned. Arild glanced over at us.

"Maybe you could get a bunch of them," I said. "You could hand them out on the street."

"No, that's not the point," said Nils.

"How'd you get this, anyway?" I turned the cap over. The words were printed under a layer of plastic. "It's off your bottle? Maybe you just need to take a bunch of Norwegian Coca-Cola. You can buy it in bulk; I bet Arild'll cut a deal for a good cause . . ." I knew I was being cruel, but I couldn't stop.

Nils wasn't grinning anymore. "It's for you," he said. "It's not for Thai girls, it's for you."

"Oh." I felt very tired. I put the cap down in the middle of the table and leaned back. But later, when Nils wasn't looking, I slipped it into my pocket. I wasn't sure why I wanted it.

Nils would be leaving in two days, going for a month of sun, beer, and beaches. Although he didn't know it yet, word of his trip had spread. Far away, in Thailand, a woman had quit her job and set up an empty bank account in preparation for his arrival.

CHAPTER SIX

"OH *ARE* YOU HERE, YOU SMALL devils? You have black on your faces and black on your feet. Why aren't you in the mountains? Why are you in the road, where you can be run over?"

I woke in the morning to the sound of Rune's voice. But the room was empty. Groggy, I pulled back the curtain and looked down on the road before the shop. The asphalt was covered with sheep, sprawled like seals on a rock. Rune stood among them with his hands in his pockets.

Rune wouldn't say it, but all that day he was waiting for me to go with him to Martin's grave. He walked in and out of the shop, not even bothering to sit down. He'd come in, look around, and go out again, sit at the picnic table under a low sky and roll another cigarette. He was angry when I passed with the lambs' milk bottles. "They never explain why half the people who get cancer *don't* smoke," he spat, then sank back into hunched lethargy. That was when I remembered my promise. I fed the lambs and came back, and Rune was happy again.

The sky was a bulbous gray, colorless to the point of absence, so the glowing church on the hillside with its glowing, swaying trees seemed perched on the edge of nothing. The seagulls weren't even flying. Rune wanted to drive to the church, though it was only meters uphill. There was a parking lot to the left of the graveyard, where traveling RVs stopped for a night of quiet and free water. "See?" Rune explained. "We can park close." He opened the little gate and shut it behind us and watched it drift open again.

Martin's grave was in the back corner, and fresh. To get there we had to walk past everyone else, names I recognized. Someone had mowed the plots short, down to dirt in patches. Each grave was decorated with flowers and little sculptures. I stayed quiet, walking. I didn't know what role I was playing here, what Rune wanted me for, so I tried to whittle myself down to presence alone.

"There's a lot of old graves here," Rune told me. His tone hinted at a coming lecture, some moral he wanted to share about the depth of history, but he was distracted and fell quiet. Scattered throughout the graveyard were white wooden crosses, markers for gravestones not yet carved. He pointed at them, counting under his breath. "Fifteen white crosses," he said. "That's a lot of new graves. It's not common to see so many at once."

Martin had a gravestone already, red marble with a half-buried pot of yellow daisies in front of it. MARTIN DAHL, 1951–2012. THANK YOU FOR EVERYTHING. Two brass birds perched on the stone, and a brass cross entwined with a rose. *I could have fucked you.* I picked up a pebble from a bare patch of grass and set it down beside the flowerpot. Rune frowned.

"That's my tradition," I said. "To put pebbles on graves." I found another pebble, for Rune, and put it beside the first.

"It's a nice grave," said Rune. "With the birds. And the flowers."

"Did you put the flowers?"

"I took care of his house," he said. "It was my job to take care of his house, until Martha got here. And I come to the church-yard. We come in winter, people come in winter at Christmas and New Year's and light candles. You would like to see it."

"I would like to see it," I agreed.

"But now there's so many white crosses," he said. "And so many old graves. There"—he pointed to the grave behind Martin's, with an engraved boat and a plot of pansies—"that's he who got stabbed in Finnmark last year, just a boy. The son of the cowboy, he Helge Jensen."

"Twenty-one years old," I said, reading.

"Mmm, twenty-one," said Rune. His eyes had moved on. "And there's Jeanette's grandparents, do you see, and there's my sister's baby daughter. And here are the Kristoffersens. It's the whole family."

Some of the Kristoffersen graves looked among the oldest in the graveyard. There was Johannes Kristoffersen, who had founded the shop and built the church; Arild's aunt Aud Unn, whose purple dress hung in the Old Store; a wooden cross marking his mother, Edel. I'd come to know Edel, albeit secondhand. She was a constant presence in the apartment, with her paintings of storm-tossed ships and fishing docks and the occasional tropical sunset, or the half-eaten candy bars that turned up in corners and drawers, where she'd stashed them after her doctor forbade sugar. Her tiny white clogs remained in a pile of shoes by the door, though Arild had set off several times to dispose of them. Edel had enjoyed romance novels, smoking a pipe, and sago pudding thick enough to slice. "Now you know me, now you can get to know my mother," Arild had remarked one day, suggesting that, if I were interested, I could peruse the dozens of wire-bound journals that Edel left stacked throughout the apartment. After that, I flipped through them on occasion, enjoying the nonagenarian's notes about her handsome young doctor or how spring's cyclists biked past the window "nearly naked." She wrote that she'd baked *krumkaker*, though her hands, still fluid on the piano, were too shaky to roll the cookies into cones. When a friend stopped by, Edel was embarrassed: not only were her *krumkaker* flat, but she'd eaten up nearly all of them.

Over the course of her final year, Edel's handwriting grew looser, and her entries shorter, until she rarely marked more than the date and the weather. The last entry followed the pattern of those before it, but was written in Arild's firm, familiar hand:

3/30 Died today. Fine clear weather, -2°C

I'd had to read it twice before I understood.

At the end of the row of Kristoffersens, beside Edel's white cross, was a grassy space with room for more graves. It occurred to me that I hadn't thought about bodies, that when I'd stood before Martin's gravestone I had not considered the fact of his body in the ground below me. I wondered if I would ever stand here before Arild's grave.

When I looked up, Rune was watching something to my left.

Two teenage girls had entered the graveyard. One had apple-red hair and the other wore a sleeveless sweatshirt with a rib cage painted on it. They stood by the gate. They were pointedly not looking at us.

"So you're coming to the graveyard," Rune called out.

The redhead whispered something to her friend, and both girls started walking the long way around the church, away from us.

"There's a lot of old graves here," Rune called. "And this year, you know, there were fifteen white crosses. Fifteen, yes, and not just old people." Rune leaned forward as he talked, like an actor reciting careful lines, but his voice still slurred. Maybe more than usual.

The girl in the sweatshirt muttered, "Yeah." The redhead pulled her phone from her pocket and started texting.

"They were in their sixties," Rune shouted.

"Come on," I said. "Let's go."

"There's a lot of old graves here," Rune said softly, as if to himself. As we pulled out of the parking lot, I glanced back; the girls stood in the far corner, by the boy who had been stabbed. In the car, Rune was happy again. "And a lot of new graves, too."

Later, in the shop, Arild sat down beside me. I thought he was hinting to me to mow the lawn, but when I stood he gestured me back down. "You understand," he said, "that Rune's favorite thing is chainsaws."

"I understand," I said.

Arild took his time pouring a cup of coffee. He sloshed the thermos—it was running low—and raised his eyebrows, so I went to the hallway to start a new pot. When I got back he continued: he had dragged tree trunks from the hill to the sheep field, but he needed them cut into firewood. Rune had been promising to do it for months. "So today I said to he Rune, 'Rune, now you must sit down and relax, because I'm going to teach she Blair to use a chainsaw.' And so now suddenly he is out there cutting wood. You can see it best from the upstairs window."

I followed Arild up the stairs. "Here's binoculars," he said, handing me binoculars. There was Rune in an orange coat, bent over a stack of logs. As I watched, a chunk of wood fell off and landed in the mud.

"I think that was pretty smart," said Arild.

I agreed that it was very smart. Did he want me to cut grass?

"No," said Arild. "Please relax. I just wanted you to see that."

That night, Arild's friend visited from the city, as he did every few weeks. His name was Nils, but since he kept a trailer on Mortenhals, Arild called him Camping Nils, to differentiate him from Thailand Nils. Camping Nils was a newspaperman in his late fifties, a soft-spoken retiree who radiated quiet, amused kindness. His favorite candy was milk chocolate with dried fruit and hazelnuts, which I knew because every time he was coming, Arild sent me down to the shop for a big bar of it.

I joined the men on the patio, as I always did with Arild's guests, but before long Arild glanced at his watch, wondering aloud if I was tired, poor *pia* kept awake with the boring chatter of old men. I faked a yawn and cleared the table, checked the lambs, slipped back into the house. When I fell asleep at last, it was to the sound of the men's inaudible conversation drifting through my window, late into the blue night.

On Saturday, Rune was drunk for his morning coffee. "Do you want to know the future?" Arild said, after Rune had stumbled out. "In a few hours, Rune will come back and buy twelve more pils. Then tomorrow, when the shop is closed, he'll call and ask me to bring him some more. I'll refuse. I'll say that I can't drive because I've had a drink myself. So Rune will call back five minutes later and say he's gotten a taxi and will soon be arriving at the shop. How far do you think from his house to the shop? A kilometer? The taxi will cost him three hundred kroner"—around fifty dollars—"but when he's damp like this, that won't stop him. Then he'll run out of money and we'll have to feed him for the rest of the month."

Three P.M., Rune walked back in. Saturday was the busiest day of the week: not only did the city folks come out, but it was gambling day. A dozen customers stood around the table, guessing randomly about the success of various foreign soccer teams, buying lotto tickets with their extra change. This afternoon Arild was in the city, meeting his lawyer, so Anne Lill managed the rush herself. I helped where I could, ringing up purchases and restocking shelves.

"So you're gambling?" Rune boomed, and then he started to laugh. He was so loud. The customers quieted. Though plenty of locals gambled, these were mostly city folk. They came to their cabins on long summer weekends to get away from the bustle of life—to remember, for a few days, what Norway used to be. Two women sat in the corner, looking at shoes. One of them lifted an enormous men's sandal. The movement caught Rune's eye.

"It's too small for you!" he bellowed. His hands fell heavily on the table. "It's only a forty-six," he said. "It's too small!"

The women seemed to shrink, ignoring him, and Rune turned his attention to the other customers—clapping their shoulders, critiquing their gambling cards. I should do something, I thought—take him by the arm, bribe him out the door with talk of chainsaws, anything. I could help. But I found myself staring at the tabletop with everyone else, oddly paralyzed. How could I confront him, what would I say? Maybe I could leave to make more coffee.

Eventually Rune stumbled to the beer fridge. He bent over, revealing a stretch of delicate butt crack, and grabbed two six-packs off the bottom shelf. Then, still chuckling, he lurched out the door.

"Is he gone?" someone asked Anne Lill.

"Yes," she said. "Thank goodness."

Anne Lill didn't approve of Rune hanging around the shop, on this day or any day. She couldn't understand how Arild tolerated him—why, even encouraged him. She preferred things orderly; she mopped every evening, and twice a year she washed the customers' coffee mugs, despite their fervent objections. Nor did she like children running down the aisles. "This isn't a cafe," she'd say to herself, following with a rag to wipe up their dirty footprints. The only children she longed for were Jeanette's, still ensnared in bureaucracy; their court date had been postponed once again, this time until September. Anne Lill seemed to take the children's absence personally, a corrupt intrusion on private rural and family life. The injustice steeled her. She told anyone who'd listen about Jeanette's skill as a mother: how Jeanette had been mistreated herself as a child, so she knew better than anyone not to pass it on. One afternoon, Anne Lill doodled the names of the missing children on a scrap of paper, surrounded by flowers and hearts. She left the note in the middle of the coffee table, where it lay untouched for a week.

Anne Lill had stood by the shop through the hard times, when it was her work—and her outside money—that helped to keep it afloat. And she'd stand by it through the current times, too, as Arild and his sister battled over rights. Anne Lill believed that Ingeborg was doing wrong, and her disdain for wrongdoing aligned her with her husband. She'd been there when Ingeborg showed up, started grabbing things off the shelves of the Old House. She'd been there when Ingeborg had burst into the shop itself, and tried to nail the door shut, and when the men at the coffee table had risen to their feet and stood behind Arild, a wall of muscle and support. She knew what keeping a shop entailed.

So when news came that Egil was stepping down, and that Martha, the American, was taking over the Sand Shop, Anne Lill snorted and fell still. She did not reflect on the end of an era, or on what the change might mean for her own business. She thought only of Martha. There was not a trace of amusement on her face. "I'm amazed she can bear it," she said.

That night my phone rang. It was Anne Lill. "Have you seen?" she said. "Have you seen what's at the dock? What is it?"

"Right now?"

"Oh," she said, "something's here now. I'm going down to look."

I was happy that she'd called. Anne Lill was never unkind to me, but she had at times seemed ambivalent about my presence, and I'd often wondered what she thought of the fact that I had essentially moved in with her husband. Lately, though, I'd sensed a shift. Maybe she'd had the time to feel me out, or maybe it was the work I put in around the shop, but she'd started drinking coffee with me, sharing gossip, catching my eye in exasperation when one of the men said something particularly vulgar. Anne Lill reminded me of girls I had admired in school, smart and self-assured and cattier than I dared to be. I was grateful for her welcome.

I got to the Old House just as Anne Lill came out the side door, and we walked the gravel road to the dock together. At first glance, it seemed the dock was empty. The boat was so low that only its top was visible, a mess of wires and poles, bobbing slightly; closer, we looked down on a long wooden skipper, painted green and blue, with two leather couches on a deck piled high with backpacks and sleeping bags. A coffee table was covered with spilled beer cans. As we watched, a half dozen teenagers skipped past us without even a hello, clambering down into the boat. One wore red-and-black-striped pants with a yellow poncho; another, a one-piece blue rabbit costume. They had come from the church.

Two young men sat on the couches. One wore a fringed leather vest and held a camera with a lens as long as his arm; he raised it lazily and snapped a picture of me. The other man wore a clean fleece jacket and was sitting quite upright with his hands in his lap. His eyes fastened on Anne Lill.

"Mom?" he said.

Anne Lill raised her eyebrows very high. But before she could say anything, a man emerged from the cabin. He wore a leather jacket and tight black jeans; gauzy curtains of curly red hair formed a sort of froth around his head and shoulders. The cowboy: Helge Jensen. He reached up and grabbed my arm, tugged me down into the boat before I could say that I could climb in just fine by myself, thank you. The deck gave under my weight; the camera boy walked over, shook my hand, and, without releasing it, led me to the couch and tried to pull me down next to him. I had to use my other hand to wrench the first free from his grip. He winked.

A gold plaque on the cabin spelled the word *Abdullah*.

Helge Jensen touched my back and followed my gaze. It seemed we were already friends, no introductions needed. "*Abdullah*," he said thoughtfully. "When I first saw it, I thought fuck, that's some Arabian shit. I don't like that. But actually it's a brand of Turkish tobacco from before the war. There used to be all sorts of shops like the one Arild's got now, and boats like this would travel up and down the coast selling them wares. So this one sold Turkish tobacco. I got it south of Bergen, after the last owner died and his wife didn't know what to make of it." Helge Jensen stared at me. He didn't appear to have any eyebrows. I waited for him to look away, and when he didn't, I turned to find the camera boy watching me, too.

"Show them the picture of the fly," Helge Jensen told the boy.

"I didn't take it," he said.

"It doesn't matter," said Helge Jensen. "It's unbelievable."

The boy swiped through his phone, and eventually held up an iridescent close-up of a housefly on a leaf. The fly was green with metallic swirls of pink and orange, like an oil slick. It had a lot of eyes.

Anne Lill giggled. Helge Jensen made her nervous.

The air on the ship was one of languor. The boy in the bunny suit sat down on an overturned bucket and began to eat marshmallows out of a brown paper bag. His eyes were unfocused; he picked the marshmallows from the bag one by one and pushed them into his mouth and swallowed and then ate some more. Somebody threw a live fish and it flew through the air and landed on the couch behind us. It gasped its gills on the black leather. Nobody moved it.

Helge Jensen glanced at the pulsing fish, then reached into a pile that I took for trash and pulled out a dried fish, two feet long and rock hard, with a gaping hole where its head had been. He held it by the tail and waved it like a wand. "Dryfish," he said. "You've had it? This one's a little strange because I left it out on the boat over the winter, but it's still good to eat. We'll hammer it flat and eat it. You can buy this but it's very expensive. A thousand kroner." He put his hand on my lower back and rubbed me in gentle circles. "This boat," he said, "she sailed tobacco up and down the coast. Turkish tobacco." More circles. I stepped away from him.

Instantly, as if filling a vacuum, two girls walked over and put their arms around Helge Jensen and he grabbed their hips and held them both tight against him. "My daughters," he said, kissing their foreheads in turn.

"How many kids do you have?" I asked him.

Helge Jensen looked around. "All of them."

Helge Jensen's son had been stabbed to death two years before, after a fight broke out at a party. Now he was surrounded by children. He closed his eyes and pushed his face into his daughters' hair; their affection seemed so intimate that I felt myself blush. Anne Lill caught my eye and we both climbed back onto the dock, waved down at the waving teenagers, walked briskly up the road to finally burst into laughter. "I've never seen such hippies," Anne Lill remarked. "And my own son!" She sounded skeptical. "It'll be fine as long as he doesn't marry one of Helge Jensen's daughters." Then she stiffened. "Don't look," she said, "but you see those houses on the hill?" They were lined up beside the church, to our right. "I'm sure they're all watching to see what's going on. And now—oh, no." She laughed and frowned at the same time. "Oh, now they've all seen us getting off Helge Jensen's boat!"

On Sunday, Arild moved his car from the shop to the Old House, so that it would be out of sight. When Rune called and asked for beer, Arild shook his head sadly. "Gee, Rune. I wish you'd called earlier. We already left for Finland."

Rune was desperate. Was Anne Lill around? Wasn't there a hidden key to the shop? Was there an open window to the basement?

Finally Arild relented and left a six-pack on the front step. When the cab pulled up, he ducked into the barn and hid.

That week, a new drama consumed the village: cloud-berry season had come early. When Arild drew me a near-incomprehensible map to show where I might find "approximately ten berries" behind the RV park, he tore up the paper after I'd seen it. Berry patches were private matters, passed down within families and guarded fiercely, and cloudberries were gold. *Northern Light* published a front-page story about a man who reported false bear sightings on Facebook to try to deter his neighbors from berry picking, but the story was just a new spin on old news. Cloudberry bears had been around for generations, and at this point, the only people who believed in them were outlanders and small children—and children caught on soon enough. I got to the patch and found dozens of empty stems and eight remaining berries, blister-swollen and salmon-colored—what Martin's mother, who was famously crude, had once compared to rosy dick heads scattered across the tundra. The berries were sour and seedy. I didn't understand what the fuss was about. He the Rich One explained it to me: nothing tasted as good as what your neighbors couldn't find.

Nobody could remember getting berries this early. But

then, they mused, it had been an unseasonably warm May. In fact, this had been a summer of records: the warmest May, the wettest June, the earliest potato harvest, the most ice cream sold nationwide. When salmon season opened, T-shaped nets scarred the surface of the fjord, but the nets were empty; the salmon had already spawned. The fields bloomed cream and magenta with fireweed and cow parsnip; though cold kept the trees small, the summer flowers were enormous, this year even more so than usual. But the tall grass and wildflowers, left on their own, were stressful. Women pursed their lips, passing, and men shook their heads. The growth meant that the land that had taken so long to clear was being left untended. Clumps formed in the grasses, saplings took root, forests closed over what had once been opened. The trees ate the land. But a cut field, with its mowed spirals, its rows of soft grass drying in the sun, was beautiful. It meant there was life in the village.

With cloudberries came haying season, for those who still hayed. Farmers drove their tractors to the shop for sodas and leather work gloves. Arild was proud that out of all the farmers on the peninsula, it was his right to hay the graveyard. After all, the shop had hosted traveling priests when he was a child, and, although he was not now religious, this connection to religious life made him more intimate than most with matters of the church. He was not even afraid of the graveyard, he bragged, so long as he had a proper reason to be there. And so it was with pleasure, humming a tune drowned out by the sputtering engine, that he left Anne Lill in charge of the shop and maneuvered his tractor up the hill. When he'd acquired a critical mass of hay, he brought me to the hay room in the back of the barn to admire it. The hay was heaped higher than my head, mounded like snowdrifts in February. An old ladder led to a loft by the ceiling. I climbed up for the view, and Arild followed.

Dust filled the air like fog, swirling in pinstripes of light that shone through the wooden walls. We looked down on the hay. "We used to jump from here, when I was a boy," Arild said. He glanced at me. "You can try, if you'd like."

I didn't like heights, but that wasn't the point. With a deep breath I jumped and fell, rolling down one of the soft mounds to land disoriented by the door, spikes of hay pricking my waist and neck and ankles. I couldn't stop laughing. "You coming?"

"Blair," said Arild, "you understand that an old man in his sixties does not jump from the hayloft."

"You're not that old," I told him.

"Thank you," said Arild, "but I am." And with perfect posture he stepped into the air.

A few days later, Rune didn't show up at the shop in the morning, or even in the afternoon. Customers came with rumors, one by one.

Rune was dizzy.

Rune had fallen by the side of the road.

There was an ambulance.

He'd been taken to a hospital in the city.

Rune was dying.

Perhaps, they said gravely, he was already dead.

Nobody seemed devastated.

At five minutes to closing, Rune came to the door, looking for beer.

"Are you okay?" I asked him.

He rubbed his hand over his mouth, his beard. "Yeah," he said. "There was an ambulance, *jo*." He giggled through his hand. Six beers.

Arild watched him shuffle out to his car. "Rune the unhealable," he said, sounding at once mournful and impressed. "He's been a dirt clod all his life."

But the next day Rune bought two apples and two pears.

Nobody had seen him buy produce before. The doctor had scared him straight.

When I rang up the fruit, Rune didn't look at me. He stood by the counter, hands in his pockets, and thrust out his chin. He gazed around the shop, his eyes skimming over the familiar racks: the shoes, the lotto tickets, the tobacco, the magazines. He handed me twenty kroner, clasped the bags of fruit in a blackened hand, and paced out.

"Rune buying *fruit*," observed a white-haired woman at the table. "He's really trying to be healthy, isn't he?" A snort burst out of her, and she breathed in and sat up straight to hide it. "I shouldn't laugh," she admonished herself. But she chuckled into her collar long after Rune was gone.

CHAPTER SEVEN

H EYYY," SAID HELGE JENSEN, ON THE phone. "I'm going to build a fire tonight and call some folks. There's some Muslims coming, some Polacks, and we've got dryfish and a few cans of beer."

I waited.

He waited.

"I'll come," I said, and hung up.

That afternoon, He the Rich One told everyone about a squirrel that he'd trained to eat birdseed from his hand. Squirrels were new on Malangen, more exotic than cloudberries, and some of the men competed with each other to tame them. No sooner had he brought up squirrels, though, than He the Rich One took advantage of the opportunity to complain about the cost of bird-seed. This Arild took as a cue to chase him from the shop. "Blair," he said, "why don't you show He the Rich One where to find some blueberries by the lake?" I took He the Rich One's elbow and led him out to his sports car.

"I like you too much," said He the Rich One, pulling onto the road. "It's dangerous."

Something inside me froze. "For who?"

"For who?" said He the Rich One. "For me! I'm an old man with an old heart."

I exhaled carefully. Of course; this was just He the Rich One. I'd spent the summer with him. We were all right. Still, once I'd shown him the berry patch, I offered to walk back to Mortenhals alone. When I got to the shop I borrowed Arild's twenty-eight-year-old Passat, which had the problem of accelerating spontaneously, and drove the fifteen minutes to Helge Jensen's house braking all the way.

WHEN THE SUMMER IN ALASKA had come to an end, Dan and I stayed together. For me, entering into a long-distance relationship was the path of least resistance—I was, at that point, pretty done with resisting—and had the major benefit of making me unavailable to date college boys I might have to see, and sleep with, much more often. Dan loved me, he said, like he'd never loved anyone else. He wanted to make it work. He gave me a framed photo of us, one I couldn't remember having been taken. He suggested that I was only going to school to please my parents, and should instead follow my heart, and live with him in Canada. I pretended to think about it. I put his photo facedown in my desk drawer and covered it with papers.

The truth was, from my new basement dorm room in central Maine—at Colby College, a school I'd chosen in part because of how far north it was—Alaska seemed very, very far away. Five months ago, all I'd wanted was an adventure. Now all I wanted to do was skate in Colby's dim, empty ice rink and watch *America's Next Top Model* on my friend's laptop. Staying with Dan felt like having a needy tropical fish: I'd send an e-mail every day or two, sprinkle on a few "I miss you's," and not think about it for the rest of the time. Later in the fall he came to visit me, sleeping in my twin bed while I snuck off to the library to study for tests that were two months away. My friends thought Dan was handsome and exotic, an older man. I thought my room felt adulterated with his presence. After he left, back to Canada to guide for the winter tourist season, I summoned the courage to tell him we were over.

Dan was patient on the phone, understanding. He explained that he'd known the whole time that this would happen—that the distance would tear us apart, because I was too immature to handle it. Without physical contact, he argued, how could our love survive? Things were just as good as they'd always been; I just didn't know it. After we hung up, he texted how much he loved me, how we were meant for each other. I looked at the phone in my hand, wondering what was going on.

In the coming months, I broke up with Dan a half dozen more times. Each time, by the next day, he wrote e-mails or left me messages with as much affection as usual—maybe even more. When I tried to clarify things, he was firm: "Look," he'd say, with the calm patience of a father, "I refuse to talk about this until we're sitting next to each other. You don't mean what you're saying. Just wait." Eventually I stopped trying, stopped talking to him on the phone. I stopped eating, too, losing forty pounds in two months, until I no longer recognized the body that Dan had fucked. I liked that he didn't know what I looked like anymore.

But he would, the next summer, once I went back to Alaska. It never occurred to me that I didn't have to go; it never occurred to me that I might not want to. Of course I'd go back to the dogs, the ice. Without them, who was I? Not the person I wanted to be.

When I landed in Juneau, expecting to be picked up by one of the company's support staff, Dan stood by the baggage claim. He greeted me with a hug, said he'd taken a day off to meet me. Of course he had. We were going to have a great summer, he told me, without a hint of acknowledgment of our months-long breakup. Though he had told our coworkers that he wasn't sure if we were together, with me Dan acted as if there was no question. I wondered if I had imagined the whole thing.

That first week, when I tried to be straightforward—"I want to break up"—he'd either bargain or argue. Just give him a month, he said; I needed time to reconnect with him. I was feeling distant after so long apart. We loved each other. Remember how happy we were? Sometimes he took the tone of a compassionate elder: He had to remind himself how young I was. How little he'd understood when he was twenty. I wasn't even *myself* yet, and on top of that, college had changed me for the worse. "No one else would ever treat you this well," he reminded me. "No one else will put up with you like I do."

"You're not the nice girl I thought you were," Dan said. I thought, I could have told you that a year ago. I briefly hoped that he would dump me, now that I wasn't nice anymore, but he seemed only more determined to fix me. During my first days back in Alaska, I had only one victory: I'd told him that I wasn't going to have sex with him, and so far he'd acquiesced.

He tried to persuade me otherwise on our first weekend off the ice. We were sitting on a foam pad in the women's apartment, against one wall of the bedroom, which I shared with a girl named Rebekah. Rebekah was a homeschooled eighteen-year-old from Indiana who had never been away from her family for more than a week, and who lived her life, in her words, guided by Jesus Christ and His teachings. Back in Indiana, she had fallen in love with the idea of dogsledding, the idea of Alaska, and saved up money from working a McDonald's drive-through to buy a malamute and a husky, which she trained to pull her on Rollerblades. But here in Alaska, she'd never even stood on a sled. Instead she worked as an assistant, tripping over the snow in her oversized rubber boots, fetching this bucket or that shovel for whichever musher called out to her first. She made an easy target for pranks—some friendly, some less so—and I recognized in her earnestness a bit of myself from the year before. We shared a tent. More than that, we shared estrangement and girlhood, but those were hardly traits to bond over. Instead, our friendship was cautious; I wasn't sure what could be gained, for either of us, by associating too much with each other.

Now Rebekah napped in her sleeping bag, a warm synthetic one from Fred Meyer that I coveted. I'd been making do with cotton blankets, and Dan had suggested that we drive to get a sleeping bag that night, since we were due to the heliport first thing in the morning.

I hugged my knees. Dan put his arm around me and murmured into my hair. "I don't understand," he said. "I feel like you're pushing me away, just because you feel like it. Why don't you want to sleep with me?"

Across the room I noticed Rebekah's eyes flutter open, then shut.

Dan petted my shoulder. "Huh?"

The carpet was faded and peeled back from the wall to our left, and from a crack a small brown spider climbed the wall in little bursts. I watched it closely. The harder I watched the spider, the less I could feel Dan's hand.

"I just don't like it," I said. I didn't have much left to say. I was just so tired.

Dan, petting my shoulder, reminded me that I hadn't given him a single good reason.

"Because," I finally said, "I'm *not attracted to you.*" That was an understatement—even thinking of Dan's touch made my whole body freeze up—but it was, at this point, one of the few things I still knew for sure.

No sooner had I spoken than Dan withdrew his arms and stood. His face curled into an expression I didn't recognize, his eyes narrow, his mouth slightly open. "Why didn't you say so?" he said. "You could have saved us both a lot of grief." He crossed the room in three steps, one hand smacking the door frame on the way out.

Was that it? Was he gone? It seemed that the very air around me had changed, grown brighter. I started to grin, hardly trusting my own relief. In the same moment, I felt a pang of regret. Maybe I should have waited until after we'd gone to Fred Meyer.

Then Dan walked back in, something shiny in his fist. With a sharp breath he flung the thing across the room, so that it crashed into the wall beside me. I flinched. The thing fell to the ground. Keys. "Feel free to use my car," he said, leaving again.

The keys had left a mark on the wall, about a foot from my face. I picked them up and held them in my palm.

The apartment was quiet. The spider was gone.

"Rebekah?" I said. "Want to go to Fred Meyer?"

She opened her eyes and glanced at the door, then nodded. Rebekah was wary of both of us. Dan had been kind to her when she first arrived, had driven her around Juneau and helped with errands. But she trusted him less after he asked too many questions about her virginity, after he touched her skin too many times. And anyway, she needed groceries.

Dan wasn't anywhere in the apartment. He wasn't on the stairwell outside. He wasn't in the parking lot, either, where barefoot children tossed pebbles at a bear cub in a dumpster. His car was parked in a far corner. We got in and I drove in silence, across the bridge, out past the heliport and the dump with its circling eagles. Rebekah had a shopping list—food for the days when she worked in Juneau alone. I bought a sleeping bag and a few jars of good peanut butter. I'd learned the hard way that the peanut butter on the glacier sucked.

A STREAM OF WATER LEAKED from Helge Jensen's driveway, staining a stripe in the road, and I parked the Passat alongside it. The gang sat around a fenced-in campfire in the backyard. There was Helge Jensen with his hair and a mug of wine, and beside him a teenage boy, still baby faced, frowning under a black hoodie. Another man, with a hook nose and a frizzy ponytail, sat on a piece of foam on a wet bench. His name was Zoran, he told me, in an impeccably courteous voice, and he was from Macedonia, and he would be delighted to share his foam with me.

His foam wasn't very big. I found another piece by a wood-pile and placed it beside him. Zoran looked hurt. He reached out and touched a hand to my hair, as lightly as a bird.

I wasn't sure if the party was over or if it hadn't started. Nobody seemed to be talking much. There was a pitcher of coffee with grounds floating in it, and another pitcher of wine, home-made from blueberries and black currants. There was a grill on the waning fire with three sooty, wrinkled hot dogs. "Take one," suggested Helge Jensen, so I broke a hot dog in half and took a bite. It tasted fine, but it stained my fingers black with grease.

Helge Jensen wanted to talk about the Sailor. The Sailor had gone to sea at fourteen, north to Svalbard on a ship of men to spend his adolescence clubbing seals. "He came back, he didn't know the rules, you understand? Not the *rules*. He liked girls, but he didn't know how to talk to them. He asked his friend how he'd got a girl to kiss him, the friend said he just carried her up to the hayloft, she liked it. But when Tormod found a nice girl and tried it, you can bet she squealed. Folks avoided him after that. But he just misunderstood, he thought that was the thing to do, to carry her up to the hayloft. He didn't know. How could he have? All he knew was boats, and to kill seals."

Two girls wandered over from the house. They looked maybe thirteen or fourteen. One of them had bleached hair and white-and-silver tiger-striped pants. The other had maroon hair and tight white pants and a pierced lip. They carried an iPod, which played tinny music—"Friday I'm in Love"—from a turquoise speaker, and they sat leaning against each other on the bench across from us. The redhead stared at me with a look of abject boredom, then rolled her eyes into her head until they were closed.

At the graveyard, with Rune. That was where I'd seen them before. Their brother's grave. The hooded boy went to stand behind them, rubbing each of their necks with one hand.

Helge Jensen glanced at his daughters, then back at me. He seemed to be trying to talk his way toward something.

"Killing seals is fair," he said. "It's fair. I don't mind it. You kill them three times. You kill them and kill them and kill them. You shoot them, then you hit them, then—why? You have to make sure they're not suffering. It's much better than what bears do. The polar bears, you see them, they play with baby seals like a kitten with yarn."

He was watching me closely, and I watched him back. There was a game here, it seemed, and I decided not to play it. Or maybe that *was* the game: proving I wouldn't react. In that case, I was a master. I picked up the remaining half of the blackened hot dog and took a bite, just to give my face something to do.

"Can you imagine?" said Helge Jensen. "Can you imagine what it would do to you to spend months at a time of your adolescence living with adult strangers on a sea of ice?"

Maybe I shouldn't have nodded, but I did.

Helge Jensen raised his eyebrows. I swallowed my bite and explained, in a few words: summers, glacier, dogs, men. When I said it I felt embarrassed; it wasn't the same at all, no, it was nothing like what the Sailor had done. How arrogant of my heart to jump at the words *sea of ice*. I looked down, wiped my hands on my pants.

"I got really interested when you said that," said Helge Jensen. "It means you have a story. You know, if you're curious, I could get a place for you on a sealing ship. I know a man who owes me a favor. You would be so strong when you came back. Strong physically. Strong *mentally*. Sealing is fair work."

"Maybe," I said.

"Maybe," said Helge Jensen. "But you have to promise, you won't be some kind of fucking veterinarian."

I shook my head. My knees were hot from the fire and I rubbed them with my hands.

Zoran was bored. "Say," he said, bringing the conversation into English. "Dryfish! You like dryfish?" He reached past me, brushing his hand against my back, and felt around the wet woodpile behind us. Then he came back with a dryfish I hadn't known was there, stiff as wood and as long as my arm. He pretended to take a bite from the side of it, then laughed and peeled off a strip instead. The girls were bent over their iPod, but they looked up, and the blonde held out her palm. The other poured them both another glass of wine.

"Dryfish," said Zoran smilingly. He pulled off a string of fish for the girl and laid it gently across her palm, then stroked her wrist with his thumb. "It gives you the penis of a twenty-five-year-old even if you're forty-five." He lowered his head and spoke into my ear. "I have been eating it every day. Ever since Helge told me to."

"He ate it and his dick became more heavy," said Helge Jensen. He seemed pleased with his English.

"Da-ad," said the blond girl, and the redhead joined in. "*Dad.* Dad!"

"Hm?" Helge Jensen turned to them.

"There's no more wine." The redhead climbed into the blonde's lap and they put their arms around each other and pouted.

"It's in the kitchen," said Helge Jensen. The girls stood and left and the boy followed a moment later. Helge Jensen turned back to me. "I like Zoran," he said. "I like outlanders. People from here, actually all they want is to eat pizza and watch TV. With them, all of life is a rerun. But some people are searchers. We want new information. We want to hear things described in a new way."

"Described in a new way," I repeated. That was interesting.

Helge Jensen leaned forward and punched me hard in the knee. "Fuck you," he said. "Who are you?"

I stared at him.

"I like that," he said. "I touched you and you didn't jump. I like to be able to touch my friends. That's fair. I like you. I can tell you, you have a heaviness to you. I can see it. It's from when you were on the ice. It wasn't always easy. Maybe some men were interested in you and you weren't interested in them and they got mean. It gave you a heaviness, which makes you still and stable. You're very stable because of that heaviness."

So I was winning the game.

The teenagers came back with a pitcher of wine and re-filled their glasses. The blonde sat down on the boy's lap, distracted, as if she had fallen there by accident, and he rubbed his hands up and down her thighs. The redhead gazed at them a moment, then walked around the fire to Zoran and sat on top of him. His pressed his face into her neck and she took a swallow of wine.

"*Bollemusfantomet*," said Helge Jensen, laughing at Zoran. "Heh? All he can think about, it's puffy pussies."

"Mmm," agreed Zoran.

"We always say Greeks are the best lovers," Helge Jensen told me. "That is, everyone says Greeks are the best lovers."

Zoran licked his index finger and smoothed his eyebrows one by one.

"But I think I am pretty good," continued Helge Jensen. "I am a good lover. Women come to me, they go home to their boyfriends and their boyfriends say, 'Helge, what you did to her?

All she wants is to fuck and to fuck.' But *you* are a neutral party. Here is my suggestion: that you shall fuck us both and say who is better."

"Yes, yes," said Zoran.

I had no answer for that, so I just rubbed my knees.

"That was a joke," said Helge Jensen. "I wanted to see how you would respond to something shocking. You remained calm and did not get nervous. I like that." He grabbed the dryfish by the tail and swung it toward me approvingly, then pulled off a new string for chewing. It took him a while to swallow. "Well," he said, "it wasn't entirely a joke."

Across the fire, the boy tucked the blonde's hair away from her cheek. "You're sexy," he murmured, leaning to kiss her. She turned her face. "*You're sexy,*" she imitated nasally, making exaggerated kissing sounds with her mouth. Both girls stood from their respective laps and went back to the house. The boy sank back into his hood and slumped forward with his elbows on his legs, but Zoran just turned and began to pet my head, like a dog's.

He was an artist, he said. He made paintings of angels. He'd made a painting of the angel Gabriel rising to heaven after having informed Mary of her forthcoming virgin birth, and he'd put it on a website and sold it to a family in Alta, a few hours north of Tromsø. But when the painting arrived, the angel's eyes had chipped off. The family was so freaked out to have an angel with no eyes that they bought Zoran a plane ticket to come fix it, and since then he'd just stayed.

"But *you*," he said. "You are an artist, too, a writer. But I don't believe it. Because where is your passion? How can you have art with no passion?"

"I have passion," I said.

"Where is your passion, then? Where is your love?" His fingers were gentle but calloused, snagging strands of my hair.

"I have plenty of love," I said. "I love my boyfriend at home." It was worth a try.

"That is so far away, it doesn't count. You're in the north now. How can you be truly in the north if you don't let yourself love here?"

Now I knew where this was going. "No, thank you."

"Will you not make love to me?"

I shook my head.

"I would like to make love to you," said Zoran.

Helge Jensen scooted close on my other side. "My friends are fair people," he whispered.

"I am just being honest," said Zoran. "I see you, you're a beautiful woman. I am a passionate man. I think to myself, I would like to make love to her. So I am honest."

"All my friends are fair," whispered Helge Jensen. "If anyone is bad to you, I'll fuck them up. You're safe now that you're friends with me."

"I have so much passion to give you. For the sake of art."

They were both in my ears at once, touching me, murmuring at me. Someone's hand was on my leg, someone's on my back. A log broke in the fire and sparks rose to the blue sky and there were voices and hands and hair against my cheek. Then something wet: Zoran had licked my neck.

"It's okay for you to touch my hair," I said, "but please don't lick my neck."

Zoran nodded. "I just don't understand how you can have art without passion," he said mildly.

Helge Jensen was telling me a story—maybe he'd always been telling me a story. Something about the military, a friend, a good friend—something about trust and meaning. A shipwreck, maybe, or was it an airplane, or was it a friend—such a friend—with meaning and learning and trust, the best trust he'd ever had, back in the military when he was a young man with a friend and love and so important.

"I'm going home," I said. I needed to leave. I put my hand on Helge Jensen's back. I could feel his spine through his sweater. I knew that the only way for me to leave was if I touched his back when I told him I was going. He nodded. He was still telling the story, or maybe he'd stopped. I rubbed his spine and thanked him for the dryfish and the evening and I said good-bye and the hooded boy sat alone and watched me go.

It was late and Zoran had work in the morning, so I drove him, too, to a yellow house at the far edge of Mestervik. I pulled half up the driveway but Zoran wouldn't get out of the car. He was talking about something. Gratitude. He liked me, he said. He was going to have an exhibit in Storsteinnes that I should attend, an exhibit made of lights made of brain waves. He was still in the car. Why was he still in the car? "It's time for you to get out of the car," I said. "Open your door." He opened the door and I pushed him until he stumbled out. He was smiling, still talking when I drove away. I drove home slow on the turns, careful, and pulled the hidden key from the fleece-lined pocket of the coveralls hanging by the door and tiptoed up the stairs, through the kitchen to my room, tiptoed to my bed where I pulled the curtains shut and lay down, so glad to be alone.

CHAPTER EIGHT

IN LILLEHAMMER I WAS A STUDENT, at the folk school I was a dogsledder, but in Alaska I would never be anything but a girl. It didn't matter how many men's clothes I wore, how many weeks in a row I stayed on the ice, how well I cared for my dogs. Dan wouldn't let me forget it. I'd enter the kitchen tent to find him scrutinizing the veterinary care I gave my puppies, or mocking something he'd overheard me say to a tourist. He talked loudly to other guides about how I was too sentimental to work with the dogs or give tours. Once, as he escorted an older couple to my sled, I heard him say, "She's good at acting like she knows what she's doing. It's too bad you didn't get an experienced musher." I didn't believe the things he said about me, and I didn't think the other guides did, either, but that didn't stop them from laughing along.

Rather than confronting Dan, I became increasingly withdrawn. If I could be alone, fine; if I could be with the dogs, even better; but most human interactions made me cagey and brittle. I even came to resent the tourists—resent them for how much they admired me—and volunteered to trade my tours for the crap chores that nobody wanted, the outhouse pumping and snow shoveling that most mushers tried to avoid. The whole thing felt less like an adventure and more like an ordeal, so that it was hard to recall what I'd wanted here in the first place. In fact, I realized, I was more miserable than I had ever been in my life. I had always been someone who woke up happy at the prospect of another day; now I woke up dismayed at the prospect of having to leave my tent. And once I did leave my tent, nothing seemed to matter; with the exception of the dogs, whom I loved unequivocally, the tours and chores and meals blended into an endless slog. I didn't want to be on the glacier, but I didn't want to be back at college, either. I didn't want to be anywhere or do anything. I just wanted to be locked in a room, preferably with some sled dogs, where nobody would ever bother me again.

My most pleasant hours, that second summer, were when I was assigned to dig a pit. Pits were in high demand on the glacier; we used five for melting water, one for cooling food, and a "modesty pit" in the kennel where mushers could urinate between tours. All of these needed to be regularly re-dug as the snow melted away and we moved the camp up-glacier. When I was digging, I could put on headphones, listen to music, and spend hours ignoring everything but the task in front of me. I could fall into a rhythm, jumping once on the shovel, heaving its contents over my shoulder. I could sink to my knees, my waist, my shoulders, until no one could see me, until I could see nothing but the mineral turquoise that ripened toward the heart of the glacier.

Usually it was raining, the raindrops a constant racket on my hood or the roof of my tent. That summer it rained, with few reprieves, for two months in a row. Several of the mushers gave up staying dry, and traded their jackets for neoprene. The rain made people crabby, and made some of the dogs depressed.

They'd curl in their houses and refuse to come out. One dog, forced to wear a cone around his neck, stared up for hours at the raining sky—"trying to drown himself," as one musher put it. A girl in my team named Stoic stopped eating, and grew so emaciated that she had to be hidden from tourists. She was a small, gray dog—mousy and delicate, soaked to the skin. The cook and I made her elaborate meals, mixing meat and rice and bacon fat into a hot gruel. She'd sniff the food politely. Her fur tufted vertical lines over her ribs. I couldn't stand it. I'd sit beside her, coax her to eat individual kibbles from my swollen, bleeding fingers. "Look," the manager told me. "Dogs don't starve themselves to death. When she's hungry enough, she'll eat." But looking at her, I wasn't so sure. Eventually she was moved to another musher's team at the far end of the kennel.

I felt reckless again, in a way I hadn't since the latter months of my stay with Far. I went for secret walks past the bounds of camp, over snowpack unprobed for crevasses. On weekends I sweet-talked my way onto bush planes and spent days in the mountains by myself. I was soggy and unhappy and, therefore, invulnerable. Nothing I did seemed to matter.

Two days of the week, I shared my tent with a musher named Stacy; but she was dating one of the male guides, and therefore seemed a member of another gender entirely. One day, during an implausible hour that somehow combined a break in the clouds with a break in tours, Stacy went out to sunbathe in a bra and shorts. She invited me along, and on a strange impulse I took off my shirt and joined her. What good had it done me to dress modestly? My skinny body looked good—smooth and long—in a way it never had before and probably never would again. The men noticed. "So, that's what you've been hiding," someone called; a few others, hearing voices, trudged out of their tents to come see. Stacy laughed and stretched her arms over her head. I laughed too, trying to copy her ease. One musher, who also worked as a photographer, took a picture of us. We grinned. "The girls of Norris Glacier," he said. "Show me what you've got." Before long Stacy and I were reclined on a pile of propane tanks in the center of camp, all abs and legs and skin between our goggles and our rubber boots. Somebody whistled. "Pervert!" Stacy yelled back. She straddled a tank, thighs open, chin cocked for the camera. The photographer suggested I climb on behind her.

That big lens over his face. I started to shake my head, but sensed movement behind me, and turned.

There was Dan. He had passed between tents, glimpsed us, doubled back, and crossed his arms. His anger was tangible over the distance: whatever I was doing, the sight of me—it hurt him. I changed my mind and slid onto the tank behind Stacy, spreading my legs, miming more sexuality for the camera than I had ever performed for Dan. I felt him watching. I felt the damp breeze off the ice, the cool metal of the tank against my thighs, the approval of the gathered mushers who had hardly spoken to me all summer. I closed my eyes and arched my back, shifting with the clicks of the shutter. Another pretty young thing. Bathed in light, or something.

Later that day, Dan spoke to me for the first time in weeks. It happened quickly. He was exiting the community tent, and I was entering, and before I climbed fully inside he'd blocked my way, stepped into my space as if challenging another man. "Why don't you ever *think* before you do anything?" he spat, and I felt filled with pride and defiance, and then I went back to my tent and crawled into my sleeping bag and zipped it up to my forehead and cried.

It never occurred to me to leave. I saw no way out but time. I had committed to a summer on the glacier, and I would complete it, no matter how miserable. Rebekah was miserable in her own way, too: she yearned for home with an intensity that I recognized but could not relate to. If girlhood hadn't been enough to bond us, longing was, and as the weeks passed I began to see time with Rebekah as the only respite glacier life offered. We had both developed a taste for apocalyptic novels, which we borrowed from the Juneau library using a fake address, read by flashlight, and traded furtively. When tours were cancelled due to weather, we'd sit on our cots with cups of trail mix, bartering M&Ms for dried pineapple, talking about Norway and Indiana. "I just want to go home," she said. "Don't you want to go home?" With just a month left in the season, Rebekah bought plane tickets for a weekend trip to see her family. She counted down the days: Eight. Seven and a half. Seven.

My own escape was internal. I daydreamed about escaping the north as much as I had once dreamed of reaching it. Perhaps encouraged by the novels I read, I developed elaborate strategies for what to do if some disaster struck the rest of the planet, if the helicopters ever stopped coming, so as not to be trapped on the ice forever. I could steal dogs and sled down the south tongue of the glacier, then walk the shoreline of the Gastineau Channel back to Juneau. I could scale mountains using gang-lines for ropes. In my deepest daydreams, the rest of the world was simply an idea, a concept that might or might not exist at any given moment—certainly not a place that could be relied upon to save us.

When the day came that Rebekah was scheduled to leave to see her family, she *still* hadn't driven a sled, so I begged an hour off and we hit the trail with enough time for a quick ride before her departure. We had just taken off when five helicopters rounded a distant mountain single file and roared into camp, coming down fast on the ice, hot rotors thumping. Moments later, nearly thirty blinking tourists stood around the American flag at the edge of the dog yard.

It was not a scheduled landing. I knew it, and all the other staff knew it, but we also knew better than to acknowledge to the tourists that anything was unusual. So the other mushers didn't even glance at each other as they corralled the tourists together with big smiles and shouts of "Welcome to Dog World!" Rebekah and I, partway down the trail, stopped our dogs and watched from a distance. The tourists seemed happy—we could hear the buzz of their excitement—and the guides ran around harnessing dogs and hooking up teams as quickly as they could. The pilots huddled behind the helicopters.

It turned out that a sudden storm, a wall of cloud between Juneau and the glacier, had blocked their usual flight path, forcing them to forgo the flightseeing tour and make an early landing. Now, from the glacier, the weather looked overcast but by no means terrible; visibility was better than it often was. The pilots decided to continue on schedule. They lifted off in a line, heading back to Juneau. In an hour, they would return to pick up the tourists and drop off the next group. The other mushers took off with their tours, and Rebekah and I continued along the trail.

For a while, at least, the ride was lovely—maybe the best I'd had all summer. It wasn't raining, Rebekah was laughing, and the tourists' voices sounded from the other trails, where other people were responsible for them. But within fifteen minutes another rumbling echoed over the glacier, and a tiny figure in an orange vest zoomed toward the dogsled trails on a snowmobile. This was Malcolm, our manager. We'd been warned about orange vests: they were used to signal urgency. In all my time on the glacier, I couldn't remember seeing one used.

Malcolm waved to the tourists as he passed them—"Stunning, isn't it?"—and came to a stop next to Rebekah and me. "We're in trouble," he said. "The pilots can't get back." His voice was higher than I'd ever heard it. "Nobody's hurt, but the tourists are trapped here now. They're trapped here."

Rebekah was jumping a little on the sled brake. "What should we do?" she said.

He told us to let the staff know what was going on without alarming the tourists. "Just tell them they'll be here longer than expected—maybe an extra hour or two until the weather clears. And, girls? Try to make it sound like a good thing."

Rebekah drove fast around the trail, and we were waiting in the kennel by the time the other teams returned. We split up to spread the word: "Great news! You get a longer tour than usual!" While the tourists cheered and rushed to pet the dogs, I sidled up to each musher and whispered an update in his ear. Chad snorted—"Nice one, Blair"—but Henry, an older guide whom I considered a friend, nodded and squeezed my arm before returning to his group. I had been hoping that Rebekah would reach Dan before I did, but by the time I'd worked my way over to his kennel she was still several teams away, giggling sharply and gesticulating to a man in a cowboy hat.

When Dan saw me coming, he led his tourists away from me, toward the lead dogs who had flopped down in the snow. "This here is Mo," Dan said. "He's awesome." I noticed that he was following instructions: Mo was short for Money, but Malcolm had directed him never to use the dog's full name, since tourists might think he was angling for tips. When I reached the group, I put on my biggest tour-guide smile and gave them the news.

"Wow!" said Dan. "Why don't you all pet Mo for a minute?" He walked a few feet off, head down, and I followed. "What's going on, Blair?"

I told him the birds couldn't get back. This was the closest that Dan and I had come to being alone together in two months, and I couldn't help noticing how familiar he was. A strong man with small features, small eyes and ears and nose and mouth. We were standing very close together.

"Okay," he said. He crossed his arms.

"Just keep them happy for as long as possible," I said. "I'll let you know when there's more information."

For just an instant, Dan looked up, and our eyes met. "Don't tell me what to do," he said. "And next time, send Rebekah. At least she knows not to interrupt me when I'm with tourists." By the time I gathered a response, he had walked away.

Back at camp, Malcolm and the cook stood around the satellite phone, talking in low voices. They had called the cruise ship to say that the passengers would be late; the captain had agreed to wait three hours, but no longer. The cook was heating a massive pot on the propane stove, preparing cocoa. Their goal was to keep things fun for as long as possible. Let the tourists hang out with the dogs, then bring them in for hot drinks. They were making plans for snowmobile rides and a snowman contest. As long as the backup helicopters arrived within an hour or so, there was no reason for the tourists to worry.

But after a half hour in the kennel, when the weather had only worsened, we took the tourists into the community tent and fed them digestive cookies. Malcolm broke the news: They were stranded. The helicopters couldn't make it in. "No," a man said, "that can't be. My ship is leaving." This was met with nods of agreement. The snow, the ice, the expanse of it all—it wasn't a possibility. Then the tourists were angry, at the guides for bringing them here, at the pilots for misjudging the weather, at the ships for not waiting. Didn't we understand that this was a serious inconvenience? A woman had left her infant child with a babysitter. A couple was worried about standing up a dinner date. A few people raised concerns about medication they needed back in Juneau—the pilots, crabby because of the constant Enya music they were required to play while flying, had passed a rule that bags weren't allowed in-flight—but their voices were lost in the general despair.

Framing a backcountry emergency as an extended luxury tour is no enviable task, but Malcolm did his best. "We have a cook," he announced, his voice confident. "We have plenty of food and water." The tourists looked grim, but he gave them a pleasant nod and then stepped outside, gesturing for the staff to follow. "I don't care what you need to do," he whispered once we'd gathered around him. "Just keep them happy. Do whatever it takes. Act like this is the best thing that's ever happened to you. And for God's sake, don't do anything that could get us sued."

That afternoon passed in a haze of card games, the tourists constantly checking their useless cell phones, the weather reports from Juneau steadily bleak, and at some point it became clear that the tourists would have to spend the night. The guides would be ceding their tents, cots, and sleeping bags to the tourists—we had extra sleeping bags for emergencies, so there were just enough—and after a meal of meat loaf, real mashed potatoes, and chocolate cake, Malcolm went tent by tent to make sure the quarters were ready. He'd decided we should call the tourists "guests," as if they had been invited over for a dinner party and just happened to be spending the night. "Put all your stuff in trash bags," he said to the staff, "and pile it outside. We want to make sure the guests are comfortable."

When he reached our tent, Malcolm made Rebekah and me take down the perfume ad we had tacked, semi-ironically, to the support beams. "We can't have guests sleeping under a naked picture of Leonardo DiCaprio," he said. "No. Don't argue. We just can't." But when Rebekah reached to take down a photo of a baby from a day-care center where she'd worked back in Indiana, Malcolm stopped her. "Put that somewhere prominent," he said. "It makes us seem human."

Rebekah surveyed the empty tent. "Where are we going to sleep?"

"I really don't care," said Malcolm.

Back in the community tent, the tourists were gathered around the three tables, playing Go Fish and Parcheesi. A few guides hung around outside, sitting on a pair of snowmobiles, not saying much. Every twenty minutes or so, one would take a long breath, stretch a smile across his face, and pass through the tent flap. "Parcheesi! I love Parcheesi! Who's up next?" Whoever had been relieved would step out of the tent, visibly deflate in the chill air, and collapse onto the empty snowmobile seat. In this way, the tourists were infused with a constant rotation of freshly faked enthusiasm.

When it was Rebekah's turn, she stepped off the snowmobile and headed toward the tent.

"Rebekah," Chad called after her.

"What?"

"Just remember," he said. "Jesus hates you."

I took my shift in the tent just like the others, but it startled me to realize, even under the circumstances, how little I cared about the tourists. It seemed that their happiness was a bomb that could detonate at any time, and my job was to keep it from doing so. I had, at that point, spent a total of six months giving eight rides a day, eight hourlong tours in which I assured the tourists that the situation I blamed for my misery was, in fact, the Best Job in the World. Of course I understood why they saw it that way. I saw it that way myself, when I tried to be objective. After all, wasn't I the girl who was obsessed with the north? Wasn't I surrounded by snow, by wilderness, by dogs—the very things I'd wanted? On my best days I was grateful for the amazement on the tourists' faces, a reminder to appreciate—to try to appreciate—the astonishing scale of the place in which I lived. But most days I played by script. It was easy to pretend, to act delighted by all things Dog and Glacier, fascinated by every detail my giddy tourists reported about the cruise—a whale that very morning!—and their trip so far and their relatives stuck at home and their new Welsh corgi.

I was still a great guide, as evidenced by the generous tips and teary hugs I received, and the grateful letters that came up occasionally, wadded in a pilot's pocket. But I had decided that my energy was needed elsewhere, or rather that I needed it more. It felt like all I could do to stand in the snow, watching the patterns of light on the mountains, noting again the oppressive smell of propane, ducking my head at another sexual remark of the kind that, without Dan on my side, I was no longer spared. "Another one, Blair," a pilot would call, letter in hand. "What are you doing, giving blow jobs?"

That night, there wasn't much to figure out in terms of sleeping arrangements. The men had claimed the community tent, the storage tent had no floor space, and the cook would have the kitchen, which left the vet tent for me and Rebekah. That was okay. It was far away, at least. I slung our trash bags over my shoulders and staggered through the snow, dumping them just outside the entrance. Then I untied the bags and began rummaging inside for blankets. I had my head so deep in one that I didn't notice when Dan came up behind me.

He was holding back a dog with each hand, clutching their collars as they stood, panting, on their hind legs. I unzipped the flap and threw my blanket on the floor. "No room for dogs," I said. "We're sleeping here. There's nowhere else." A rule-follower at core, I had already checked with Malcolm, who advised me to take the dogs from the vet tent outside.

Dan pushed past me into the tent. When I followed him in, I saw that he had kicked aside my blanket and was tying his dogs into the small floor space.

"Why are you doing that?" I said. "We need to sleep here."

"The dogs are sick," he said.

"The dogs are fine."

He didn't answer.

"Dan," I said, "why are you doing that?"

There had been times in our relationship when Dan and I had talked, really talked—about the dogs, about Alaska, about what we wanted in life. He'd put his dreams into mushing—put everything into it. And I loved it when he told me about that. I felt like a child in whom a grown-up had confided: special, chosen. Trusted. It never occurred to me to question the imbalance; it never occurred to me that I had anything worth confiding.

And now, in the vet tent, I found myself reaching back for those moments. It struck me that I'd never been afraid of him, not even when he had pressed himself onto me, when he'd hushed my objections. I'd been resigned, unhappy, but never afraid. I wasn't afraid after the breakup, either, when I saw his anger. I understood it, or thought I did, which is as close to forgiveness as I've come. Even now, with thirty stranded tourists and a world of unknowns hanging over the morning, I wasn't scared. Unhappy, yes. Resigned. And here was Dan. It all felt familiar.

Dan had loved my naiveté, he told me once—loved me for it—and it was easy now to find that same part of myself, to speak from the one place that might reach him. "Dan," I said, more softly. The voice of a nice girl. "Why are you doing this?"

The dogs had settled down, but they looked up when I spoke, and their collars jingled. Otherwise it was near silent.

"Don't sleep here," Dan said. "Sleep with me. We'll find a place."

"I can't," I said.

"We could fix all this right now," he said.

I thought about it. What would be harder, what would be easier.

"I miss you," he said. He was crying, and the sight of that

shocked me more than anything else that had happened that day. "You're different now," he said. "I miss who you were. You were a better person before. Don't you remember how happy we were? We could have that back. It's up to you."

It was up to me—if only I would sleep with him. The unspoken standing offer, now made clear. In light of the rest of the summer, it didn't seem so terrible: the idea that things could change, that the animosity, at least, could be over. That I could belong again. I tried to remember the feeling of Dan's mouth on my ear, the heat of his skin beside me. Whether those feelings were more or less tolerable than the silence, the muttered comments and cruelty from coworkers, my constant prickling awareness of Dan's whereabouts. It was hard to say.

"I told Rebekah I'd stay with her tonight," I said. "Besides, there's nowhere else to sleep."

"We could say we need the kitchen," Dan said, smiling, and I was caught off guard by an image of the cook wielding ladles to defend her territory, and for a second everything dissolved, and we were two people laughing. Okay, I thought. Then, quickly, the moment was over.

"Fine," he said. "But it's not going to get better. When you want it to, come find me."

Later, after the tourists had gone grumbling to bed, Rebekah and I hooked Dan's dogs to a cable staked outside the vet tent. We spread our blankets in the small rectangle of floor between plastic chests and stacked dog crates, boxes of Neosporin and Cipro and tea tree oil. There was a folding table with zinc cream, rolls of stiff new booties, and mascara to shade the dogs' eyes from the sun. A propane heater hissed in one corner, and the rafters were draped in dark, insulating blankets. Within a few minutes of lying down, curled beside each other, the tent had warmed enough to release the strong smell of piss and menthol. It burned the inside of my nose.

I had always liked nights on the glacier—the thin buffer of time between leaving the dog yard and falling asleep. Most evenings I spent an hour or so grooming trails on a snowmobile, gunning the engine constantly to keep the metal grader from catching in the snow. It was an optional job, cold and loud at a time of day when most of the others were settling in after dinner, but I volunteered whenever I could. I'd realized early on that driving the trails was the only time I could be alone. I loved it when a fog came in, when I couldn't hear voices or the dogs and couldn't see anything but white opening up in front of me, white closing in behind. When I finished the rounds I'd pull up to an empty camp, a silent ghost town with just the faint glow of flashlights showing through tent walls. My tent was the farthest away, about a hundred yards from the base of a triangular mountain we called the Guardian. I'd peel off my clothes carefully, draping the rain shells and long underwear over the dozen lines strung from the central rafter. I hung my boots up last, upside down, catching the toes in loops of string so that moisture drained overnight. Then I'd tiptoe through the jungle of clothes and fast-spreading puddles to fall into my cot, zip my sleeping bag, and exhale.

Now, in the vet tent, Rebekah was not asleep. I could hear her turning, could make out the tiniest of whimpers. It was black in the tent, the snow's glow blocked by the insulating blankets— the first darkness I'd seen in weeks, and even that was unsettling. I whispered, "How are you doing?"

"My flight," she said, voice muffled by her pillow.

I'd forgotten. "Your parents will understand."

She sighed. That wasn't the point.

"I'm sorry the guys are so mean to you," I said. It was the first time I'd acknowledged it aloud. "I wish they weren't."

"What do you mean?" Rebekah, more audible now, must have turned her face toward me.

"You know," I said. "When they make fun of you. Jesus stuff. Everything."

"They're just being guys," she said. "That's how they do things."

"But it shouldn't be like that. You shouldn't have to go home because of them."

"I'm going home because I miss my family," she said.

We lay in the darkness.

"They're meaner to you than they are to me," Rebekah said. "I mean, if I can say this—Dan is the worst." She told me how she'd met him at the beginning of the summer, before I'd arrived in Juneau, and he'd said "all sorts of stuff" about me. "I was pretty nervous to share a tent with you, actually, after what I heard. Then I met you and within five minutes I was like, what was he talking about? 'Cause you were so friendly."

"No," I said, thinking. "That can't be. He still wanted us to be together."

Rebekah didn't answer. I had the odd, sudden feeling that she was embarrassed for me.

I thought: We were never happy. Neither of us. Of course.

It took me a long time to fall asleep. I wondered how many of the tourists were also awake, twisting in their borrowed sleeping bags, blinking their eyes against the constant, unfamiliar glow of the ice. In the morning I went to the kennel early, moving team by team, working to get all the dogs fed. I wasn't used to caring for the other guides' dogs, and when one of them nipped my arm, I felt like throwing down the food in frustration. But reaching my own team felt like coming home. I took my time with each dog, rubbing ointment between their toes, kissing the dips between their eyes. I took pride in brushing them sleek and stretching their muscles with my thumbs.

So maybe I could relate when Dan found me at the vet tent later that morning, where I was rolling up a blanket and—yes, a little—lingering in the quiet dark to feel whatever it was I couldn't understand enough to identify, a big feeling, something growing, and he said he was angry about the dogs. That's how he said it: "I'm angry about the dogs." And he had a point: he'd put his dogs in the vet tent, and I had moved them. For a moment it didn't matter that we both knew the dogs were fine, that they'd have been happier outside anyway, that there'd been nowhere else for me to sleep. The mushers had a tacit agreement not to interfere with each other's dogs, and I had broken it. I apologized, then turned back to my blanket. But Dan was still there.

"I'm angry about the dogs," he said.

"I'm angry that you talked about me to Rebekah," I said.

For that moment, there in the dark, all that mattered was the fact of his body before me, the fact that he did not—and could not—touch me, the thoughts I couldn't find in my own head. We talked as if we were human beings, as if talking was even an option. The one dog had a sore, Dan explained; he needed to keep his foot dry. And now he'd been in the snow all night and soaked off his scab.

And that was where I finally let myself disagree with him, and told him so. Whenever a dog in my team had a scab, I rubbed it with a toothbrush until it came off, until the skin underneath was pink and silky. When the scab re-formed, I scrubbed it off again. Sometimes I'd need to open the wound a dozen times before it finally healed over smooth. But if I did it right, it hardly left a scar.

That was the last gift Dan and I gave each other: a disagreement over dog care. Something real. But then he started to yell, and I to cry, and we hated each other with utter passion and an equally utter lack of discrimination—I hated his hat and his small hands and his stupid Canadian accent, and he hated my braid and my men's Carhartts, and we shouted things that

neither of us quite understood about dogs and love and responsibility.

Later, during that second day's Go Fish and poker and
snowman contests, I would not forget that moment with Dan.
It stayed in my head as I watched the sky, the fog and drizzle
and clouds rolling in and those same clouds pulling apart again,
through the hours stuffed with laughter and nerves and false
cheer. One of the tourists, an insulin-dependent diabetic, was at
risk of slipping into a coma if he was stuck on the ice for another day. But nobody could know, Malcolm decided: the tourists
mustn't worry, absolutely not. They were busy pining for their
ships, and we were to keep it that way.

I'd turn to the tourists beaming, and play cards and tell tall
tales that I swore up and down were true—it didn't matter what
I said, so long as I kept the smile. The pretense felt familiar,
easy. Every hour brought whispered rumors of rescue attempts
from Juneau, mountain climbers scaling cliffs with insulin in
their packs, helicopters bringing skiers to the edge of the icefield
before turning back, caught in a cloud. It was nice that they were
trying, I thought vaguely. The rescuers seemed fake to me, like
people who had died before I was born. I knew we were on our
own. We had always been on our own.

Rebekah spent the day in the kitchen, washing pots and
chopping vegetables. For my part, I hung out with the tourists,
driven less by a sense of duty than a desire to appear purposeful
while avoiding my increasingly agitated coworkers. For close
to two hours I spoke softly to the diabetic man, who I guessed
was in his midfifties. He sat on a cot, breathing slowly, radiat-
ing a calm I envied. I tried to tell him the stories I'd perfected
over months of tours, but they felt empty to me, forced. Halfway through a secondhand story about a polar bear encounter,
which was one of my standbys, I found myself wishing that I'd

never started telling it at all. Instead I took a piece of paper and drew a picture of the man, taking my time. I tried to capture the angles of his broad face, his soft skin. When I finished, he admired the sketch at length, then tucked it into his breast pocket. He took my hand. "I'm honored to be spending this time with such a lovely young woman," he said. I squeezed his hand and felt like a liar.

When the man fell asleep, I left his tent and went outside. The guides were sitting on snowmobiles, facing away, looking out over the icefield. It took me a moment to realize what they were watching. There was a figure in the distance, heading away from us. "He won't get far," someone said. "He'll either get spooked and come back, or he'll fall into a crevasse."

"Who is that?" I asked.

"Chad," the guides said in unison. One of them added, "Either he's gone for help or he just lost it."

"Lost it?" someone else said. "What's to lose?" They all laughed.

Chad waved. He was so small; the idea of watching him horrified me. I thought about going into the community tent, but instead I went to the guest outhouse and locked the door. It was, we were frequently told, the cleanest outhouse anyone had ever seen, with a vase of silk roses beside the toilet seat. It smelled nice in there, like biodegradable cleanser. I stood with my eyes closed, leaning against the door. But at some point I noticed myself, a sad, foul-smelling girl hiding in an outhouse, and once I'd noticed that I couldn't un-notice it. I squirted sanitizer on my hands and trudged back out into the snow.

The clouds to the north had sunk low enough that only a strip of mountain was visible, black stone between white and gray. I stared at the dark line, thinking of my body, my location in space, in a way that I hadn't for months. Here I was, in the middle of nothing and everything. Here I was, in Alaska. I didn't know if I was running toward my life or away from it.

It was late afternoon when the rescue helicopters made it in. We hadn't known they were coming—hadn't let ourselves hope for it—and we had begun preparations for a second night, had gathered the tourists in the community tent to break the news. That was when we heard the thin rumble, so quiet that I thought, at first, it was in my own head, and everyone froze, listening, and then began to cheer. The tourists rushed outside, clutching their jackets as the birds landed. I stepped back and watched from the kennel, sitting on a doghouse as some guides ushered the diabetic man into the nearest helicopter. Rebekah and the other tourists climbed into the other four.

I don't remember whether any of the tourists hesitated and looked back. It's true that earlier, a few had made remarks about wanting to stay. "I can't believe you get paid for this," they'd said, declaring that if they could take the summer off, they'd love to come work here. This Malcolm noted as a success. But in the moment, midrescue, the dogs were in a frenzy, yelping and leaping at their chains, and snow rose and everyone's clothes snapped in the wind, and the pilots were shouting, and the noise of the rotors drowned out everything else.

I remember this, though: When the helicopters first came into view, all of the guests, as if by instinct, raised their arms, reaching. And without realizing it, I did, too.

For years afterward, Dan would maintain that I had changed, gained some new or darker side that was, as he once explained in a letter, "without a doubt, not beneficial to who you are." I was young, starting college; of course I changed. I changed my clothes, my eating habits; I made new friends, tried yoga, worked as a telemarketer. But the change Dan meant was less obvious: the fact that I no longer went limp and let him touch me; the fact that, when forced to choose between the bitter protection he offered and the exhaustive work of shielding myself alone, I knew that I could not be with him. And yet the decision burned. Turning down Dan—choosing jurisdiction over my own body— felt like choosing exile from the very things in which his approval had granted me legitimacy. What role did I have, really, on the icefield, or even in dogsledding? Who had I been there? I didn't remember. Though I couldn't explain it at the time, leaving Dan felt like leaving everything I'd been working toward, all the ways I'd been trying to prove myself. And for a while, that's exactly what it meant. I left him and I didn't come back.

The change Dan lamented was that I had started to trust myself. But the way I saw it, I had flunked out of the north.

CHAPTER NINE

IN AUGUST, ON THE FIRST CLOUDLESS AFTERNOON in weeks, Jeanette made hay. Rune stopped by the shop for a six-pack of Tuborg and a bag of potatoes, then drove a dirt road into the forest to work his chainsaw in the warm summer air. Helge Jensen took *Abdullah* out fishing and boiled fresh-caught cod on the shore. The Sailor drove to the Polar Zoo, the northernmost zoo in the world, where he admired the albino grizzly bear, Salt, and his brown brother Pepper. Anne Lill took her grandson to Storsteinnes to watch monster trucks destroy each other. He the Rich One looked for, but did not find, cloudberries. Arild and I closed shop at six, then drove to the island of Sommarøy, west of Tromsø, where I gathered pink shells along a white coral beach. We made it back to the city just in time to buy sweet rolls for the drive home. The mountains were nearly pastel in the soft night sun, and patches of fjord boiled with herring, seagulls circling above. The lambs were wailing when we arrived. They were stuck in the garden, and dinner was late. "One thing I'm glad I'm not," said Arild, "that's a nursing lamb in Mortenhals." But I thought, as the lambs gulped their milk, that there were plenty worse lives to be had.

Sometimes I asked Arild that—what life would he want, if he were not the firstborn son of the shopkeeper in Mortenhals? Where would he be? He would not, he said, be anywhere but here. But he allowed that he might not want to run a shop.

"You could be a dogsledder," I teased. "You could be a seal hunter."

Arild fixed me with the long stare that meant I was being particularly foolish. He would not drive the ugly dogs, who had on occasion escaped from the folk school and eaten his sheep. He had never tolerated the smell of seal.

Though his choices were narrow by birth, his decision to run the shop had not been passive. He had loved driving trucks, loved knowing the roads and farms and people for hours around. But when the time came for him to take over the shop, he had chosen to give it all up. If he lived his life as a truck driver, what would outlast him? He'd leave behind an old vehicle, rusting by the side of the road. Sometimes, on drives, he saw a man driving the very truck he'd thought about buying. They nodded a greeting from the drivers' seats, then passed each other by. "You know him?" I'd asked, the first time this happened, and Arild's answer was uncharacteristically solemn. "I know him well," he said.

Sometimes he wished he had traveled when he was young, while his friends worked ships around the world; as it was, he'd rarely ventured farther than the Finnish border, where during his military duty he drove busloads of NATO officials to peer, breathless, into the dangerous mosses and boulders of a pawn of the Soviet Union. But Arild was largely content with the path of his life. In Mortenhals the things he'd built, the things he'd sustained, would last long after he was gone. He could give them to his children, his grandchildren. Though tradition granted his firstborn son, Henning, the right to take over the shop, he secretly hoped that Henning wouldn't be interested, and his youngest daughter, Emma, could take his place. He was close with Emma—she called to chat, he played the lottery for her every week—and she worked in retail herself. Emma managed a clothing franchise in southern Norway, and in her first year as manager, Arild bragged, her franchise had been the most profitable in its district. Henning may have been his firstborn son, but Emma, who'd gone to business school, had the soul of a shopkeeper. Her gift swelled Arild's heart with pride.

Then there was the RV park, the sheep, the Old House. Even the Old Store, which was not just his legacy but the whole community's—something he'd kept for them before anyone even knew they wanted it. That was his role: to anticipate needs. To provide. He was moved by his customers' loyalty, their appreciation. Of course, there were also customers who had left him during the hard times. Customers who borrowed from him when they were broke, but shopped in the city when their wallets were full. Customers he'd lost in the divorce. But there was little point in thinking about them.

"If I didn't have the shop," he finally allowed, "then I would have more sheep."

But as shopkeeper, he was part of a legacy that extended in both directions.

"And you?" he said to me. "If you didn't have to be a shopkeeper, what would you be?"

"I don't have to be a shopkeeper."

"Mm," said Arild. "Is that so."

At first, when we'd talked about my life in the United States, it was in the context of larger things—politics, government, the American educational system. But I'd begun to tell Arild more and more. He rarely responded in the moment, so that sometimes I wasn't sure if he was listening, or cared. But I had begun to realize that he remembered all of it, memorizing my life just as he did for his customers, for everyone he'd ever met. Sometimes he brought things up—asked about my hometown, or about my mother. Sometimes he bragged to customers, and I overheard details I scarcely remembered mentioning: "She American *pia*, she's not the worst. She had a letter to the editor in the *New York Times*." And I'd blush, somewhere between embarrassed and pleased.

Arild cared about my parents, and asked about them often. He approved of my father's work in tobacco prevention; Arild himself ran a similar campaign on a smaller scale, dispensing moral judgment with each cigarette pack he retrieved from behind the counter. When I mentioned that I wanted to get a sweater for my mom, he went into Edel's closet and pulled a folded, hand-knit beauty off his mother's shelf. Would it fit? It would. His eyes shone.

For a few years after Lillehammer, I'd felt acutely what I considered to be my parents' betrayal. I didn't know how agonized they'd been back at home, how they'd priced out plane tickets, how my mother had written her angry e-mail while caring for her sick father and his wife, and regretted it immediately. Still I had sensed, as my anger faded with time, that the betrayal was not theirs to commit. It belonged to the world itself, which was not as safe as they'd once made it for me. And as the years passed—as I moved on to folk school, to Alaska, into Dan's arms and out again—I'd grown comfortable with the idea that the danger had never been theirs. That my parents' job was to love me, and in this they were transcendent; it was my own job to protect myself.

As impossible as that sometimes seemed.

BACK IN COLLEGE, AFTER LEAVING ALASKA, I had studied environmental law and coached the synchronized figure-skating team. I taped pictures of sled dogs to my walls, promising myself that it was only a matter of time before I'd be back on the runners. I wrote about the Arctic for my classes whenever I could, and eventually started writing about it for magazines, too—another chance, like being a guide, for me to make myself an expert. I thought often of the dogs I had loved: Saddam and Condy, Jaxon and Stoic. Sometimes I pretended to strangers that I was Norwegian, only visiting the States for a short time. "Call me Målfrid," I'd say, with just the right touch of accent. The north still governed my thoughts, my daydreams; only this time, whenever I thought of going back, I had a dozen reasons to put it off. I couldn't afford it, or I had to take this job, that opportunity. Not once did I let myself think that I was simply afraid. The north was supposed to have fixed my fear.

"Should we go back to Alaska?" I asked Rebekah each spring, on the phone. We'd sit in silence, pondering our excuses, before deciding that this was not the year. Maybe next year. Maybe the year after that. But soon Rebekah was married, pregnant, settled in a way I could only marvel at from a distance. She said, "I would never let my daughter do what we did."

For those years I was serious, devoting myself to school and work; upon graduation, my class would vote me Most Likely to Be Found in the Library. I did not date. I did not go to parties. I did not drink at all. I told myself that I didn't like that sort of thing. That my aversion to alcohol had nothing to do with the last time I'd gotten drunk, at a bonfire in Juneau, and leaned on Dan the whole way home.

It would be two years before I slept with anyone else, before I met a shy boy—in the library—whose lips I thought about at night, who kissed me gently before the first time we had sex and whispered, "We don't have to do this if you don't want to." I almost cried. It hadn't occurred to me that even then, lying naked beneath him, I still had a choice.

Besides, I wanted to.

It was this wanting that astonished me more than anything. That I liked sex. That whatever had happened with Dan had been something he'd done to me, rather than something we'd done together. It wasn't like this, wasn't two people drawn to each other and discovering how close they could get.

Two years later, when I went to graduate school, I met Quince. He had dark hair and pale blue eyes and a dangerous, direct way of talking—to peers, to teachers, to anyone—that made him somewhat polarizing among the other students: he called bullshit when he saw it, particularly if that bullshit had to do with justice, or gender, or art. He was a writer and sometime cowboy who had recently ridden his horse across South Dakota, and lived on a farm in northern Wisconsin, in a light-filled house made of logs that he'd skidded from the forest with a team of horses. He loved the cold, loved the Wisconsin winter. In the two-dimensional world of academia, his friendship was a balm, a reminder of what felt real. Soon after we met, he invited me to pick up his horse, which an aging cowboy had just driven four hundred miles and dropped off at a local McDonald's. Over the next weeks Quince taught me to ride bareback, up and down the road in the dusk of the prairie night; eventually he climbed on to ride double behind me. His horse's body language seemed foreign, impenetrable, compared to the easy expressiveness I'd learned to read in a team of dogs. It didn't help that with Quince's hands on my hips, I had trouble thinking at all.

With Quince I found a balance that I hadn't known I was missing, someone who moved easily between worlds I'd felt alone in straddling. His relationship to nature was at once awed and utilitarian. He was a hunter and veteran who wrote for a magazine about nonviolence; he split his time between New York City and the Northwoods, and praised equally a friend's award-winning symphony and a neighbor's technique for canning tomatoes.

He was also transgender, and had transitioned three years earlier—at age thirty—from female to male. It's too easy to pin personality to gender, particularly for trans people, but in his case, I believe one result was this: a lifetime of knowing that his truth was not what the world saw had helped him form a vehement moral system, one that didn't necessarily align with social rules. Chief, to him, was friendship—supporting the people he loved. He delighted in surprises, postcards and packages that he sent constantly to his dearest. If you were his friend, he would turn up from across the country to celebrate your accomplishments; if a family member died, he would be there washing dishes; if you were depressed, he might give you some challenges—*eat almonds on Mondays*—to get you through the days. He thought nobody above or beneath him. If he believed something was right, he found a way to do it.

Quince had always been masculine, but testosterone brought out impulses in him that he did not recognize, that we both struggled to understand. One night, soon after we first slept together, he held me in the dark, kissing my forehead and my hair. "I adore you," he whispered. Then his arms hardened around my shoulders. "What is it?" I asked, and when he spoke again he sounded genuinely surprised: "I want to *kill* anyone who hurts you." I stiffened at the violence of the words, then relaxed into them. How to describe how safe that felt, to have male strength—the ferocity of it, an anger I'd never understood—poised at my defense? And sexy—it was definitely sexy. What did that mean? About me, about him? What I feared most was men, and what I feared for was my body, and yet my body *wanted* men, and there was no answer for any of it.

No, that wasn't right. There was an answer for some of it. And that answer, I felt certain, was somewhere in the north, if I would only go and find it.

I still wanted adventure. I had always wanted adventure—

wanted the thrill and the stories and the identity that came with it. But I'd become acutely aware that adventure was a kind of violence, too. It was there in the mountains and the ice and the deep cold, the speed of the dogs and the changing weather. It was there in Dan. Of course, I knew that Dan was not Alaska. But he was part of it, represented some hard masculinity that seemed to thrive in the north, and that I didn't want to be shoved up against. Not again. I wasn't sure if I could handle it.

But at the same time, I wasn't sure I'd feel safe—anywhere, really—until I had proved to myself that I could.

CHAPTER TEN

IVE YEARS AFTER LEAVING ALASKA, I came up with a new plan for going back to Norway. I had not been there since graduating from folk school. But now an editor had put me in touch with some reindeer herders who would let me join them, and their herds, as they crossed the tundra in the annual migration out of Kautokeino, in northern Norway's barren interior. The twin jobs of reporting and writing a feature story would give me the structure and courage I needed. I imagined myself fording rivers, taking notes around a campfire, riding an ATV over a sea of sunset-colored mosses. I bought a return ticket for two months later.

Ten days before I was supposed to leave, I received a message from the reindeer herders. They had set off earlier than expected, and were already deep in the wilderness. I was still welcome to join them, they reassured me; but even I knew that the task of setting off alone onto the tundra in the hopes of possibly running into a particular herd of reindeer with a two-week head start was not a realistic one.

Still, I never considered canceling the trip. The momentum propelling me toward Norway—the ways I'd been mentally preparing for it, running through scenarios, getting used to the idea—seemed to exist independently of any particular plan or goal. I didn't know where I would go. I just knew that if I waited any longer, I would no longer be able to buy my own excuses, would have to face the fact that I was no longer connected to the self that I'd built there. Quince held me all night before I left. I couldn't stop crying. "What's wrong?" he kept asking, but I could only shake my head, overwhelmed with emotion that would drain into numbness as soon as I stepped onto the plane. Returning north, once more alone, seemed like the most terrifying and the most inevitable thing I'd ever done.

The strangeness hit me as soon as I landed in Oslo. For one thing, everyone spoke Norwegian, which was a language I regularly thought in but hadn't heard in years. It had begun to feel like a private language to me. Now everyone was walking around, speaking the words from inside my head. The streets were clean and the people were well dressed. They were almost all white. They almost all wore Nike sneakers. I went to a thrift store and bought a wool sweater and then I went to a 7-Eleven and bought three sweet rolls and ate them all in a row. Then, because it was only noon, I went to the National Gallery and sat on a leather bench for two hours. Across from me was a painting by Edvard Munch called *The Dance of Life*. Couples were dancing on a shore, but one of the men was a green monster with a red mouth. His partner in white looked away, his arms around her waist. The moon shone on the water.

My latest plan was to start in southern Norway, see some old friends, and then hitchhike north, avoiding Lillehammer. For the first few nights, I stayed with Natasha in Oslo. Natasha had a fancy apartment and a Portuguese boyfriend. We drank absinthe and watched a reality television show in which participants painted themselves to look like undersea creatures. A human turtle submerged himself in a tank and all his makeup came off.

Natasha was still skeptical about Norwegians. "Do you want to understand them?" she said. "They're the kind of people who, if you call them because you're not safe and you need a ride, they'll say yes, but only if you pay for gas."

Maybe, I thought, my problem was that I didn't like Norwegians.

I felt more comfortable when I left the city. Farms spotted the green valleys and forests shrouded the mountaintops. Everything was green; it was late May. I took a bus, and then another bus, asking the driver for directions. "I'm not from here," I explained.

The driver sighed. "Obviously."

It was nice to sit on the bus, watching out the window, moving forward without doing anything at all. I could have ridden for days. But after three hours, I came to the end of the line: a brown-and-yellow log building on top of a hill, Valdres Folk School, where the former principal of 69°North now worked with his wife. The principal's house was traditional—too traditional, the neighbors muttered, with its black-painted log walls and grass roof, its reindeer-fur boots by the doorway. But it reminded me of northern Norway. I knocked on the door. I'd sent a note to say I was coming.

The inside of the house was entirely birch: walls, floor, ceiling, cupboards, table, chairs, like some sort of elaborate sauna. It was disorienting. The principal, who looked like a happier version of Brad Pitt, put some *joik*—Sami throat singing—on the stereo. He scooped vanilla ice cream into bowls and sprinkled nuts on top. This was his favorite brand of ice cream, he said— very creamy. He closed his eyes when he took the first bite. I liked how much pleasure he took from the ice cream.

I asked him if it was different, running another folk school. "Look," he said. "It doesn't matter where I am. The most important thing I can teach my students is how to be cold."

How to be cold?

"How to live," he said.

I thought of him in leather pants, with binder clips on his nipples.

At 69°North, every student had been required to complete an *årsprosjekt*, a yearlong project that they designed themselves. Something they'd always wanted to do. One girl had knit a sweater. Another built a dog agility course. Several students made knives. Several students learned to play the guitar. One boy taught himself to hunt. Three years later, he died in a hunting accident. The other students went to his funeral, but I didn't, because I was in America.

For my *årsprosjekt*, I wanted to write a book, but I didn't have a computer. So the principal gave me the key to his private office. Every night, when I wasn't dogsledding, I'd enter the teachers' wing of the school building, which was locked and smelled like lemonade. Students weren't allowed in the teachers' wing, let alone the principal's office, which had a small window overlooking the common room. Every night I sat there. I loved opening the file, typing the first words, my thoughts filling the quiet space. The book was about a girl from California who discovers that she's a changeling, and that her true home is in northern Norway, and that everybody knew it but her. So she goes to Norway and learns to dogsled. Along the way, she solves a centuries-old murder involving an evil identical twin. The twin part was based on a ghost story that Tallak told one night around a fire. Since Tallak said it, it was obviously true.

"That was huge for me," I told the principal now. "The fact that you let me use your office? It made me want to work harder to deserve it."

He took a bite of ice cream.

"You were an interesting case," he said.

He was as much a psychiatrist as an administrator. Analyzing each student, trying to figure out what they needed. Folk schools, he said, traded less in puffed-up self-esteem than in uncomfortable self-awareness. Students learned that they were bossy, that their outspoken confidence was obnoxious, that they were too selfish with money, that they collapsed under physical discomfort. "You liked yourself because you were good at things," he said. "But your challenge was to like yourself for just *being*. Because one day you were going to fail at something big, and if you'd based your self-worth on accomplishments, you were going to be shattered. You were brave but you didn't trust your own instincts."

I thought of Alaska. Failing and leaving.

"You're teaching people to be happy," I said.

"I don't care if they're happy," he said. "I just want them to be successful in all things."

That night, I slept alone in the empty folk school. It was raining. I read a book that the principal lent me, about animals eating each other in the darkness. In the morning, before I left, he asked my schedule. I didn't know. "The soul of a Northlander," he observed. "Don't know where you're going, don't know how long you'll be."

I thought I knew where I was going. I was going to see Oda, with whom I'd once dogsledded across Finland through a blizzard. She lived in a village about thirty miles away called Bromme. There was no bus. I started walking. I held out my thumb.

A few cars slowed, but none of them stopped. A woman in a red Volvo met my eyes and accelerated. I watched her car shrink away down the road. "I'm Norwegian," I said aloud. "I'm in my car. I don't *like* strangers." But it didn't make me feel better.

I walked all morning and all afternoon. A river joined another river. The road joined a highway. By midnight my thighs were twitching, and the wind of each passing RV caught me like a shove.

That was the point at which my trip changed.

In fact, it was exactly the situation I had imagined: traveling by whatever means available, sleeping wherever I stood when night happened to fall. That was the kind of freedom I needed in order to come back to myself, to really figure out how I fit into this country. A wanderer—no, an adventurer, following nothing but whims. How exciting, I told myself, to be spending my first night on the road, even if that road was a highway shoulder. It was still light. I waited until no cars were passing, then ducked through a thicket, passing into a clearing on the other side that looked suspiciously like a backyard. I pitched my tent on a pile of moose droppings and climbed inside.

It was cold, a sharp cold that came up through the ground and wracked my chest with shivers. The sound of each passing car rose and fell as if it were swooping overhead. In the yellow half-light of the subarctic night, shadows played across the tent fly. Swinging branches, birds that wouldn't sleep. I didn't know where I was. Nobody knew where I was.

I didn't realize I was panicking until I tried to take a deep breath, and tried again, and choked.

I remembered stories I'd heard from other women who camped alone: men who circled their tents, pressed the dark outlines of hands to the fabric, whispered threats like sweet nothings or else loudly considered their options. And those were the stories that ended well. There was no limit to the ways in which someone could hurt me.

I would not see them coming.

How could I sleep? Surely a driver had seen me duck through the bushes, had seen that I was alone, was even now standing at the edge of the clearing with his hands in his pockets. I lay with a hat over my face, blocking the twilight, but with my eyes open; I held a great tight balloon in my chest and sensed that if I gave in to just one whimper or tear, it would explode. And I realized, with a certainty that was almost comforting, that I could not travel like this. I had tried my plan and it had failed. I shook and shook, waiting minute by minute until the sun rose and caught me in its glow. By 3 A.M. I was back on the shoulder with my shadow stretched before me.

As long as I was walking, I was safe. The only vehicles were trucks, driving the night shift from Oslo to Bergen, and a traveling carnival that passed, piece by piece, over the course of several hours—now a Ferris wheel, now a stack of bumper cars, trembling slightly under colorful ropes.

Later, describing the night to Quince in a letter, I'd summarize it in three words: *I got spooked.* I didn't tell him how, to calm myself, I'd imagined his arms around me, his voice in my ear. *I love you. I'm proud of you. I love you. I'm proud of you.* Repeating for hours. But he must have understood, because soon after that he e-mailed that he was sending me a package. "Please open it privately," he wrote, "as you would any, um, intimate thing that you might not want immediately seen by others." I thought it was probably a vibrator or a gun.

It was still early when I reached Bromme, which had a single gas station. I bought a hot dog for breakfast. "How did you get here?" the cashier asked me, and when I told her, she gasped. "Heavens!" she said. "You're a tough girl."

I swallowed my hot dog and asked if she knew where Oda Evensen lived. But she shook her head. "There's no Oda Evensen here."

As it turned out, Oda lived in the opposite direction from where I had come. But there in the well-lit gas station, my stomach full, talking with a woman who was determined to help me, I couldn't bring myself to care. All that mattered was that last night was far behind me, that the cashier knew a trucker I could hitch a ride with, that I was no longer on my own. I felt so infused with community that, as I waited outside for the trucker, I asked an old woman in her garden if she wanted help weeding. "Uh," she said. She squinted at me, and I saw her eyes register my face: a stranger. "I prefer to do it alone."

That night I stayed with Oda. She had forsworn her lesbianism to become a Jehovah's Witness. She was between homes. We drove switchbacks up a mountain with guinea pigs in our laps, looking for a place to sleep, while two border collies moaned in the backseat. Oda missed having a girlfriend, but she didn't have long to wait before the end of the world. "I have the animals," she pointed out. We stopped at an abandoned barn on top of the mountain and ate store-bought almond cake for dinner. The dogs licked our fingers clean.

Oda would have welcomed me to stay longer, but despite the fact that all my plans so far had fallen through, and that I had been back in Norway less than a week, I itched with the odd sensation that I was running out of time. I didn't want to stay in the Southland. I wanted to go back to the Arctic.

Still, I couldn't quite puzzle out why it felt so vital to me. I loved the language of the north, and the remoteness thrilled me; the nearest gas station could be not just a few hours' but a three-day walk away. But then I imagined walking along a road and a car pulling up beside me, a man inside, and I felt a flash of panic that made me want to just cash in the trip entirely, stay in Oslo with Natasha, lie on a towel in the sun. That's what I had wanted during that panicked night on the roadside: I wanted out. I wanted to be done with the whole thing. It didn't seem worth it. And then I had kept going and people called me a tough girl and I was so comforted by that, like I could almost believe it, although I hardly knew what it meant.

I had intended to hitchhike to the top of the country, but I bought a plane ticket instead—a concession I allowed myself—and flew to Tromsø in a late-May blizzard. "We are now descending into Troms—" the stewardess announced, snow whipping against the windows, and then she caught her breath and cursed, "Oh, fucking cunt. Cunt!" With a scrabbling sound, the microphone clicked off. I looked around. The other passengers were reading, or else leaned back with their eyes closed. No one acknowledged the outburst. Nobody seemed to have heard it. The plane landed smoothly. I got off with weak legs, hoisted my backpack, and walked out of the airport, into the parking lot, where the wind nearly knocked me over. I turned around and walked back inside.

At least the airport was warm.

It was early afternoon, which gave me plenty of time to avoid my next decisions. I bought another bag of sweet rolls at a 7-Eleven and set up camp on a bench by the baggage claim, reading and rereading a stack of brochures that seemed unchanged from when I had first encountered them six years before: Arctic Jeep Safari. Arctic Sea Cruise. Arctic Kayak Day Trip. Arctic Yoga. Arctic Plumbing. Arctic Sex shop.

The Northernmost Water Park in the World.

The Northernmost Tea Shop in the World.

The Northernmost Burger King in the World.

Arctic, I knew, meant nothing to the people who lived here. *Arctic* was for tourists. But northern Norway—being *nordnorsk*—ran in the marrow of their bones.

Planes landed one by one. The small airport emptied, then filled, then emptied. Outside, trees bowed, snapping upright between gusts; the snow didn't fall so much as rearrange itself in midair. In every direction, sharp white mountains faded into dark sky.

After all the buildup, after all the *significance* I'd assigned to this trip, it was hard to admit to myself how lost I felt. I was a planner by nature; in the past, I'd always traveled with a mission, or at least a role—to be a daughter, a student, a guide. Now, I didn't even know where I was going, let alone what I would do when I got there. I looked into the coming weeks and recognized nothing. I wanted to keep moving until an answer presented itself, making my way toward Kirkenes, the northernmost town in mainland Europe—because if north was good, then *as north as possible* was even better. But what if the answer never came? And how would I sleep? I wasn't eager to relive my tent experience. I would gladly have taken a job, but I wasn't sure where to find one. Maybe I could find a dogsledder who needed help.

It was Sunday and, although I didn't know it, a national holiday. Everything was closed. The snow hardened into sleet. After several hours of stalling in the airport, I wrapped myself in a garbage bag and walked alone through the downtown, crossing empty streets, catching my hunched reflection in the dark storefronts. The only thing that seemed alive was a cruise ship at the dock, its windows bright through the storm. It looked dry. I walked toward it without really thinking, then, in a burst of purpose, strode up the ramp and through the open doorway. "Hold on," the guard said, and I froze. But she just gestured at a dispenser on the wall. "Be sure to sanitize your hands."

With a mumble, I sanitized my hands. Then, heart pounding, I climbed three sets of stairs, hid my backpack behind a chair, borrowed a book from the lending library, and found my way to a communal sitting room with pillowy armchairs. Outside, sleet thudded on the window, and waves rose against a dark sea. Inside, two women were knitting. I tucked my legs under me and tried to read.

An announcement, a captain's voice: the ship would be leaving port in forty-five minutes, at 7 P.M.

One of the knitters glanced at me.

"Do you know if this room closes at night?" I asked her. I grimaced, as if trying to remember. "I've been up weird hours. You know, with the jet lag."

"Oh, no," she said. "It's open all the time." She was American. I wondered if she took a lot of cruises, if she'd ever cruised through Juneau.

Thirty-five minutes.

I knew myself well enough to know that to pull off a stunt like this, I'd have to trick my own conscience. I couldn't just wait here, counting down. But I could fall asleep, wake up—regretfully—at sea, and spend the night reading in the sitting room that never closed. Sneak off in the morning. I didn't care where I ended up; I just wanted someone else to make the decision for me. I lay back and closed my eyes, thinking about what a good place I was in. How dry it was. How safe.

How much trouble I would get into if I was caught.

Two minutes before the ship closed its doors, I grabbed my backpack and walked back out into the storm. The guard tried to stop me but I broke into a run.

The dock and the streets were empty. The bus yard was closed.

How could I stay in a hotel? Hotels in Norway, especially in the city, are exorbitantly expensive; one night would have used a third of my budget for the summer. But my reluctance went deeper than money. Staying in a hotel would have forced me to acknowledge that the trip, as I'd conceived it, had backfired. I was already failing at every hope I had brought into the journey: that I was brave, resourceful, tough in solitude. That I could, by some combination of will and fate, force myself to belong.

So I went to the only place that I knew was open, because Oda had told me it would be open: the Kingdom Hall of Jehovah's Witnesses. Inside, the hall was bare and clean, a large room with rows of seats before a low stage. A few men and women looked up at my entrance. The women wore lace; the men, three-piece suits. I wore baggy pants, greasy hair, and a face full of mosquito bites from my night on the mountain. "Come in!" they said. "What's your name? Where are you from?" They brushed the snow from my coat and I let myself be tended. During the service I sat in the back row, pressed between two soft, smiling women as the storm throbbed against the walls around us. Afterward, an older couple came over and took my hands in theirs. "We've been discussing it," they said, "and we've decided you should stay in our spare room."

In fact, I stayed with the couple for almost a week, each day that the snow lasted. They gave me a small room with a cot, a stationary bicycle, and blackout curtains, and I was sure I had never slept anywhere more luxurious. My rent was to wash the dishes and ask questions about Jehovah. I paid it gladly. I'd like to believe that the deception of my stay—the fact that their religion, though interesting, did not move me in any spiritual way—was what finally drove me out. But my reasons were simpler: the sun broke through the clouds, and I had a package to pick up.

It seems strange in retrospect, but I had not really thought about going to Malangen. The way I saw it, everybody I knew there had already left: all the students, and even the teachers, because the folk school staff turned over regularly. I figured that going there alone would only be depressing. But Quince had asked for an address and, at a loss, I'd given him the address to 69°North. It wouldn't be hard to swing by and pick up his package. Now that I was headed there, though, I felt more optimistic the closer I got—I figured I could hang out with the dogs, chat with some current students, and open the mystery gift. Quince always gave thoughtful gifts, and whatever this was, I had a feeling it was good. Sexy or funny. Physical proof that somebody knew what I was doing, and cared. Maybe it would be just what I needed to get my mojo back. I thanked the Witnesses, left them some maple syrup as a gift, and caught another bus.

It is very hard to describe what happened to me when I reached Malangen.

It was an understanding, I guess, but it hit me with the force of shame, or joy—something chemical, like the first spring sun after darkness.

First thing was the mountains. We weren't even close yet, but the shape of the landscape changed. There was a certain silhouette to the mountains, that meltedness, and the sight of it gripped me with a shock that froze me solid. So, first thing was the mountains.

Second thing was the sagging fish racks on the pebbled shore.

Third thing was the spacing of the farms, and the stretch of snowy bog that surrounded the road. Cloaked, with colors underneath.

How hadn't I known that this place was the point of everything? That it had been the point of everything all along?

Just a totally normal thing, getting off the bus in Mortenhals. Not a big deal at all. Just a normal thing to walk up the driveway to the folk school, find two small packages on the steps, make my way into the woods. Obviously the woods were familiar. Obviously they were perfect. Obviously I was safe here. I sat down and opened the well-sealed boxes. Obviously I was carrying a knife.

The boxes were full of camping supplies. Chapstick. Gloves. A sweatband. A flashlight. A magazine. Some sort of charger. Some sort of nylon holster, which was empty. A contact lens holder. Two bandannas. A fanny pack. I looked for a note and found one scrap of paper with a torn edge. Quince's handwriting, in marker, in misspelled Norwegian: "Happy Trails!"

Something was wrong. I didn't even wear contacts. I unzipped the fanny pack and found it empty. I reached inside the gloves. I spread everything out on top of my backpack.

Please open it privately, as you would any, um, intimate thing that you might not want immediately seen by others.

My eyes fell on the flashlight. It was silver metal, still in its clamshell packaging. But the photo on the case showed a red plastic flashlight, not a silver metal one. Looking closer, I saw that the packaging had been opened. The flashlight was big, about ten inches long. I pulled it out. It had metal spikes on the end. It had a button marked with a lightbulb, and another button marked with a lightning bolt. It had a socket for a charger. The charger had come in the second box. The flashlight fit in the holster.

I was in Malangen. In Malangen I could do anything.

I picked up the flashlight with both hands, pointing it away from myself, and pressed the lightning bolt.

Quince told me later that, when he said he was shopping for his girlfriend, they tried to sell him a girlie stun gun. A pink one, little and cute—the kind that could fit in an evening bag. But I had said I was scared for my safety, and if there was one thing Quince understood, it was that people knew better than anyone else what their position was in the world, what their struggles were. If I said I felt danger, he believed in that danger. If what I wanted was safety, and he could help, then he would. So he didn't want to send me a cute mini-weapon. He wanted to send me something powerful, something I could decide whether or not to accept. He chose that particular million-volt stun gun because, when the saleswoman demonstrated it, when the crackling electricity filled the room, she peed her pants.

Me, I just screamed and dropped it. Then I picked it up, strapped it into the holster, and tucked it into the bottom of my bag. It was heavy, but I didn't mind the weight. I was in Malangen and Quince loved me and I had received my first piece of mail. I had finally arrived.

CHAPTER ELEVEN

NILS WALKED INTO THE SHOP AND grinned, like everyone was watching. They were, of course, though they hadn't looked up. "When's today's *Northern Light* coming?" Jeanette said, flipping through her phone, and before Arild could respond, Odd Jonny interrupted: "The newspaper's like death," he said. "You know it's coming but never when." A well-worn joke. They took long sips of coffee. Nils settled at the head of the table and crossed his arms. He knew everyone's questions were burning under their nonchalance, and, as the man with the power, he fully intended to wait them out.

Nils looked good. He was fit and glowing from his weeks on the beaches of Thailand, his skin a deep bronze, his sleeves rolled up to show that the sores on his arms had healed over, leaving patches of soft pink. He cracked open a Coke.

Jeanette didn't wait long. So: was there a girl?

There was a girl, Nils allowed. He hadn't met my eyes yet. Odd Jonny looked up.

Who was she?

Her name was—well, something with a *K*. Nils couldn't pronounce it, so he just called her Gi.

And where?

Well—

Nils turned the bottle cap over in his hands. No writing inside. He batted it across the tabletop with his index fingers. Well, the thing was, he didn't need any girl. That was what he'd found out. He'd had a good time, drunk beer and enjoyed himself, hung out with the family of his friend's ex, who were welcoming but miffed when they learned that Nils's friend hadn't brought them money. There were girls everywhere in Thailand. Girls driving two and two on mopeds, whistling at him. Like he was hot shit. Girls asking to come home with him. But Gi, she had been there from the start. She'd been waiting for him. And he liked her all right, and thought maybe something would come of it. But she was so jealous, Gi. He'd go dancing and she'd follow, he'd talk to girls and she'd follow, she'd accuse him of avoiding her and just blow right up. "Anyway," he said, pleased by the room's attention, drawing out the dregs of his story. "Anyway! What I figured, you know—she didn't even like me. Or, she liked me *jo* all right, but she liked me before she even met me, right? She just thought Norwegians were rich." So he told her it was over, and came back to Norway alone. "I do just fine," he said, leaning on his elbows, sweeping his eyes around the table to grin at everyone in turn except me. This was flirting, this avoidance. I had no patience for it. "I have my own farm. I don't need to share it with *anyone*."

"Except dear Blair, of course," he finished, his eyes darting at me quick, a flash.

"Except for me," I said, staring at him until he looked back at me. A moment's smile. A truce. But Jeanette had followed his gaze; Nils should stay in the spotlight. "How'd you break it to her?" I asked. "Gi."

"Be patient," said Nils. "All details with time."

"There's no time," I said. "I'm leaving next week."

Nils drank some Coke. "I just told her so," he said. "Why are you so interested?"

"Not," I said.

He laughed. We were okay.

When Helge Jensen called me to go fishing, to sail out onto the lit night fjord, I said I'd be there in half an hour. So folks said his ship didn't float? I could swim to shore. I borrowed Arild's car and braked my way back to Mestervik. When the car broke down, I walked the rest of the way to the fishing dock. Seagulls swung over me as if on strings.

Once more, Helge Jensen helped me onto his boat, holding my hands just a bit too long after I jumped down on the deck. It seemed like the crowd had already gathered. A few empty beer cans lay tossed on the ground. There was a quiet man named Markvard, and Helge's cousin Svein, and Svein's date Katrin, who was visiting from Ukraine. Svein wore snug jeans and a faded track jacket with a silhouette of a trawler on the back. Katrin was slight, with blond curls pulled back in a braid and dainty ballet flats. As *Abdullah* churned from the dock, I settled into one of the leather couches on the deck. Katrin sat down across from me, crossing her legs at the ankles, and Svein dropped down beside her like he'd been waiting for his chance. She stared away from him, into the sun.

Svein smiled at me, like we were sharing a joke. "It's only her first visit," he said. They'd met on the Internet a year ago, and already things were great. "Look at her," he said, and then he waited until I did to continue: "Look how she takes care of herself. They all do, in her country. It's a poor country, okay, but the women are still *women* there."

His words hit some part of me—*the women are still women*—and I became aware of myself, in my cargo pants and wool sweater, and smiled weakly. Svein seemed not to notice. He reached around with his free arm and rubbed Katrin's knee, like he was tousling the head of a child, and then left his hand there. Katrin tucked her long fingernails under each other in her lap, clicking them back and forth. Svein beamed at her. "Norwegian women," he said, lowering his voice, "they're not exactly something you'd want to collect. Anyway, she loves it here. She loves all of it. Right, Katrin?"

Katrin, clicking her fingernails, didn't respond.

"What does she love?" I said.

"Fish," said Svein. "It's all she wants. She can't get enough of it. It's fish and more fish for every meal. Fish for lunch and fish for dinner and roe for breakfast, on bread." Katrin raised her eyebrows. "FISH," he explained in English. "YOU IS EATING FISH."

"Oh," said Katrin. "Yes, fish."

"She's moving here?" I said. It was gross, speaking Norwegian past her. It was the easiest thing to do.

"Well," said Svein, "you'd have to ask *her* that. But between you and me, I'll just say it's going very well." He leaned against her and laughed suddenly, loudly. "Right?" Katrin looked at the sun and closed her eyes.

Somewhere a faint radio played a jazz standard, the sound of horns drifting over the sounds of the engine and the waves. We churned down the center of the fjord. The mountains on either side of us were traced with white lines, creeks draining the last of the summer snow.

Helge Jensen came out of the cabin, leaving Markvard to steer, and sat down on my couch. His body didn't touch mine, but his fluffy hair tickled my cheek. *"Abdullah,"* he said, looking around at the skipper. She'd never sunk, *Abdullah,* though his other ships had, too many times to count. One January, he told me, he'd been hauling a freight of fish heads around Lofoten with a friend and a German shepherd. When the boat sank offshore, they climbed onto a little islet, a rock outcropping. But the coast guard helicopter wanted to fly them to Bodø, which was where their boat had been heading. If they got to Bodø by helicopter, they wouldn't have gotten there *fairly*. "No," Helge Jensen remembered saying, "we'll go to land." So they swam, and while it was tough to convince the dog to leave the islet, they all made it back to shore. Fair as fair.

"Was that when you taped your lighter to your head?" I asked.

Helge Jensen squinted at me. "You've done your research."

There was a light onshore now, a fire at the water's edge with two figures standing by it, one shirtless and one in a red bra. Helge Jensen smiled. That was the Sailor and his lady, enjoying the night. He pulled his phone from his pocket and dialed.

Behind us, Svein and Katrin had started fishing. Katrin held a pole, lifting it in a bored rhythm, while Svein stood behind her with his hands on her waist. I found another pole in the back of the boat and came to join them. There was a breeze from the north, and we faced into it. Onshore, the figures came to the edge of the water and shaded their eyes, looking for us. Then they returned to their fire.

Suddenly Katrin squealed, and reeled in a cod. She laughed as Svein unhooked it for her, and posed for a cell phone picture holding the fish by the gills in one hand and making a peace sign with the other. She giggled as she dumped the fish into a blue plastic barrel.

Svein looked into the barrel, then winked at me. "One has to be well rested to get fish," he said. "So you understand, I rested her *well* last night." I tried to think of a response but the pole jerked in my hand, so I began reeling instead, winding in slow motion until another cod broke the surface. It gasped its big mouth as Svein unhooked it. Then Katrin got a second cod, and Svein lifted it by its eye sockets and kissed its lips. "Katrin!" he said, his lips moving against the fish's. "Photo! Look, photo! You can kiss." There was blood in the lines of his knuckles.

Katrin stood back, flicking through pictures on her phone. "*You* can kiss," she said.

It was hot and we were drifting shoreward. When Katrin got a third cod, Svein said, "You can bet she got rest last night," and when my second fish was a thin, undersized herring, he burst into laughter. "You got a herring because you're so *nice*," he said, tossing it back into the water.

Nice. There it was again. Just like Dan had said: that I was the nicest girl he ever met.

I looked at Svein carefully. He wasn't drunk. So he just had a terrible sense of humor.

I wondered what I'd done to make him think I was nice. I guessed that I'd smiled a bit. I thought then that I could probably become quite mean to Svein, and that if I smiled the whole time he wouldn't even notice. That maybe *nice* was a word men called women they didn't bother to get to know. When I caught my next fish, I handed it to him and watched, disgusted, as his stained fingers worked the hook free with a sucking, cracking sound.

There was a splash; Helge Jensen had dropped into a dinghy and was puttering toward shore. Katrin produced a wet wipe and dabbed fish blood from the railing, then the handle of her pole. Svein watched her. "Look at that," he said. "City girl." My line was knotted and Markvard came from the cabin and untangled it for me, as delicately as if he were painting a face on a doll. But the reel was broken, so he handed me his own pole, and for himself used a can of Mack's Refreshingly Norwegian Arctic Beer with line wrapped around it.

The four of us were quiet, lifting and dropping our lines. We'd drifted close enough to shore to bump against an anchored boat, which was small and wooden, painted in a uniform shade of blue. The boats squeaked where they rubbed together. I'd mostly fished with my grandfather before, during my childhood summers in the Puget Sound, and whenever my line tweaked I heard his deep voice in my ear: *Set the hook, Blair. Set the hook!* But the force of that movement, the sudden lift, embarrassed me, and nobody around me seemed to be setting their hooks, so I reeled quietly instead, and loosened whatever seaweed had caught on the line, and cast again without a word.

Then the Sailor climbed aboard, beaming at me and smelling of garlic, and his lady Lily followed with her red bra shining through a thin gray tank. Before I could talk to them, Helge Jensen beckoned me to the helm. "It's yours," he said, staring at my eyes with his lips twitching. "Ride it like a bull. You'll *feel* it. Take us to the Brygger"—the resort between Mortenhals and Mestervik. He thrust a lever to start the engine again. He was still staring at me hard, and I looked down and put my hands on the many-handled wheel. It hardly turned when I pushed; I had to lean my whole body against it to shift it to the left, even slightly. Helge Jensen was gone and I watched out the milky windshield as he joined Lily on the couch, sandwiching her against the Sailor.

I hoisted myself onto the tall bench and sat with my legs swinging to the rhythm of the engine, starting to enjoy myself. After a few minutes, Katrin wandered in. She sat beside me, then reached out with one hand and touched the wheel. There was only one other boat on the water, a dinghy straight ahead of us with two Germans standing in it. I tried to turn, but the wheel was stuck. We were going fast now. Katrin whimpered. Without speaking, we shoved together, to the right, and with a great scraping sound the wheel gave and *Abdullah* turned sharply, charging around the dinghy in an arc. Helge Jensen looked up at us and smiled. Katrin and I, glancing at each other, broke into giggles.

Up close, Katrin's lips glittered with pink and silver sparkles, and her top and bottom lashes curled sharply away from her eyes. She hugged herself with thin arms. I asked where she was from. Mykolaiv, she said. Two hours from Odessa.

"And you're liking Norway?"

Katrin wrinkled her nose. "It is . . . boring. What people do? Yesterday I'm drill all day." She mimed drilling into a wall, her hands trembling. "We drill all day, Svein's house." She rolled her eyes.

I liked sitting in the cabin with her, swinging our legs. It occurred to me that I hadn't spent time alone with another young woman all summer. I felt that we were thinking the same thoughts. I wanted to tell her that I saw Svein for what he was, so that she wouldn't have to be alone in that knowledge. I thought that she probably felt lonely.

What I said was, "Do you like him?"

"He has good . . . character," said Katrin. She was playing with her fingernails again.

"Are you moving to Norway with him?"

"What?" Katrin's hands froze. "No, no. I'm . . . holiday. Two weeks. Then home. Home, I'm dance, salsa, Latin. I'm take class in the city. What people do here? No, I no like."

Then Svein was in the cabin, squishing onto the bench beside us, and Katrin's face went blank. He looked at us and laughed and took Katrin by the hand and pulled her with him outside. I watched them leave, and watched the calm sea splitting around the boat, the sweet red houses along the shore. Markvard came in and sat down beside me, where Katrin had been a minute before.

Markvard's calmness, his ease on the bench, caught at something in my rib cage. *You got a herring because you're so nice,* I heard in my head. I wanted to prove Svein wrong. I wanted to prove Dan wrong. "It's ugly," I said. "It's ugly and horrible. Everything is just disgusting." I thought a moment. "And I hate it. It's ugly and horrible and I hate it. Everything is stupid and everyone is awful."

I smiled at Markvard and waited.

"Sure," he said. "Of course."

Then: "Don't worry. We're only stopping at the Brygger to steal toilet paper and pick up the bachelor party."

It was true: It wasn't my fault I was nice. I could say whatever I wanted. I wanted to grin, to laugh. Without responding, I walked past Markvard and out on deck, to the back of the boat where Helge Jensen and the Sailor, arms around each other, asked me to take their picture. After I did, the Sailor unbuttoned his pants.

"He wants to take a dick pic," said Helge Jensen.

"Yeah!" said the Sailor. He was drunk.

I waited with the camera. I could wait all day. The Sailor changed his mind and buttoned his pants again.

"*We* were in a shipwreck once," said Helge Jensen, punching the Sailor's thigh. "Long ago. The boat was stuffed full of herring and it had trapdoors in the deck. So it ran into a berg, and the pressure made the doors pop open like champagne corks, and all the herring just exploded up and covered the deck. And the captain, he just stood there and fingered his collar. He didn't even know what was happening, because something was wrong but the boat wasn't sinking."

"But he was *jo* near death already," said the Sailor. "He drowned overboard a year later."

We were quiet, considering. The back of the boat, where we stood, was full of mess that somehow felt clean in the sea air. A Norwegian flag, tattered into strips, fluttered over the wake.

There were two trunks against the back rail for storage, and across from them, against the cabin, a heap of stuff: tarps, ropes, gas cans, a chipped basin, a cardboard box labeled "Eggs" that contained plastic bags and empty Tuborg cans, a broken fishing pole, a broken folding chair, and, resting on the chair, a dryfish, which Helge Jensen occasionally peeled slivers from as if he were peeling threads of string cheese.

Lily came over and the Sailor pointed at her, beaming. "*We've* been together for twenty-five years."

Lily leaned back against the railing. "We're not together," she said.

"Twenty-five years," said the Sailor.

"No," said Lily. "It wasn't twenty-five." She turned around to face the water.

The Sailor caught my eye, licked his finger, and snuck behind her. He jammed his finger up between her legs. Lily jumped, then turned and scowled. "You're dumb in the head," she told him.

"We've been together twenty-five years," he said proudly.

Helge Jensen watched, amused. "Even if it was twenty-five years," he said, "you were at sea the whole time. You were constantly at sea. You know"—he turned to me—"we were young, and he was supposed to have all of Christmas and January off, at home, and we even had a Mustang we were going to drive. And it's not even the first day of Christmas before he says, 'Oh, they called me, I have to go.'"

The Sailor smiled.

"You thrived at sea," I said.

"One had to," said the Sailor. "Anyway, my money grew like grass. When I was in Iran . . ."

Lily looked at him. He sat down on a trunk and crossed his legs. "When I was in Greenland, I came back after six months with a long gray beard, and I went to Lily's house and was talking to her father, sitting at his kitchen table, and she didn't recognize me. We sat there the whole evening . . ."

"I sat *jo* and flirted with another guy all night, and then I went home alone," said Lily. "I still can't believe you let me do that."

The Sailor kicked his feet. One of his clogs half-dangled, exposing a bare heel. Later he'd pull me aside and whisper: *I was a spy. Lily doesn't know.* But for the moment they looked at each other fondly. Helge Jensen poured a bucket of guts overboard, which spread in an underwater cloud. We drifted past the far end of the Brygger, empty glass-front cabins lining the shore, and then we pulled into their marina and I clambered up the stone wall and crossed the clean, elegant foyer to the ladies' room, where I filled my pockets with toilet paper for *Abdullah*'s depleted head.

When I got back, there were eight new men climbing down onto the boat, and they were all the same. They were young and sometimes handsome and carried a suitcase and wore things like nautical shirts and high-top sneakers and a pin-striped jacket with shorts. They covered the leather couches and passed around a bottle of cognac and said, "We should fish some dryfish, that's tasty," and "This here is *jo* a fantastic boat. It really is a fantastic boat." Lily was sitting in the middle of them all and one man kept asking her name.

"You look like a Lily," he said, when she told him. "And you look like your last name is Larsen."

"It's not," she said.

"People on Malangen can have whatever name they want," someone said. Someone else said, "This is really a fantastic boat."

It turned out that Helge Jensen had promised to take the bachelor party across the fjord, to a cabin on the other side. But the boat wasn't moving. Its propeller had caught on a black plastic boom, a thick tube floating around the marina to block waves. This didn't seem to bother the partiers. Helge Jensen kept gunning the engine, and they cheered and sat on the couches and patted Lily's shoulders. I stood to the side. The Sailor pointed at me. "You!" he said to the men. "She's American." The men looked at me and shook their heads, doubtful.

"Say something in English," one of them suggested.

"I'm American," I said in English. "I'm not from here." Then I smiled. I knew that my foreignness was just another drunken idea nobody believed.

They scoffed.

"No, really. I was born in California," I insisted, my American accent harsh against the smooth night. "I'm staying with Arild Kristoffersen"—mispronouncing his name on purpose, the r's hard and unrolled—"in Mortenhals. I'm not from here at all."

I had, in my life, pretended to be a Norwegian, and an experienced dogsledder, and a girlfriend, and an adventurer, and brave—roles to prove my place, to show that I could belong. But tonight, when I could be whomever I wanted, I pretended to be myself. Blair Braverman, the Californian, sitting on Helge Jensen's boat. The least likely character of the bunch.

The groom-to-be, in his pin-striped jacket, stood up. "She's a li-ar," he announced in slow and happy English. Norwegians liked to speak English when they were drunk; now a few others joined in. But the boat rocked violently and the engine whistled off, distracting them. The groom-to-be peered over the rail. "I'll take over," he said to no one in particular. I followed him back to look at the boom, which was caught underwater. When we got close it rose like a whale, sending up a splash, and I ducked.

Svein and Helge Jensen and several of the men stood regarding it, and after the boom settled Svein climbed down to stand on it in the water, holding the boat for balance. He gripped the rail and leaned back, looking solemn. I thought that standing in the water made him feel important. Helge Jensen tried the engine again, back and forth, but we were still stuck.

I went to the cabin, where I found Katrin sitting alone. We sat and felt the boat shift with new and fruitless efforts. It was late and the water was gold. The sun was behind the mountains, where it would set for the second time since May.

After a while the voices outside got excited, so we went to see what was up. A man had rowed to shore and come back with a drysuit, which was yellow and looked unused. He stripped to his boxer briefs to put it on; the Sailor found me and covered my eyes with his rough hand. When the man was dressed again, his wrist and neck elastics snapped into place, he climbed down into the water and everyone leaned over to watch him. It was cold now that the sun was gone. The new theory was that an anchor rope had caught in the propeller, and the man intended to swim under the boat and look for a tangled rope and then cut it with his rusty knife. He went under.

We waited. The man burst from the water blade first, gripping the knife in his fist. He grinned.

"I'm cold," said Katrin.

There was a scuffling, a collision: Svein and two other men had tried to put their arms around her simultaneously. Svein won, mostly. He squished up behind her, hugging her waist. One of the men satisfied himself by rubbing Katrin's forearm between his palms, and the other stepped back and rolled a cigarette. After a moment, Katrin shrugged away and came to lean against me, hooking her arm through mine. I took off my coat and wrapped it around her shoulders. I was tempted to catch the men's eyes, to gloat, but I didn't even need to rub it in.

The blond hair of the man in the water was plastered photogenically to the sides of his face; he shook it a little, to reattract everyone's attention. He urged his friends to take pictures of him in the water, holding the knife, and post them online. Several friends did. But when Helge Jensen tried the engine again, the boat was still stuck. The man had cut the wrong rope.

Markvard stood off to the side. "Let's go forward," he kept urging. "Come on, let's go forward."

"I think that's the point," I said.

"You can just keep saying that to him," the Sailor said. "Just tell him again. It won't help. He's deaf." He pointed to his own ear, widening his eyes until they bulged from his face.

Markvard looked at us looking at him. "Sure," he said, nodding. "Of course."

It took another hour to free the boat, and I'm not sure how they did it; I'd long since stopped paying attention. By the time we started moving, the sky had turned pastel, warm blue and pink that reflected in pink stripes across the rippled water. The mountains were shadows or clouds on every horizon. The party men took turns driving and Helge Jensen sat on a couch with his legs up on the coffee table and directed them with the smallest of gestures, a tipped head or twitched finger that steered the whole ship home. We left the Sailor and Lily back on their beach, and left the bachelor party at a rickety dock across the fjord, where they hoisted their duffel bags and waved thanks and puked into the water. When we finally docked in Mestervik, Helge Jensen gave me a ride to Arild's car. He kept one hand on the steering wheel and the other wound in his hair. "You and me," he said, "we're not some of those mass-produced people, are we. But we recognize that in each other. We don't even need to say it aloud." The summer before I would have taken this as a compliment. But now I was just thinking of how to tell the story back at the shop.

The next morning I recounted it at the coffee table, drawing on Post-it notes to show the route, the stuck boom, the arrangement of boats at the marina. He the Rich One shook his head in wry disapproval. Odd Johnny said, "Helge Jensen was sober, wasn't he? That's the kind of thing that would never happen if Helge Jensen was drunk enough." The Sailor sat beside me and pinched my ankle with two fingers to give it a shake, saying nothing at all.

CHAPTER TWELVE

ALL THAT SUMMER I KEPT THE OLD STORE open on weekends, and all summer people came, travelers from neighboring fjords and families on their way back from church and strangers who liked waffles. A man brought records to play on the gramophone. A woman from Tromsø brought her mother, who had Alzheimer's. She smiled as she walked through the familiar shop of her childhood.

Two girls from the RV park showed up one morning, and then the next, and before long they joined me daily, often appearing from across the pasture the very minute that I turned the skeleton key. The girls were almost disconcertingly well mannered, pretty and big eyed and loyal to each other; when an adult addressed them, they would convene—sometimes in whispers, sometimes with a glance—before one or the other stepped forward to answer the question in full sentences. Sometimes I gave them jobs, sweeping the floor or arranging the children's clothes. But mostly I tried to get them to play. I gave them milk to feed the lambs, whom they called Cool One and Grass. I hid new artifacts on the shelves and promised the girls ice cream if they could spot the additions. At first they drifted about carefully, lifting the ice skates or the bottle of gelatinous orange aquavit, but as the hunt took hold of them they began running around, pointing at random. "This?" they said. "This? This? This this this this this?" I gave them ice cream anyway, and they had the decency to look astounded.

I enjoyed their company. The younger girl liked to wind the gramophone so that it pulsed a scratchy waltz, and together we'd dance around the room, melting to the floor as the music slowed and faded. The older girl liked to stand before a warped mirror and laugh as her face twisted in strange directions, and to read aloud classified ads from old magazines: " 'Sailor with own car seeks girl or widow, age twenty-eight to thirty-eight.' " She wore a purple sweatshirt with Justin Bieber's face on the back. "I don't wear this every day," she announced regularly, though no one had commented. "I don't even like Justin Bieber anymore. I like Isac Elliot now."

The visitors loved them, these polite children. "You must be interested in history," they'd remark, and the girls would glance at each other, and one or the other would step forward and say—

"I am sort of interested in history, but not really. I am more interested in lambs."

On rare weekends when the girls didn't show up, the Old Store felt different. Creaky and shifting. Not unpleasant—just laden. Months later I'd hear a psychic describe haunted places: they were always cold, she said, and seemed to shimmer, and were often filled with the belongings of people who'd passed. It made sense. Ghosts or no, the shop was full of stories, and in quiet times I sat there and tried to hear them. I'd sit on a corpse chair and tear bits of waffle apart with my fingers, listening for car tires, watching out the window at the unchanging sea. I'd flip through the guest book, reading the names of people who had passed through.

Toward the end of the summer, Arild took me to the city for dinner. I knew, as soon as we entered, why he'd chosen the restaurant. The pizzeria was decorated with old things: skis, records, coffee grinders. The walls were lined with dark wood, labyrinthine with bookshelves that formed private nooks. Couples and friends in well-tailored neutrals murmured to each other by candlelight. When I touched the leather-bound books, I found they were glued together.

A lanky waiter seated us by the window, under two accordions. Outside, a man threw handfuls of torn-up pastries onto the sidewalk, attracting a cloud of seagulls. "Look at the birds," Arild said. "Anne Lill would hate that, but I think it's nice."

"It *is* nice," I said, and he almost smiled. "Do you come here a lot?"

"No," said Arild.

We ordered a Chicago–style pizza to share, with sour-cream dressing and a Coke for him. The Coke came first but he didn't drink it.

A couple in matching raincoats passed the window and took a picture of the Middle Eastern grocery store across the street. "They must be from a cruise ship," I said.

"Yes," said Arild. "That's what I would have guessed." He seemed unusually curt, distracted.

The waiter passed with a pizza, but it wasn't for us.

When the pizza finally came, it was meaty and rich and tasted like MSG. "Pretty edible, right?" Arild said. I agreed. For a while we chewed in silence, but then we started to get full. Arild wiped his mouth and exhaled. "Blair," he said. "I hope you're not disappointed with your stay in Malangen. I know that it's not full of excitement every day, and there aren't as many visitors to the Old Store as we expected. I hope you don't regret coming. For my part, I think it's been very pleasant to have you here, but . . ." Arild had recently read a newspaper story about an American student, a girl, who was helping some Sami with their reindeer. She'd called the experience "exclusive." Ever since then, he'd been worried about the experience he was providing me. He had sheep, not reindeer. His life was not exclusive at all.

"Arild," I said. "It's perfect. There's nothing I would change. Really."

"Well," he said, straightening a little. "Well, that's good to hear."

I took a sip of water. Our eyes met but we both looked away.

"One thing that's nice," Arild said, "is that other diners might notice us sitting here and think that we're father and daughter. But if you were Thai, for example, then they would notice us and think that I was an old man who had bought himself a wife."

I thought about that. "In a way," I said, "you are my Norwegian father." I was nervous to say it.

"Yes," said Arild. "I know."

Arild couldn't pronounce Quince's name, so he called him Mr. Q.

I didn't talk about him much, but that didn't stop everyone at the coffee table from knowing about Mr. Q, and asking regularly when he would show up. In fact, I had found, as the summer wore on, that I thought about Quince more and more. He came into my head while I walked in the mountain village, when talk at the table grew dull, when I curled into the orange bed and tried to sleep despite the glow through my eyelids. But these weren't thoughts so much as fantasies, daydreams, more obsessive than pleasant. I ran through them in careful detail, over and over, until I was calmed or satisfied.

The first was a fantasy. During our trips to the Northwoods—familiar to Quince, but new to me—we frequented country bars in small towns, the kinds surrounded by snowmobiles in winter and four-wheelers in summer. I'd imagine myself entering some new bar, or maybe perched at the counter, and noticing that Dan was there, too. He'd be sitting there, nursing a beer, maybe focused on a game on the screen. I could see it clearly. Although I'd been too young to join Dan in bars while we were dating, I had the idea that he was quite at home in them. Once, early on, he told me that he occasionally got in bar fights in his hometown, usually with visitors who acted too much like they owned the place. He seemed thoughtful, relaying this fact, and the contrast was exciting: a man who punched others and confided in me.

Which is to say that it wouldn't surprise me, encountering Dan in a strange bar. It was his terrain, and the Northwoods was not so far from Canada. In fact, the possibility crossed my mind every time I entered such a place, and my antennae grew stronger the closer I was to the border, as the accents thickened and I found myself glancing around at the odd overheard phrase with familiar intonations.

In the fantasy, Quince was with me, but this was where I left him. "Be right back," I'd tell him. Then I'd walk over to Dan and stand there until he noticed me.

Our reunion would be warm. We'd hug, fondly but briefly, and then Dan would point at the door and ask if I wanted some fresh air. "Sure," I'd say. I would follow him out.

Outside we'd sit on the curb, not touching but not too far apart, and watch others come and go. Maybe a couple would be arguing in the parking lot, and we'd look away, embarrassed. We'd ask questions about each other's lives, and be moderately interested in the answers. Then, after a few minutes, we'd hug again and go our separate ways.

I suspected this fantasy was about putting Dan behind me for good. After leaving Alaska, I had struggled to make sense of all that had happened between us. And for a time, I tried to rewrite our relationship as a positive one. Dan was a good guy, I decided, citing evidence: He drove dogs year-round; he was generous with his car; he was Canadian, and Canada had universal health care. I knew I'd been miserable while we were dating, but I told myself, in retrospect, that I'd blamed him too much for my feelings. It weighed on me to have parted with such vitriol. I felt that I could sense Dan's long-distance hostility.

And so, a year or so after we broke up, I wrote him a letter. I wanted to apologize for how I had wronged him—that I had turned cold toward him, which seemed in retrospect unthoughtful—in the hopes that Dan would, in turn, offer his own apology. After that, maybe we'd be able to leave our grudges behind. Dan accepted my apology warmly, but he knew, he said, that he himself hadn't done anything wrong. *It became very obvious to me last summer,* he wrote, *that you really need to get a better grasp of what the world is.* And yet, he said, he wished me well. How could I disagree with him? We were, it seemed, friends again—a status that put to rest some of my anxieties, if not as many as I had expected.

It was only in dating others and recognizing the contrast that I could no longer sugarcoat my time with Dan. If Dan had been so kind, I asked myself, then why did I sometimes have reactions I couldn't explain, particularly in sexual situations? Once, making love to the boy from the library, I found myself paralyzed when he turned me over and kissed my back. Because I couldn't see him, I became convinced that I couldn't be sure of who he was. More recently, with Quince, I had to suppress feelings of panic when one of us was turned on and the other wasn't; the discrepancy seemed unspeakably terrible.

If Dan had been so kind—a generous lover, as I'd once, incredibly, described him to a friend—then why did I find myself combing over our sexual encounters, recalling again the burn of his sweat on my skin, or his hands pushing my knees apart, arranging my body to his liking? The memory of one incident in particular filled me with shame, and yet I often thought about it, testing the bruise. We had been in a bed, not a tent, though I couldn't remember where—maybe in my college dorm room, the fall after my first summer on the ice. After he came, Dan sat up between my legs and grinned. "I'm glad that worked," he said. "I was going to suggest that you needed a pillow under your hips."

That was all: two sentences. Innocuous—that sex had been no worse than other sex we'd had. But the memory scathed me. I had failed, even at being raped.

No, I corrected myself every time. I hadn't been *raped*. That word, hovering in my consciousness, brought with it an avalanche of self-doubt. It hadn't been rape, because I could have stopped it. Of course I could have stopped it. What was I, helpless?

The thing was, nothing that had happened to me—not Far, not Dan, not anything—was beyond the normal scope of what happened to women all the time. Some harassment by an authority figure, a few sexual remarks, pressure from an insistent boyfriend? What woman *hadn't* experienced those things? It made me the same as everyone else, and luckier than many. It was just a natural result of being female and living in the world. And if you added up the moments of fear, the comments, the touches—well, they certainly weren't traumatic. Not for me. Not for a tough girl.

On the other hand, if I'd accepted the word *rape*, maybe I would have discovered other words, ones that could have helped me make sense of my earlier experience: dissociation, counterphobia. Maybe it would help me understand how being back in the north sometimes slipped me into a watchful passivity, a state where others acted around me and I could choose whether or not to respond. What good was a reaction to lines like *I could have fucked you* or *You're safe now that you're friends with me*? From where inside me would such a reaction come? That organ seemed to be missing. Flirting at the coffee table, talking about dryfish with Helge Jensen—situations whose arcs I could predict—felt like surfing the waves of an ocean that had once pulled me under. As long as I knew what was going on, everything was okay.

These men carried their desires on the surface—not hidden, which was where they scared me. "It's okay for you to touch my hair," I had told Zoran, "but please don't lick my neck." I was getting better at putting my own desires on the surface, too—negotiating a precision of permissions. This power thrilled me.

My second daydream was a memory, a recollection of an evening with Quince that had been perhaps our most troubling. And yet the memory, each time I sank into it, was comforting. It calmed me like nothing else.

This one started, like the other daydream, at a bar—this time at a country bar about two miles from Quince's farmhouse. It was a busy night, a Friday, and I'd traded my usual root beer for a whiskey ginger while Quince worked the jukebox. The bar was packed, but even as we chatted with neighbors and strangers, Quince and I were linked by an electric sexual tension; behind every side conversation lingered a brilliant suspense for all that we would do back at home.

But then something, or a series of things, shifted the mood slightly, so that even I didn't notice when the tune of my excitement changed. At one point we slipped out the back door to make out, and noticed only after several minutes of kissing that a strange man was rubbing Quince's back; Quince had assumed that the hands were mine. Later, somebody bought us drinks—hot pink shots—and I felt obligated to drink the alcohol, even though I was already tipsier than I wanted to be. Finally the drunk man on the next bar stool, after we declined giving him a ride, bent over to reveal a pistol tucked into his boxers.

By the time we got home, I was in an odd mood—drunk, turned on, and more agitated than I realized. I kissed Quince hard in the hallway, pulled him toward the bedroom. I felt numb to his mouth, numb to his hands in my hair, though I was hardly aware of that numbness. What I wanted, I decided with the half of my brain that seemed to be functioning, was sex— mindless, all-encompassing physical comfort, with the deep love and safety that I always felt when Quince and I were together. It was only the intensity of his skin, his body on mine, that could bring me back into the moment and shake whatever odd thing had crawled up into my throat. There was no way but through. With this thought, I stripped off my clothes and climbed into bed, pulling Quince after me. But Quince didn't get in. He stood by my piled clothes and looked down at me. His white T-shirt covered the skin that I wanted so badly against my own.

"Take off your shirt," I said.

"You want me to take off my shirt?"

"Yes."

"Not yet," he said.

"Please," I begged. "Take off your shirt."

He shook his head.

The more he resisted, the more I begged him, until I felt myself shrinking. Everything in the room seemed to grow up around me, so that my naked prostrate body was at the mercy of Quince's standing clothed one. He was so tall over me. I could hear myself repeating the same request; I couldn't form any other words to explain what was happening. Finally, exhausted and horrified, I turned away from him and curled into a ball.

Instantly Quince was beside me. In the daydream, this was the moment I returned to: the moment when everything shifted, when the room went from dangerous to safe, and his body from a threat to a comfort. I was trembling; he wrapped his arms around me and held me still against him, whispering words I couldn't understand. Gentle words. *It's just us,* he whispered. In the morning we'd talk about it: how confused he'd been, how he'd interpreted my requests to remove his shirt to mean that I felt good, that I wanted to have sex, but he'd not wanted to move forward when it was so clear that something was wrong. That night, though, we didn't talk about anything. We just held each other until we fell asleep.

At times, the comfort of this daydream disturbed me. Was that really what I wanted—to be rescued by some guy? And yet I returned to it again and again. For everything that scared me, the memory reassured me, there was an ending. For everything that scared me, there was another side.

A few days after our dinner in the city, Arild invited me down to the Finnish grillhouse in the RV park. The grillhouse was a little hexagonal building with benches along the walls and a central fire pit, built from a kit by one of the residents, whose name was Henrik. Henrik and his wife and daughter were already sitting on the benches, resting on blue plaid cushions and rolled sheepskins in a haze of smoke. The grillhouse was new— everyone was getting one lately—and they were still working out the kinks. For instance: smoke pooled under the ceiling, and when they tried opening a window, the smoke blew into their faces. But that was a small inconvenience, everyone agreed, for the sense of coziness that the grillhouse provided. Henrik offered Arild some cognac, which he cut with a few drops of diet Fruit Chimpanzee, a local soda that had changed its name from Fruit Champagne after threats of a lawsuit from the French champagne industry. I accepted a lump of chocolate cake on a paper saucer. A fat golden retriever, who was exactly the same color as the birch walls around us, licked my hand compulsively.

Henrik's daughter was studying leadership at the university in Tromsø. She wore a pink bow around her ponytail and had tucked her jeans into turquoise socks. She scooted closer to me. The trick to leadership, she explained, was to offer people something they needed but didn't know they needed. After that, they would need *you*. It made sense. She lit a cigarette and handed it to me, but I gave it back. I was supposed to be like her, I thought, but she was a different species. We sat politely beside each other until she left to drive back to the city.

Nearby, Henrik was talking politics. He thought Norway was having problems, the gist being that everyone was on welfare instead of working, and even if they did work, the outlanders worked three times harder for the same salaries. Then they quit, the outlanders, and went home to their lousy impoverished countries with Norwegian unemployment and Norwegian child support and lived like small kings—with servants and mansions!—on the taxpayers' dime of the few Norwegians who actually *were* working. He'd read in a men's soft-porn magazine that Norway had a democracy of 3 million but supported 180 million people. As soon as the oil ran out—BANG, Norway would collapse. Like Spain, he said. His mouth twitched into a smile whenever he stopped for breath. Arild sat leaning toward him, but Henrik's wife, who was knitting a purple chenille blanket with her feet tucked under her, didn't even look up. Smoke swirled around her face.

Arild finished his drink, and Henrik made him a new one. He offered me one but I shook my head.

Outside, threads of whitecaps rose on the water. It could have been any time of day or night. Lowering his voice, Henrik confessed that his family was having more immediate problems, too. Their house was haunted.

When he said it, his wife looked up from her knitting for the first time all evening. She sighed.

The trouble had started years ago, when they moved into their new home on Kvaløya, near the city. It began with the usual, windows and doors opening on their own, silent untraceable phone calls, the sound of breathing in dark rooms. A blond boy ran into the kitchen, noticed Henrik, and vanished into the air. His wife woke repeatedly to the feeling of being held down by unseen hands. Their daughter heard voices. She was afraid to sleep alone.

Finally they found a psychic willing to diagnose the problem. When she entered their house, even the psychic got scared. She explained that they lived over an ancient trail that souls still followed, and that a blacksmith had once raped a woman in what was now their living room. Did I know what the word *rape* meant? Henrik asked me.

Before I could answer, Arild interrupted. "Rape," he told me. "I'll show you later." He laughed loosely. The others groaned, but I stared at him. Arild was the only man here whom I trusted not to think such things. My heart pounded and I petted the dog for comfort, concentrating: soft head, soft ears. Soft head. Soft head.

It was quiet now, but Arild seemed not to notice. He took a sip of cognac and smiled.

Henrik cleared his throat. Anyway—and this was the thing—anyway, once they accepted the ghosts, things got better. It seemed that the ghosts just wanted to be acknowledged. And it took the family a while, a few years, but they learned that the sound of breathing was only bad if you let it be bad. It made sense, if you thought about it, for souls to stick to a place. After the body was gone, where else could they go? The soul was like water—it couldn't be broken. I asked if they'd thought about moving. He said it wouldn't help. At this point, the ghosts were riding their shoulders. The ghosts had been riding their shoulders for years.

"But you'd undo it, though, if you could?" I said. "You'd rather live without it."

Henrik and his wife looked at each other a long time. Finally she shook her head. "I don't know," she said. Her voice was deeper than I expected. "We're so used to living with it."

Arild's face was blank again. "There's a lot we don't know between the earth and the sky," he said.

How could he be so calm now? I couldn't bring myself to meet his eyes.

It was late, almost 3 A.M. I thanked Henrik for the cake and excused myself, leaving the others to their drinks and stories. It wasn't until I stood in the grass outside, squinting against the wind that whipped off the water, that I could breathe properly. When I walked the gravel road to the shop, my feet seemed to roll beneath me, as if I were a passenger in my body. I was grateful for the light.

The next morning, at 11 A.M., Arild called my cell phone to wake me up. It was Sunday, so we drank our coffee at the kitchen table. "Speaking of last night, I saw a terrible thing today," he told me. "Five bicyclists rode past the shop—and they were headless. The worst part was that the last one, he was singing." Arild watched me until I laughed.

I didn't laugh at the joke. I laughed, after a long moment, because whatever hardness, roughness, I sensed in the men of the Arctic, Arild knew it well—and it didn't quite fit him, either. Sometimes he messed up the script. But nobody belonged in the Northland more than he did.

From any of the other men in Mortenhals, Arild's comment in the grillhouse would have been nothing, a dumb joke to roll my eyes at. But from Arild it had stung. And yet I had never felt threatened by him, not once. In fact, Arild was the reason I had finally gotten rid of the stun gun the summer before.

For weeks after arriving in Mortenhals, I had kept the stun gun in the bottom of my backpack, strapped into its holster, buried under my dirty clothes. I could feel its weight when I hoisted my bag, heavy and reassuring, and could snake my hand through my laundry to double-check that it was there. I was always aware of the weapon, but I felt no need to keep it easily accessible. It was protection enough to know I had it.

Arild had said that I could spend time in his apartment

whenever I needed a quiet space, even if he wasn't home. One rainy day I took him up on it, reveling in the full bookshelves and the wide windows overlooking the fjord. And there in his mother's living room, surrounded by her paintings, I pulled the stun gun from my bag and felt ashamed. The people I'd met had welcomed me, had offered me what I needed; and in carrying the stun gun, it was I who harbored violence, not them. The gun was one man's fist in another man's house, and I didn't want any of it.

The problem was, I didn't know how to get rid of the stun gun. For one thing, it was illegal, and it had a serial number etched into the bottom, which meant it might be traceable. But mostly I didn't want anyone to get hurt. If I threw it away, or hid it somewhere deep in the woods, there was still the chance that someone could find it. I thought of borrowing a boat and dropping the gun into the middle of the fjord, but what if it electrocuted the water? Was that even possible? It seemed a foolish risk. So I carried the stun gun into the mountains, to a place where a cliff gave way to boulders. I climbed to the top of the cliff and threw the gun as hard as I could toward the rocks below. Then I climbed back down to examine the damage.

Apart from a few small scratches, the stun gun was unharmed.

I sat down on a rock and tried to think. Alpine blueberry plants clustered by my feet, their berries small and pink, and a few orange ants climbed among them. A stinging nettle grew behind the rock, its leaves curling upward

The way I saw it, there was only one solution. I lifted the gun, held it in front of me, tried to steady my arms. Then I pressed the lightning button and didn't let go.

The sound exploded; electricity shot from my hands and dissolved, crackling the air in front of me; the gun pulsed with the force of it, a strange, strong pulse that traveled up my arms and into my chest. I squeezed my eyes closed, steadied my arms, willed the popping and the lightning and the charged air to pass.

And then it did. With a last flicker, the stun gun fell still.

I scraped off the serial number with a hunting knife. I wrapped the depleted weapon in eight layers of duct tape and left it in a trash can. And I kept the charger.

CHAPTER THIRTEEN

T HOSE LAST DAYS IN THE MUSEUM before I returned to the States, to Quince, were strange. Loose and loaded. I ran the shop while Arild hayed, leaving at intervals to help him fork the dry hay into the barn. In free moments, I cataloged and photographed the artifacts of the Old Store, counting hundreds of stockings and bottles and radios and bells and hairpins. I needed to trust that I would come back, that this home would stay for me, and it helped to make myself as useful as possible. I found myself wanting to leave *things*: my work boots, my mug on the shelf by the coffee table. Often, when I saw Arild, I had the urge to tell him all that he had become for me, but instead I turned back to the work at hand, pitching hay even harder. Behind us, the lambs with their fat bodies wailed for milk. Arild whispered to them sweet nothings: *Hey you, lookit you, yeh want some milk? Some good milk? Lookit you, your tail wagging, hey you you you. . .*

In the afternoon, while the shop was quiet and I worked the counter, two men and a woman came in. City folks. The men wore plaid shirts with pearl buttons; the woman had dyed-black hair. When she walked in the door, she gasped, grabbing both men by the shoulders. "Oh my god," she said. "Look at how old-fashioned it is. I didn't know places like this still existed." She brought a hand to her mouth and bit her knuckle, eyes wide. "Look, there's even shoes."

"And coffee," said one of the men. He walked to the table and ran one hand over the mugs.

The woman paced over to the shoes and grabbed some that were purple and suede. "Bjørn, weren't you looking for new boots?" She turned in a circle, distracted; her fingers grazed the table, the box of sugar cubes, and then she vanished with both men toward the back of the shop. Their laughter rang down the aisles. It sounded like they were taking pictures.

Finally they came back with two bottles of iced tea, and paid in cash. "We thought this place was closed," Bjørn said.

"It's been open the whole time," I said. "It's been here forever."

The woman cracked open her iced tea. "You don't understand," she said. "Every time we drove by, the building was empty."

That evening, when I called the lambs for their milk, they didn't come. I checked the barn, the shop, behind the RV park. Finally I spotted one in the pasture, standing fat and alone. The other lamb, the one the girls called Grass, lay behind a hay bale, his eyes waxy. I dragged the dead lamb into the barn while the live one trotted after, touching his nose to his brother's head. He would keep Anne Lill up all night with his moaning.

In the fall, after I left, Arild sent the remaining nursing lamb to slaughter. He could not shake the memory of the last time he'd given it milk: how the lamb came to him, full of trust, right before he sent it away. But that's how it was; male lambs were not meant to live. He distracted himself with other animals. A cat chased a young fox around the barn. Arild fed them both. The fox stuck around, and as the first snows fell and gathered it grew tame enough to eat hot dogs from his hand. One day a reindeer showed up outside the shop. It was wary, and startled easily. With patience Arild trained it to come for rabbit food.

His e-mails to me were brief and informational: It was -30 degrees. He had purchased two rams from a Sami man in Skibotn. He had lost his car keys. Today the Sailor bought twelve beers and Rune bought only six. *Maybe Rune is sick.* The sheep called Blair had grown fat.

He wrote: *I heard the fox howl but it has not eaten the food I left for it.*

He wrote: *There are many who wonder if you're coming back to Malangen but not me because I know that just as surely as death is coming so too are you coming back to Malangen.*

At graduate school, I scrolled through the e-mails on my phone, feeling as if nothing was quite real. I was so far away. Again. And yet Arild missed me, and expected me back. That my absence in Mortenhals was noticed proved that I had a place there; the news buoyed me. I wrote back, echoing Arild's minutiae: It was raining; I'd made soup for dinner; I missed him.

In December, I moved to Quince's farm in northern Wisconsin, in a town with thrillingly cold winters and a population of eight hundred. We kept horses and bees and chickens, living beside a national forest where wolves loped at dusk and a network of snowy trails stretched hundreds of miles. I started training dogs for a local musher, and my letters to Arild grew longer, more animated, as I recounted long runs and tough tangles. Who was a city-*pia* now? I teased him. Meanwhile, Arild's letters grew shorter. Finally he sent one so morose that I could not ignore it:

Blair has gone to the USA.
The fox was shot.
The reindeer went to the mountain village last week.

I called eight times before Arild picked up the phone. He did not enjoy phone conversations; we spoke for only three minutes. The news was swift. He had lost the court case against his sister, although he planned to appeal; for now, he had to vacate the apartment above the shop. Further, his firstborn son, Henning, was moving to Mortenhals to take over the business. Arild would be retiring early.

I arrived in April for a five-week stay. Arild greeted me formally at the airport: "Thank you for your last visit. It was very pleasant." He wore, with his usual faded clothing, stylish blue-soled oxfords acquired during a recent shopkeepers' convention in Oslo. I threw my arms around him.

By then, most of the changes were already in place. Henning, his wife, and their two young children had moved into the apartment temporarily, though they would be required to vacate by summer, and planned to move into the Old House at that time. In the meantime, Arild was staying in the Old House with Anne Lill, a situation that suited neither of them. They adapted to the proximity by using the kitchen in shifts and commanding adjacent living rooms with separate television sets. In the kitchen, Arild's half-thawed meat competed for space with Anne Lill's low-carb breads.

Given the cramped housing, I considered staying in the Old Store, then changed my mind. It wasn't that I believed in ghosts. There were just a lot of stories there, too many to sleep with. That watery cold. That purple dress swinging with no breeze. So instead I moved into a spare bedroom in the Old House, with a window that overlooked the fjord, a soft mattress that nearly swallowed me. Clean and white. The room was almost too comfortable; it made me uneasy, felt rare and undeserved. I did not come to Norway for comfort.

This shuffling of living spaces gave Anne Lill an excuse to leave Arild, and Mortenhals, while saving face. As soon as the snow melted, she planned to move back to her family's house in the mountain village. It was bittersweet to leave the shop that she had spent the last decade tending, that she had poured her money and time and sanity into keeping afloat. But shopkeeping required diplomacy, and Anne Lill—unlike some mail-order bride, purchased for her lack of opinions—was happiest when she could speak her mind. She consoled herself with thoughts of the people she would no longer have to be nice to.

First on the list was Henning himself. Though technically the shop still belonged to Arild, and would for many months, Henning had wasted no time in demanding changes. Over the past year, Arild had stocked three additional wares: smoked whale, seal jerky, and an assortment of birthday postcards acquired below cost from a dead shop. Henning's tastes were varied, and pricier. He bought crates of pine nuts and fresh asparagus, French meringues and espresso, seamless boy-short panties, sweet-and-sour sauce, and Corona beer. New products crowded the aisles and piled up in the hallway and expired in storage before ever making it onto the shelves. Shipments arrived almost daily; money went out four times faster than it came in. Within weeks, Henning had drained the shop's savings. But the bills kept coming.

I passed the doorway of Anne Lill's living room one evening soon after I arrived. "Blair," she said, muting *American Idol*. "Do you think it'll go all right with the shop?"

I had seen the shipments but chosen not to think about them. "What do you mean?" I couldn't help looking over my shoulder, though Arild wasn't home. This didn't feel like a conversation I should be having. The shop was supposed to be a solid thing.

But Anne Lill only shrugged and turned up the volume.

Later that week, she cemented her departure by paying for her groceries with a credit card. Arild was stunned. The shop was also hers. Regardless of where she lived, he intended that Anne Lill should have free groceries for the rest of her life, and her own shop key in case she was ever in need. But Anne Lill planned to cut the cords fully. If it was just Arild, that was one thing, but she could hardly bear to be in the same room as Henning, whom she regarded as destroying all that they had built. Soon she would abandon Johannes Kristoffersen's Descendants completely. Of course, she would not get her groceries at the Sand Shop, so she drove all the way to Mestervik for food. For the moment it was awkward to bring her grocery bags into the Old House, but she stood firm, and anyway, it wouldn't be for long. She could not forgive Henning. She could hardly forgive Arild for not speaking up.

For his part, Arild believed the best of his son, and denied that he had ever doubted him in years past. He told himself that Henning's extravagant purchases were part of an ambitious strategy to persuade summer folks to do more of their shopping on the peninsula. Summer folks had expensive tastes; they preferred to bring fancy groceries from the city rather than shop for the basics at their local near-store. Maybe offering espresso and Brie in Mortenhals would draw to the shop a whole new class of customers. Of course, the theory wouldn't be tested for many weeks, but he held fast to its comfort. As evidence he took Henning's wife, Tuva, a sweet, overwhelmed woman who had, for the past several years, been ambiguously unwell. Tuva despaired of her new life in the country and drove biweekly to the city for sushi and "coffee from a machine." If Tuva liked the new wares, it boded well for her absentee peers.

Besides. It was the job of the older generation to know when to step aside.

Luckily, springtime was full of diversions. In addition to being available at the shop whenever Henning wanted him to take over—usually for several hours a day, on short notice—Arild had a flock that needed shearing, and expected upward of a hundred lambs to be born in the next four weeks. The other farmers had their sheep sheared in winter, when traveling Icelandic shearers passed through the region, but Arild was proud to shear his sheep himself. Sure, it took him thirty minutes per sheep to the professionals' three, but that wasn't so bad given that he worked alone. He saved money. More important, the sheep knew him. To be sheared, roughly and rapidly, by a team of strangers? That, he thought, must be torture.

It was still too cold to open the Old Store, so on this visit I had no guise of a role. I was in Malangen because I should be, because I could not imagine a future in which I did not come back and continue to come back. I wasn't here as the museum director. I was here as myself. And for the month, *myself* was assistant shepherd.

The shearing was fraught with problems. The clippers were rusty, the first lambs came early, and the sheep were stupid. We sheared the oldest and calmest first, wrestling them into a neck vise in the center of the barn. Arild peeled back the mass of wool inch by inch as the animals blinked and flicked their tongues, affronted. I gathered clippings off the ground, plucking out berries of shit, and stuffed the wool into feed sacks by assorted quality. When Arild got tired, we took turns. The handheld shearing machine was heavy and vibrated hard enough to numb my arm. He showed me how to dip into the fleece along the animal's neck and press my hand into the hot greasy pocket between skin and wool, pushing forward blind. I clipped cautiously, afraid of cutting the sheep, and as a result left behind a sloppy underlayer of fleece. Then, when Arild wasn't looking, I gave a few of the sheep Mohawks. By then we'd moved on to younger ewes, who kicked and struggled against their restraints. "Don't worry," Arild reassured me. "They're just ticklish. And afraid for their lives."

With ten sheep down, we went to the shop for a snack, collapsing at the coffee table. The Sailor crept up behind me and pinched my waist, chortling. He the Rich One was still in Spain for the winter, but Nils was there, dirty and flushed, and he looked on in amusement. I got him an ice-cream sandwich as a peace offering for our failed marriage, which he accepted graciously. Nils was in a good mood. He was keeping the news quiet, but he had a second date that night with a girl from the city.

As Arild and I finished our ice creams, Henning mopped his way across the shop. He stopped beside us and wiped his hands on his shirt, which featured a picture of an orca whale and the words "BARBECUE WILLY." Henning's homecoming had not been triumphant—I heard he'd been fired from his job driving trucks down south—but he was determined to do things right this time around. He glanced over me—despite efforts I'd made to get to know him, Henning seemed to find me largely invisible—and turned to regard his disheveled father.

"I don't know why you shear yourself," Henning said. "Everyone else gets sheared when the men come through, and it's so much faster."

"The men come through in January," said Arild. "Then the sheep have to spend the winter in the barn."

Henning frowned. "But it's such a waste. It takes ten days. Look, I don't care about the money for hiring someone. It's the *time*. In two days you could clean the barn and have a clean, sparkling barn. But instead you spend ten days shearing."

Henning's four-year-old son, Joar, ran down the aisle. He wore gardening gloves and a bike helmet loose on the back of his head. He shoved me with both hands. "You wear diapers!" he yelled, before sprinting away.

"Ten days," Henning said. "That's so much time. Think of all you could do. Like, if you mopped the shop, it would only take twenty minutes. Twenty minutes a day."

"It's better for the sheep," said Arild, but his voice lacked conviction. He caught my eye, and together we stood to leave.

The weather that day was strange, thick flurries alternating with bright sunshine. The nearest mountains glowed, but a gray mass was sliding up the north end of the fjord. I zipped my coveralls high on the neck and followed Arild to the barn, where the sheep had enjoyed our absence.

That week, on the twenty-eighth of April, Arild turned sixty-five. In the middle of the night, before his birthday, I tiptoed downstairs and decorated the living room with crepe paper and balloons that I'd brought from the States. I wanted to make something cheerful for him. We ate a breakfast of bread and boiled eggs amid the balloons while snow fell outside. The windows were half-covered with the dark shades that Anne Lill favored. "When she leaves," Arild said, "those will be the first thing I get rid of."

Though he tried to be positive about the separation, anger sometimes crept into his voice when he spoke of Anne Lill. Arild was no great romantic, but he liked the idea of a functional partnership, and with Anne Lill's move to the mountain village and retirement from the shop went his last real hope of such a companion. The couple would not divorce. There was no point; neither intended to marry again. And although both husband and wife remained fond of each other, neither would admit it to the other's face.

Anne Lill took full responsibility for the separation. Her treatment of the matter was characteristically brisk: she had simply lived too many years of her life alone to be happy living with someone else. Now, without adequate space for the couple to live separately, they could not be together at all. Sometimes she wondered what was wrong with her, that she was so incapable of sharing domestic life; but the fact seemed such a fundamental element of her character that questioning it did little good. "Arild's done nothing wrong," she told me one day in the kitchen, as she re-cleaned the stovetop that she had already cleaned the day before. "He's kind. He doesn't beat me." She hoped he would stay a friend, and for his birthday gave him a bottle of Bailey's Irish Cream, his favorite, which he could sip from a teacup as he watched the evening news. But that night, when Anne Lill joined Arild for his birthday dinner, a meal of meatballs and béarnaise sauce that represented a rare break from her careful diet, a bitter weight settled over the table and snuffed out all polite attempts at conversation; and, by the end, the couple's only words were to ask the American in the middle to pass the potatoes from one end of the table to the other. "I hope you'll take these things down soon," Anne Lill remarked, upon clearing her plate, about the streamers and balloons that adorned the dining room. Arild responded, with sudden conviction, that in fact he intended to leave them up indefinitely.

The decorations remained in place eight days later, when I turned twenty-six. As a surprise, Arild enlisted Jeanette to bake me a cake of Ritz crackers—newly popular in Norway—which she mixed with meringue and topped with whipped cream and berries. She delivered the cake to the coffee table midmorning, covered with lit candles, to the delight of the regular crowd. "Make a wish," Jeanette announced. Her oldest son, blond and shy, sat cross-legged on her lap, and when he looked up at her she poked him on the nose: "No, you felt ball. Not you." Her own dearest wish fulfilled, Jeanette's contentment seemed to spread around her. The court had returned her children. The judge, she claimed, had been so horrified by the dissolution of a family that should clearly have remained intact that her case was now used as a cautionary tale in the training of child services workers, a reminder of how impressions could go wrong.

I had a lot of wishes, too many to pick a favorite on the spot, so I settled on the one closest to the surface: *let the shop be okay.* When I took a deep breath, and blew out the candles, two remained lit.

"You have two boyfriends!" crowed Jeanette, in accordance with tradition, and when the table erupted—"Only two? Let's see who they are!"—I decided it was high time to cut the cake. The crackers had fused into a chewy, salty crust. Everyone ate seconds except the Sailor, who preferred coffee, and Rune, whom nobody had seen—or missed—in weeks. Rumor had it he was hanging around Martha at the Sand Shop.

After a while the crowd dispersed, and I slipped away to the back room of the shop, where I found an e-mail from Quince.

> *Happy birthday to my favorite person in the world. I wish I could be with you.*

I stared at the screen for a long time, thinking about how to respond. We had talked, for a while, about Quince joining me on this trip. Bringing him to Norway seemed like one of the most intimate things I could offer, more private than any secret, more vulnerable than my body. It meant everything. I wanted him to stand in the landscape that felt better to me than anywhere else, and for the people I cared for to meet each other. But money was tight, and Quince, who worked freelance, was offered a job in May that he couldn't afford to skip. Now, looking at his e-mail, I felt a flash of anger. So he wished he could be with me. Well, what if I didn't need him?

The force of the emotion startled me. My relationship with

Quince was one of the things that I was most grateful for, that I believed in. We were talking about marriage. I understood that he couldn't make the trip, and once he'd been offered the work, I'd in fact encouraged him to stay home. But these thoughts, this memory of love, felt dull to me. Who was this person far away? What was my duty to him? We had nothing in common.

When Henning walked in, I shut the browser quickly and stood, embarrassed that he had caught me in a moment of emotion. But he passed by me as if I weren't there at all.

That week, the folk school year ended. A poster hung outside the shop: a year-end revue, open to the public, at 6 P.M. on Friday. I went alone, walked with a herd of visiting parents into the familiar musty gymnasium, handed fifty kroner to a cool girl in pigtails in exchange for a paper ticket. The folk school had struggled over the past decade. It seemed that not as many young people wanted to learn arctic survival anymore. In a desperate bid to stay afloat, the principal had hired a celebrity adventurer and produced a reality show about his students, which showed in Norway and Russia; the prize for the best student was a trip to the South Pole. But the prize trip was illegal, and three people had drowned, and the school had been thrust into an unflattering spotlight that it did its best to back out of, even as the winning student fought prominently in a successful campaign to save folk schools when their national budget fell under attack. Now, after its brief fling with fame, 69°North was returning to its roots. Forty students, a year in the wilderness, everything the same as before.

The students were eighteen and sixteen and nineteen and they were just like I had been, just like all the students I had gone to school with; they were tough and wild and skied down mountain faces and ate raw meat and lived in the snow. They sang songs about the Northland, and performed skits about their teachers and Malangen, including a roast of Arild in which a suspender-clad fellow approached audience members with offers of coffee and relentless questions about where they were from. I sat in the back of the room, invisible in a crowd of strangers, and thought about how I was no longer this, how the students were no longer me. They were leaving. Once I had been that tough. Now I had sheep to shear.

When the show ended, someone touched my arm. It was the enthusiastic German organist. Come to her house, she said—she was hosting a dinner party right now. I followed her up the hill. She lived in the tall black house with a grass roof, right beside the church, where the former principal had lived before moving south.

Her house was clean and spare and her guests were well dressed. I did not recognize most of them. They were Egil's customers, or they shopped in the city. They wore stylish scarves and praised my accent and asked polite questions about jet lag. For dinner, the organist's husband, also an organist, made a delicately spiced fish soup, and for dessert our hostess offered sugar-free gluten-free nut balls. Where was I staying? the guests asked, and when I answered they said, "Oh," and smiled a little too late. Johannes Kristoffersen's Descendants—wasn't that where the farmers sat all day, doing nothing?

"I don't think so," I said. "I think you're mixing something up." As soon as it was late enough, I excused myself. I passed the graveyard and pulled my arms tight against my chest. The snow-covered graves looked like sheep. The graveyard was cut with well-worn paths and scattered footprints.

The next few days were busy. The first lambs had been born, and the trick was to shear the rest of the mothers before they birthed. Every few hours Arild and I walked the pasture in search of new lambs, who were usually hidden in the farthest corners, trembling in piles of yellow slime. Then we'd carry them to the barn and encourage their mothers to follow. Even when they could see their lambs in our arms, the mothers would turn and run back to the places where they'd given birth, circling and re-circling the empty ground while their newborns wailed. When we could, we chased the sheep who were about to give birth into the barn, too. There, the lambs were safe. They chirped and grunted and cried like babies. Arild installed a security camera that broadcast sound and video into the back room of the shop, so he could keep tabs on the nursery.

If we didn't find the lambs fast enough, then the crows got them. The first time they beat us, they left a lamb with red holes for eyes stumbling in the mud, bawling for milk. There were live lambs everywhere, yellow and bloody, and this one seemed no more grotesque than any other. Arild killed it fast with the back of an ax while I waved my arms to distract its mother.

We'd lost three ewes that week, birthing. The last we got to in time to call a vet, and I held her neck while the man shoved loose, dangling organs back inside her. She didn't moan, just huffed her breath, her eyes wide and white and her head sinking ever lower. He threaded a shoelace under her tail, tied it in a bow, and said to untie it in a few days. She was bleeding like a faucet. It'll stop, he said, but it didn't, and the next morning the barn was full of crows that filled the air when I walked in, and smacked all at once against the windows, and the sheep was dead and her eyes gone, too. Arild and I dragged her body out on a feed sack, heaving in unison. We had to heave twice over the door frame. "Some people have cows," Arild said, panting, and we both laughed.

Two days later, another lamb, worse: its flesh and bone pecked out through a neat hole in its belly, its fleece still so clean and white. It was a bag of lamb, perfect but for its hollowness, and when Arild lifted it up I felt sick, the crows all around, watching. Even that morning, Arild had fed them bread behind the barn. It was his compulsion: he had to feed everything. Now he dropped the empty lamb into another empty sack. Henning leaned out the window with his father's rifle and shot twice, and nobody jumped but me.

One morning four enormous strangers walked into the shop, burly men in leather jackets with tattoos crawling out their sleeves and up their necks. They split up and walked the aisles, back and forth with their hands in their pockets, and didn't seem to notice that everyone at the coffee table had fallen silent. Finally the men, after consulting in Russian, converged at the checkout counter. The tallest stepped forward, his arms crossed over his chest. Arild greeted him with a nod.

"Excuse me, sir," said the Russian, in thick English. He frowned and turned back to his friends, who encouraged him. "I look for a casserole, and small wood."

Arild handed a Post-it pad and pen across the counter. The man drew a bunch of dots on the paper. "For to smoke fish."

"*Sagflis,*" said Arild.

"Sawdust," I offered, from my seat cross-legged on the floor, where I was attempting to make shelf space for the thirteen varieties of menstrual pads that Henning had recently acquired.

The Russian nodded.

"We do not have it," said Arild, "but I know who have it." He picked up the phone and called Rune's number. When nobody answered, he drew on paper a map to Rune's house. "Listen," he said, amusement flashing in his eyes. "This man shall not open his door. He is probably asleep." He mimed taking a drink, and the Russians nodded. "So you must just walk into his house. Do not knock."

Everyone at the coffee table was paying attention.

"Do not knock?" the Russian confirmed.

"No," said Arild. "You four must walk in, he is sleeping, you wake him up. Then you say that Arild sent you for sawdust. Good luck with your fish."

The Russians thanked him politely. Arild gave them a casserole pan from his own kitchen and waited until they left before he started to laugh. He laughed for a long time.

In gratitude for the casserole, the Russians returned with a bottle of expensive vodka. Arild thanked them humbly. After they left, he called a customer who worked at a farmer's co-op and arranged to trade the vodka for a large quantity of frozen tenderloin. He sorted the meat, wrapped the choicest steak in several plastic bags, and drove two hours south to Finnsnes, where, in the parking lot of a soccer stadium, he handed the bag-wrapped package to a man in a gray van. The man handed him a key. The key unlocked the back door of a dead grocery store, where Arild collected a number of shopping carts. The carts were so large that they would hardly fit down the narrow aisles of Johannes Kristoffersen's Descendants, but this Arild viewed as a virtue: it was a fact, he said, that giving customers big carts made them buy more.

On impulse, he also retrieved from the grocery store an assortment of vinyl-strip curtains, which he intended to hang over the refrigerated display of salami, fish, and vegetables along the back wall. He was pleased with the find; such curtains were expensive, and they would save both money and electricity. But when he showed the curtains to his son, Henning was disgusted. The curtains were old. The vinyl, once clear, had yellowed. Henning hauled them down to the basement and dumped them by the cleaning supplies. How could his father be so careless with appearances?

Later, when Arild was reading his newspaper, Henning sat down at the table but didn't lean back. His mouth was pressed in a line. He stared at his father until Arild looked up.

"Listen," Henning told his father. "I have to talk to you.

You *cannot* go commenting on what people buy. You can't make people feel judged for their purchases. You can't say, 'Oh, you're getting those cancer sticks again.' You can't say, 'Odd Jonny likes such-and-such beer,' 'Ingvarda likes such-and-such toilet paper.' That's not how it's done. People need to feel like they can come in here and leave without getting talked about."

Arild blinked. He glanced down at his newspaper and then pushed it slightly away. He'd been reading about dead miners in Turkey. Earlier he'd read his horoscope, which suggested that today he was likely to make mistakes. He'd shown it to me, since we were both Tauruses. Double trouble, he said.

"Here's the thing," Henning said. "You sit at this table and you talk about your customers and nobody feels like they have any privacy. Everything you say here, everyone knows it by the end of the day. They know everything anyone says here! It all gets around. Anne Lill complained so much when those children were taken that child protective services had to come talk to her."

"She was writing things on Facebook," said Arild. "That's public."

"*This* is public!" Henning shouted, grabbing the edge of the table. "When you sit here, you're a public figure. You have to understand that nothing that's said at this table is private. Egil doesn't gossip about his customers. If you go to the city, no one is gossiping about their customers. No one is teasing them. The things you say are entirely inappropriate. The other day you said to a child, 'It's wonderful when you arrive, and wonderful when you leave, too.' To a child! If Blair worked at Eide Handel, would she say that to a customer?"

Arild didn't answer.

"Answer the question," said Henning. "If Blair were working at Eide Handel, and a customer came in with their child, would Blair say to the child, 'It's wonderful when you arrive, and wonderful when you leave, too?' "

"I guess not," said Arild.

Henning let out breath. "People are talking. There were customers here ten years ago who aren't here now, and I need to know why. This is about me. This is supposed to be my salary now. I need to know why people won't shop here. I need as many customers as possible."

A tractor pulled up by the front door and cut its engine.

"After the divorce from your mother——" Arild began, then trailed off. "People took sides."

"You made it easy for them," Henning said, "by being so unprofessional. Honestly. Sitting here commenting on purchases? Keeping track of how often they buy beer? Asking——"

Behind him, the farmer Eilif Idar walked into the shop, grinned, then stopped smiling. He turned and started examining the candy rack. Arild raised his eyebrows pointedly. Henning glanced over, but kept talking.

"——asking personal questions, and then telling other people the answers? It's no wonder you're losing customers——"

"Good day, Eilif Idar," said Arild.

"And the worst thing," said Henning, "is that you just keep doing it. As if you simply don't care——"

Arild stood up. He nodded at Eilif Idar. "There's coffee," he said, "but I have to go check the lambs." Eilif Idar had sheep himself; he would understand.

A sharp wind from the north blew snowflakes into flurries outside, and Arild walked quickly, pulling his knit hat over his ears. His knee was acting up, and he limped slightly as he strode past the gas pumps. The air stilled as soon as he entered the barn, with its warm scent of hay and wool. To his right, the youngest lambs rested against their mothers' bellies, their bodies sprawling, nearly liquid. To his left, forty or so sheep stood and chewed cud. A few turned their heads and observed him. They were mothers-to-be.

Arild lifted the cord for the security camera and pulled out the plug. A faint buzzing stopped abruptly.

"Watch out," he told the sheep. "Here comes Arild, scary Arild, who runs his mouth too much."

He walked over to the lamb stalls and peered along the row, making sure everyone was alive. There had been some hard births; he'd overfed over the winter, and the lambs came out big. But they were hardy, too. Arild reached down and lifted a limp lamb by the back of the skull, a move he'd learned recently when another farmer did it on TV. The lamb bristled awake and he dropped it back down, satisfied.

One lamb in particular was special. Half of his face was black, and the other half was white. Arild had named him Black and White and tagged his ear with a round number, 40020. Sometimes he got fancy lambs like that—black faces, black spots—because he'd used a half-black stud ram from a farmer up in Skibotn. It made their wool worth less, but he could always recognize his own sheep when he passed the summer flocks grazing in the mountain village.

"I *think* he's overreacting," Arild told Black and White. "Half the people who don't shop here, I could move to Africa and they still wouldn't come. I don't think there's anything I can do about it."

Black and White closed his eyes and breathed quietly.

"It's hard to change when you're old," Arild said, "but I can try."

The snow melted into patches and away, leaving fields caked in damp grass. The river and creeks flushed plates of ice into the fjord, where they lingered into nothing. Around the country, farmers protested the new right-wing government's proposed subsidies for small-scale farms, which they deemed inadequate. Farmers drove tractors down the streets of Oslo and dumped loads of manure in front of the capital. They threatened to blockade the nation's egg supply, just in time for Constitution Day, May 17. For a week, front-page news around the country lamented the farmers' wrath: Did they have no compassion? How could they deny their countrymen cakes? Arild's loyalty to shopkeeping was greater than his loyalty to farming; he followed a rumor about a nearby distributor's abundant eggs, and purchased dozens of cartons so that his customers wouldn't have to go without. But right before Constitution Day, the farmers called off the blockade, and Arild had to sell the cartons cheap to make room in the cooler.

On the morning of the seventeenth, villagers gathered in the Malangen church for a service. Arild refused to go, so I went alone and sat next to Jeanette's father, a ruddy and cheerful ex-sailor who bred Swedish mountain cows in the mountain village. He had recently flown to Oslo for a day to join the protests, and was responsible for a number of protest signs around the peninsula and Tromsø, which he decorated with empty milk cartons. If he really wanted to make a point about the end of farming, I suggested, he should decorate the signs with dead lambs; I knew a reliable source. As he considered how to best decline my offer, the organ blared to life, its vibrations setting a model ship hung over the aisle swinging from side to side.

After the service there was a brief ceremony, during which the enthusiastic German organist's solemn daughter lit candles in the cemetery for Malangenites lost at sea and war, and then local schoolchildren gathered to parade to the Sand School. They wore bright *bunads* and waved flags and somebody played a trumpet; the procession, congregated, stretched halfway around the graveyard. But the whole thing saddened me, particularly when I thought of Arild sitting at home, avoiding the community that streamed from the church his grandfather had built. So I slipped back down the hill and didn't join the parade. Back in the Old House, Arild had baked a chocolate cake with some of the extra eggs. He seemed happy about the cake, but I was worried about him. Between Henning's scolding and Anne Lill's impending departure, he'd seemed down lately, spending more time than usual in front of the television. His limp, which appeared on and off, had been constant for weeks. Even at the shop he was unusually quiet, and sometimes leaned on a shopping cart to get around. It was only with the sheep that he seemed content. So when, after a lunch of cake, he suggested driving to the school to catch the end of the festivities, I was all for it.

The parade had reached the school, and we drove slowly, inching along as children sprinted across the road with ice cream smeared on their faces. An older woman had dressed her poodle in a vest. Someone was handing out hot dogs, someone else playing an accordion. And then we had passed them, and there was nothing more; the potholed road curved uphill toward the mountain village, past two red houses, which belonged to Rune and to Arild's ex-wife. Arild watched the crowd in the rearview mirror. Then, with a sniff, he pulled into Rune's driveway. He had brought no gift, no excuse for the visit, but it was no matter. Sometimes he liked to spy on Rune, to tease him. Despite Henning's discouragement, he was not getting out of people's business quite yet.

There were no fresh footprints in Rune's soggy yard.

I figured Rune didn't know I was back in the country, so I went to the door alone, anticipating his surprise. I knocked hard and stepped back. But nobody answered. I knocked again, and waited. Finally I tried the knob—unlocked—and cracked open the door enough to stick my head in.

I was hit, instantly, with the smell. Sour and rotten. Something awful—I recoiled before I could think, shut the door again, and motioned for Arild to get out of the van. My heart was racing. I waited until Arild was beside me and took a deep breath before pushing the door again.

The hallway was lined with piles of sticks and trash; a beer can on its side had spilled and dried, leaving a puddle of stain on the wooden floor. "*Hei?*" I said to the house. "Rune?" Silence.

Then, as I stepped inside, something moved. A figure shuffled into the light.

Rune was so thin that I hardly recognized him. He seemed to have lost half his mass; his shirt hung from his shoulders in such a way that the front of his body seemed concave. His hair and beard had grown into a matted curtain. But his face cracked into a smile. "No, hello!" he slurred.

"I see you're on a diet," Arild said. He had taken a step back, for the smell.

"There's no food," said Rune. "I haven't eaten."

"When?" I asked. "Today? This week? This month?"

Rune giggled.

Arild's eyes traveled around the room—over the piles of wood, a heaping bag of empty cans, littered cigarette butts and porn VHS tapes stacked on a shelf. "Why didn't you call?" Now he sounded angry. "You know we would have brought you food."

"My phone's out of money," Rune said. "My car won't start."

We helped him out to the passenger seat of the van. I crouched in back as we pulled onto the road, slowly parting the crowds of dancing children and flags and *bunads* and dogs in sweaters. Rune watched the revelers happily.

"The seventeenth of May," he said. "We have to celebrate this country. It's not everyone who gets to live in a country like Norway."

Back at the shop, we unlocked the door and turned on all the lights. I filled my arms with loaves of brown bread, day-old sweet rolls, and the Danish pastries that Henning baked in excess every morning. Arild got cartons of milk and butter and goat cheese and five packs of expired sliced ham. Together we packed the food into bags. "These are for you, you Martha-lover,"

Arild said, although he let Rune pay for his own tobacco and Mack Polar Bear beer.

Rune leaned against the counter and bit into a sweet roll. He swallowed, his eyes closed. It took him a while to open them again.

"You'll be around," he said to me. "We'll see each other again soon."

"Of course," I said, glancing down at my hands. I'd taken a Danish for myself, but I didn't want it anymore.

"Let's have a fire on Midsummer," Rune said. "St. Hans. It's the twenty-fourth of June. We can do it ourselves, without Martin. We can get cider. I know you like cider. We'll build a big fire on the beach."

"She'll be around," said Arild. He didn't look at me, but he didn't need to. I'd be leaving, back to my other life. He knew.

"Yeah," I said softly. "I'll be around."

Rune smiled. He gathered the bags of food in his arms. As he started back toward the van, I grabbed a Norwegian flag from the display by the shoes, the kind of cheap flag that all of the children outside were waving, and tucked it between his beers. "Here," I said. "It belongs to the richest country in the world." But Rune handed the flag back to me.

"Don't worry," he said. "I already have one."

That night, lying in bed, I felt again the surge of anger I'd felt on my birthday, reading Quince's note, only this time my anger was directed not at his words but at his very being. I didn't need him. I wanted a great wall to descend across the Atlantic Ocean, cutting off all connection. Fuck you, I thought, with your farm and your chickens. Fuck you with your letters, claiming you miss me. Fuck you with your log house and your horse and the sexy muscles in your arms. I don't need you at all. I don't want you.

Again the emotion came suddenly, forcefully, seizing at

something in my gut. I sat up in bed, pulling the blanket around my shoulders, and lifted the blind from the window. The bedroom faced south, toward Sand, but all I could see from here was a decrepit white house in a field, the broad pale sky over the water, the twin peaks of Vassbruna Mountain. The sight slowed my pulse. I tightened the blanket around my neck and the bottom half of my face, feeling petulant. *Fuck you*, I thought again, an aftershock of anger, and my face curled into a frown so exaggerated and childish that it broke the spell, amusing me despite myself.

"What's happening?" I whispered. "Why am I alone?"

But I wasn't alone; I knew that. I was loved, and I was, in all rational moments, supremely grateful for that love. I had parents who cared for me beyond words. I had a partner who challenged and supported me in equal measure. In Norway, finally, I had a second home and community. I had Arild.

And yet here I was. Furious at Quince for reasons I did not know. Overcome with a brittle aloneness that was less lonely than defensive.

It felt familiar.

Familiar.

The word seized on something. My anger, I realized, wasn't about Quince at all. I saw a sleepless night in a long-ago bedroom, a hand tracing down a pebbled wall. The shocking conclusion that home had abandoned me. It was so long ago. With the recognition came a flood of exhaustion. I lay back on the bed, my eyes sinking shut even as I closed the blind, and fell quickly into sleep.

That night, I dreamed that I left Malangen and went to my host family's town, where Far stood in the audience at a public choir concert. I walked up and stood beside him, not saying a word. When he noticed me he kissed me tenderly on the head. I thought: I am going to stand here and not respond to anything he does, and then I'll know. I thought: this is an experiment; nothing could hurt me now. Far started stroking my back, gently, continuously. I stood still as ice, alert. He ran his hand over my ass, cupping it lightly, and then trailed his fingers to my waist. Kissed my head once more. He seemed so happy and soft and eager. In the dream I knew he'd been waiting to do it. And then I surprised myself and started to run. I ran down winding, charming streets, small houses and cobblestones, but each turn brought me back to the crowd; each time, I turned and ran in a new direction. Finally I found a house where I could rest.

When I woke up, I was struck first with disappointment: it had only been a dream. Even now, it had been such a relief to not doubt my instincts. Had Far touched me? Had he not? But, I thought, it didn't matter. He touched me now, as had anyone who had ever made me feel that my body, my life, was not under my control. Far's touch had come in the years after I left his home, when I wondered and remembered, when I let those memories chase me.

My second thought came with surprising strength. I had been certain, for a decade now, that I could not return to Lillehammer. It was a promise I'd made to myself upon leaving: the year was over; I never had to think about it again; I never again had to go back to the town by the lake. But maybe, I thought now, the question wasn't whether I could go back. It was whether I could leave it behind.

My last week in Mortenhals was busy. The enthusiastic German organist arranged for me to lead an Ask-a-Jew session for the fifth-graders at Sand School who, along with their teachers, had never seen a Jew before. Each of the students prepared a question on a sheet of lined paper. I explained about the high holy days, and latkes, but mostly they wanted to know how to recognize a Jew when they saw one. "You look normal," they observed.

"That's the point," I told them. "Jews are normal people." But they insisted. Put on the spot, I pointed out five students at random and suggested that they looked as Jewish as anyone else. This made the chosen students very happy. Then I wrote all their names for them in Hebrew, an alphabet I only vaguely remembered from religious school, with the confidence of someone who knows that her mistakes will never be found out. The session was such a hit that the seventh-grade teacher wanted me, and so did the ninth-grade teacher, and by the end of the week I had come back a half dozen times and spoken to nearly all the students in the school. I felt like a lousy ambassador but a good citizen.

When I returned to the shop after my final session, the coffee table was crowded with men, talking and laughing. They glanced up when I walked in. Rune and Nils and Odd Jonny and the Sailor and Quince.

And Quince.

He sat at the end of the table with a cup of coffee in his hands. Then he stood up and wrapped his arms around me. I let myself melt into him. The men cheered.

He had come during the night, a surprise: rented a car in Tromsø, taught himself a single Norwegian phrase—"Where is Blair?"—and followed the fjordside roads toward the incongruous silver gleam of the Brygger resort, stopping only to ask a few farmers his only question. *Hvor er Blair?* They all knew, of course; they answered in Norwegian; and he followed their gestures until he came to Johannes Kristoffersen's Descendants. Though he'd never seen it, Quince recognized the shop immediately, and Arild knew him at a glance. "You're here, Mr. Q," said Arild, pouring him a cup of coffee. And so it was.

As it turned out, Quince had been e-mailing Arild for weeks, trying to plan the trip, without ever getting a response. In his trash can, Arild unearthed a series of e-mails with the subject line "Important message from Mr. Q." It seemed that, for reasons none of us could parse, Henning had deleted the e-mails as quickly as they arrived. He left the room when I tried to ask him about it.

Luckily, Arild did not seem the least bit flustered about his surprise international houseguest, and wished only that the visit was longer. Over the four days of his stay, Quince worked in the barn and sat at the table and joked with Nils and made appropriate facial expressions when the men showed him pictures of mail-order brides. He ate open-faced sandwiches and fried whale, and on his last night, he went with me and Arild to the pizza restaurant with the old things. He would fly home the next morning, and I, a week later.

The waitress was British, though she had lived in Norway for years. She looked us over—the white-haired man with his stilted English, the American man with excellent posture—and turned to me, the woman in the middle.

"Let me guess," she said. "It's the first time they've met."

"Yeah," I said.

She pointed at Quince. "You met him in America, and now you're bringing him home."

We looked at each other, the three of us, and nodded.

"Congratulations," she said. "That's just like me, except the other way around. I fell for a Norwegian, and here I am." When the pizza was ready, she gave us sour-cream dressing on the house.

My last week passed like all the others, and the sky was bright, early morning, as Arild drove me to the airport. Summer's thaw was rising up the mountains, so that mossy fields and wildflowers grew toward the white peaks. We drove the tunnel under Malangen fjord and then, a half-hour later, crossed the fjord once more to reach the island that made up old Tromsø. I was already slipping into the cool, numb state of travel, the one I'd felt when

I came to Norway, except that now I was leaving again. Something felt more final this time. I would come back, but probably not for a whole summer. I was growing roots at home as Arild, retiring from the shop, was letting go of his. When I looked up from the horizon, I saw that Arild was crying behind his glasses.

"In English," said Arild, "one doesn't say 'love,' right? One says 'fond of.'"

"It depends," I said. "The word *love* is used more loosely in English. Like, you can love your friends. People say that."

Arild stared at the road. "I was under the impression that love was what is between you and Mr. Q."

"Well," I said, "that's love, too. That's romantic love. But love can mean—I mean, in English, it's used to mean strong affection. Like for family. If you care about someone a lot. If they're important to you. I've heard it used—" I was babbling, and stopped myself. Something in my voice had grown tight.

"I see," said Arild.

We fell into silence. The bridge arced high above the water. Looking down, I saw the patches of clear turquoise that lined the shallow shoreline, and the turquoise of underwater pillars that held up the bridge itself.

"Arild," I said, "were you going to say that you were fond of me?"

"I had thought of doing so, yes."

"But we know that *jo*," I said. Then, after a moment, "You know I'm fond of you, too."

We had crested the bridge. The road curved down to the right, toward the watchtowers and gray buildings of Tromsø-Langnes Airport. By the shore, a few men were at work erecting a *lavvo*, a lure for tourists who had recently disembarked. Arild changed the subject. He had given me a duffel bag's worth of raw wool from his sheep. Because it was a livestock product, I wasn't sure if the wool was legal to bring into the country. We discussed possible reactions on the part of United States customs until he'd pulled into the drop-off zone and I stood on the sidewalk with my luggage around me: my backpack, a small carry-on, the enormous duffel bag of wool. I'd also packed some chocolates and *lefse* from the shop, and he inquired about these now. Did I have enough food? Would I be cold on the flight? Had I remembered my passport, and a knife that he'd given me from the Old Store?

Finally, having run out of logistics, we stopped and looked at each other. Arild was crying again. He took off his glasses and rubbed quickly, almost violently, at his eyes.

"I'll have some peace and quiet at last," Arild said, "finally free of that American *pia*, she who plagues me constantly."

"And I'll be free of the old man," I told him, and walked away before I cried, too.

Late that summer, I got sick with anaplasmosis, a tick-borne illness. For weeks, exhausted and feverish, I hardly left my bed. Although I vaguely registered that my letters from Arild had dwindled, I was too weak to think much about it; the frequency of Arild's correspondence had always waxed and waned depending on how busy he was with the shop and the farm, and based on the few notes he did send, life in Mortenhals seemed fine enough.

But in September, I received an e-mail from his youngest daughter, Emma. *I'm writing because Papa wanted me to . . .* she began. *Henning has a real temper and says ugly things and is psychologically breaking Papa down.* She explained that Henning was gone for the weekend, and perhaps I could call Arild as soon as possible. I needed to set up an account to call long distance from my computer, and the setup, though it took no more than ten minutes, seemed to last an interminably long time. I couldn't find the right buttons to press. Finally, I called the shop's number, feeling nervous and shy. I needed to hear Arild's voice, but I didn't know what to say.

"Hello," said Arild. His shopkeeper voice.

"Hello," I said. "Do you sell milk?"

The joke was a gift for both of us. I could have come up with a better joke if I was thinking better.

"Yes," said Arild. "We sell milk."

"Can you deliver milk to America?"

He laughed, a laugh of sudden recognition and delight, and when I heard his pleasure I relaxed slightly. "Yes so," he said. "It's you."

"Emma wrote to me."

"Yes."

"What's going on?"

"No . . . He has a temper, he Henning." A moment's hesitation, polite distance, before he poured forth a litany of grievances. How Henning forced Arild to sleep in the grimy basement of the shop. Forbade him from eating meals at the coffee table, then even in the back room, so that Arild had to take his bread in the basement, too. Kicked over a bucket of water when Arild was mopping. Pushed him down, breaking his glasses. Grabbed him by the neck hard enough to leave bruises. Drove the shop into debt but made Arild take out the loan to save it. And when Arild bought *lefse* to sell at the shop, and paid with money from the cash register, Henning threatened to report him for stealing.

Arild's voice was calm, but it quavered as he talked about his customers. Recently, he said, an old woman came by at 8:45 A.M. to buy diesel, fifteen minutes before the shop's official opening time. As Arild unlocked the door for her, Henning wrestled him away, knocking him to the ground. "At least that time I was able to save my glasses," Arild said. "But it's clear, to do that with a customer on the stairs . . .

"But last Monday," he added, "Henning was gone from one

to six, and then I received feedback from customers that it was pleasant to have me back in the shop."

Now he had a window of time—a few days, while Henning was away—and he was acting fast. Just that morning he'd written a letter to his lawyer, attempting to terminate Henning's right to the family business, firstborn son or no. When Henning returned, Arild would confront him, backed by his most formidable customers. "He has tried to push me down as much as possible, but I have had sufficient troubles over the years that I am fairly strong. I have a good psyche, and all that—" He cut off; his voice changed. "Do you see this here *pia* with two lambs?" He was showing a picture of me to a customer. "She is in America, and it is she that I'm talking to right now . . . No, I certainly hope that she never comes back."

I laughed. I was laughing too much in the conversation—laughing every chance he gave me. I just wanted to keep him talking.

But the moment had passed. It was time for news: Was I well? How was Mr. Q? And the weather? The only other update, Arild said, was that next week he would be sending the summer's lambs to the eternal hunting grounds. Even his favorite—Black and White, the lamb with the special face.

"Because Black and White is a boy?" I asked.

"He's a boy lamb," said Arild. "And boys, they're a piece of shit."

When I hung up the phone, my whole body was burning. I searched for plane tickets to Tromsø immediately, thinking to leave that very afternoon, and went as far as to enter my credit card number before realizing, with a wave of dizziness, that if I was too sick to walk across the room without falling over, there was no way I could handle traveling to the Arctic. Arild wanted my support, had gotten his daughter to ask for it, and yet I couldn't get to him. I had never felt so helpless.

Over the next weeks I talked to Arild almost every day, frustrated and proud as I pieced together what was going on. When Henning returned from England, Arild confronted him with Odd Jonny as a witness, meeting Henning in the doorway of Johannes Kristoffersen's Descendants and chasing him back out again. Then he began the slow process of rebuilding the shop, budgeting carefully, luring back those customers who had drifted away. They came willingly. As one woman put it, "It's Arild who gets people to come together."

Henning and his family did not leave Mortenhals. They retreated into the Old House, drawing all the curtains closed. Since he was now shut out of both his apartment and his house, Arild continued to live in the shop's dank basement, in a small cement room that he furnished with a rocking chair and a television; at night, with a slab of *lefse* or a can of Pringles, he could sit back and watch TV shows about farmers finding love. Once I referred to the room as his "bunker," and Arild adopted the term with amusement. "I have endured enough difficulty in my life that I am not easily broken," he often reassured me, or maybe himself. He bought a red motorcycle from a folk school student. He thought about getting a sheepdog. It was a lemming year, and the yellow rodents left crisscross tracks on the new snow.

"If you poke a lemming with a stick, it pops," Arild told me over the phone, proud to offer this bit of trivia. I said that didn't sound right, and he admitted that he'd never tried it himself.

With Henning gone, Anne Lill returned to the shop daily, mopping the floors and rearranging the displays of food and magazines to be more symmetrical. She swatted flies and cleaned coffee mugs and retired at night to her candlelit childhood home in the mountain village. When her back ached, Arild brought her groceries and installed white cabinets in her empty kitchen. He'd retrieved the cabinets years ago from a half-burned house in Tromsø, and kept them in his boathouse ever since, certain that they would one day be useful. His thrift pleased both of them.

In November, the first week that I was well enough to travel, I flew to Norway for a short visit. It was dark, but the shop glowed with light and people, men lounging in half-zipped snow-suits, children eating ice cream with their mittens on. There was no room for me in Arild's bunker, so he arranged for me to sleep in Camping Nils's trailer, which sat empty in the campground. The trailer was cozy, but I didn't like walking by the Old House to get there; I felt that Henning's face might suddenly appear in a darkened window. Someone had put a life-size cutout of Justin Bieber in one of the upstairs windows, and it startled me every time I passed.

That week, Arild and I drove. We drove to Finland, to the Meat Hall just over the border that sold cheap reindeer and beef and pork and venison, and where a traveling choir performed songs about Jesus. We drove to Tromsø for pizza and brownies. We drove to Finnsnes for no reason at all. And on Sunday, the day the shop was closed and we could leave early, we drove to Kaldfjord—Cold Fjord—where, the *Northern Light* reported, the water was boiling with four hundred minke whales, who had followed herring farther north than ever before. Everyone at the shop was talking about the whales, and Arild was determined that we should see them with our own eyes.

The road by Kaldfjord, normally as still as that in Morten-hals, was packed with minivans and bicycles. Children ran on the ice-glazed beach and slid on frozen tide pools, fathers in expen-sive parkas sipped from thermoses and glanced at their watches, couples reclined on reindeer skins. Kayakers and fishing boats dotted the fjord. The noontime sunset cast the water in shadow but lit the mountaintops gold.

Arild had a new car, a twenty-year-old Subaru, and it inched through traffic, past a paraglider landing in a mess of cloth and ropes, past a handwritten sign promising COFFEE, CAKE, AND A CHRISTMAS ATMOSPHERE. But so far, the water was smooth—it looked hard, impermeable. Trying to cover his disappointment, Arild handed me a pair of binoculars, urging me to watch for a few more minutes. Surely something would happen. Something exclusive.

I turned the binoculars toward the beach, to a child fixing his shoe. "Do you think they're enjoying themselves?" Meaning the people.

"Of course they are," said Arild. "They're out in the fresh air, in the country. They're not staring at screens."

He had pulled over, but neither of us made a move to leave the car, for which I was grateful. It was enough to look out the window, to sit together in the warmth. We waited ten minutes, half an hour, enough time to eat sweet rolls and licorice and listen to the radio news: a murder in Bergen, protests in the United States. Finally, as the last beams of daylight faded, something splashed, quick and typical—spout, head, that last curling tail. The people on shore crowded together, pointing at where the whale had been.

"Huh," said Arild, handing me the last sweet roll. "We'll say at the shop there were at least two hundred."

I took the roll and agreed.

AFTERWORD

TWO WEEKS AFTER LEAVING MORTENHALS, two days before Thanksgiving, I got an e-mail from one of my old coworkers in Alaska. Mike and I had never talked much—he was quiet—but I'd always thought of him as one of the kindest souls on the glacier, committed to his wife and his dogs. He was an accomplished racer from a legendary mushing family; the other guides held him in high esteem. Now Mike had moved to Wisconsin, and his wife had just had a baby, so they were downsizing the kennel. He wanted to sell a small team of dogs, trained and ready, a mix of yearlings and veterans. A turnkey operation, he called it.

Quince and I had been talking about getting our own dogs, had even set up a dog yard in the garden, but so far we hadn't taken the plunge; and yet here it was, a sign from the universe, a team of good young dogs just waiting for us. We drove four hours northwest to Mike's kennel to check them out. The dogs were beautiful and generic: three yellow dogs, one light brown, one dark brown, one black. They were fast. I didn't know anything about them. Mike named an affordable price. Quince and I bought all six and drove home, parking in the barn, where the dogs staunchly refused to get out of the truck. Later I realized that they'd never been inside a building before.

I wanted to give the dogs good lives. I wanted to spend all my time with them. I learned who liked meat and who liked kibble, who enjoyed learning complex commands and who would rather keep their lessons simple. The dogs formed friendships and rivalries just like any group of creatures, and their relationships evolved with time. The shyest dog became less shy. The youngest showed the most promise as a leader. My favorite thing was to sit in the middle of the yard while the dogs ran loose around me, playing and sniffing and sprinting wild, half-airborne laps around the edge of the garden, crowding around me and slithering onto my lap, where I'd wrap them up in my arms and kiss their sweet grinning faces. I didn't have to go anywhere. They always came to me.

It was different, dogsledding with no boss, no Tallak or Noah or Dan to grant or withhold their approval. Quince threw his full support into the team, building doghouses out of barrels and lumber scraps, organizing fund-raisers, and researching strategy in the small hours of the morning when insomnia kept him on the couch. With his horse and cold-weather experience, plus a certain physical daring, he took to mushing more quickly than anyone I'd seen. Our neighbor, a carpenter, repaired used dogsleds that we found on Craigslist; the local butcher donated hundreds of pounds of deer carcasses; the taxidermist gave us fish meat and bear fat; local kids stopped by to learn the basics. Arild mailed me a pair of seal-fur boots, so that I might stay warm on the trail. I gave rides to neighbors and kids, teaching everyone who wanted to learn; the more people who loved the dogs, the happier I became. But despite the community that formed around the team, the fact that remained—that, at times, astonished me—was that I knew more about dogsledding than anyone else around. When trouble came, I had to be my own authority. And as weeks went by, I came to recognize the obvious: that dogsledding, the life of a musher, had no gatekeeper. In fact, I was doing it. This life was as real as that of any musher I'd admired.

Ten years after leaving Lillehammer, eight years after attending folk school, I made my own north.

This is my life, for now: waking up in a house that was built by the man I love, against a field smooth with snow, in a town of eight hundred at the edge of the Northwoods. Looking out the window at my dogs, stretching their delicate legs as they climb from their houses in the garden. Roosters and guinea hens calling the hour. Wisconsin will never be northern Norway, but here are Quince's roots, and here, for now, are mine. A place where I can be as tough as I want, but I don't need to be.

I entered small races, to start. Twenty, thirty miles with six-dog teams—races that would qualify me for longer ones, one or two hundred or a thousand miles a few years out. The last race of the season was the hardest. Forty-two miles in the dark, and a good pool of mushers. My parents flew out from their new home in Oregon to cheer me on.

That night, I decided to run a new leader, a yearling. Jenga was my shyest dog, scared of everything—people and snowmobiles and strange noises, lumps in the snow and moving shadows: she flinched and hissed and crawled behind my legs. But something happened, I had noticed, when I put her in lead. She stood tall; she paid attention. She never glanced back. In the starting chute, as my countdown began, I jogged up to her, kissed the dark stripe above her nose, kissed Quince good-bye. With three seconds left, I ran back to my sled. The dogs leaped against their lines, and when I yanked my snowhook we took off at a sprint, through the bundled, cheering crowds of downtown Calumet and, a minute after turning off the main road, into the silence of the woods.

Jenga set a quick pace, and the trail was packed hard, so the first turns were tricky, slick and careening. I had a new sled, light and wobbly, responsive to the slightest lean, and I threw my whole weight into the turns, sending up sheets of snow each time I skidded around a corner. My headlamp lit a ring on the dogs and the snow just ahead of them, so for a while—half an hour, maybe—I saw each turn as it came and had only moments to prepare for it. Then a light through the trees ahead—another dog team, musher silhouetted against the glow he cast onto the trail. When I came up beside him our dogs looked at each other, two teams sizing each other up at a run, twelve tongues bouncing, and then I called to my dogs and their legs churned harder and we were alone again. The sky through the trees was lit with stars.

We crossed roads, sliding through rows of silent volunteers who crouched in unison like football players preparing to tackle. We passed what seemed to be a lake, with hard wind blowing across it, so the dogs had to lower their heads into the gusts. We passed another team, and another, and then we passed two teams that were running close together, and just as we came around the second one, we fell into a pit.

I saw it coming. We all did, the dogs and I: the right half of the trail fell away into darkness, and for a moment we were all scrambling, the dogs leaping away, me wresting the sled to the left, but it was too late. The dogs slipped first and I sailed over the top of them, landing with the sled in the middle of the team. For a sick, horrible moment I thought I had crushed a dog, and I flailed in the powder, feeling around beneath me. My headlamp had been knocked sideways, and I pulled it forward again and counted my dogs. They were knotted together, neck deep in snow. Six grinning faces. Six wagging tails. I didn't know how I'd untangle us, or get back onto the trail, but it didn't matter: we were okay.

One of the teams I'd overtaken stopped beside us. A woman's voice, the glare of a headlamp shining from above. "Do you need help?"

I squinted up. "Um," I said. "No, I don't think so. Thank you."

She took off again.

A logic puzzle: you have six dogs, ten feet of rope, a knife, a ski pole, a snowhook, a handful of zip ties, and a bag of bear fat. Now: how do you get out of the pit? The powder was so deep that righting the sled was nearly impossible. As soon as I wrestled it upright, it rolled over again and slid forward, leaving me swimming on my stomach through the drift. I tried to set the snowhook, but it wouldn't hold. I'd worn two parkas for warmth, which made it hard to move, and in wrestling the sled I had already sweat through my long underwear. I willed myself to radiate confidence; the last thing I needed was for the dogs to see me anxious. The thing to do, I figured, was get the sled somehow steady, then move my way along the team, untangling the dogs and checking for injuries. Then, finally, I would work on the challenge of getting us all out. Maybe I could lift the dogs one by one. Figure out somewhere to tie them so they wouldn't run off while I reassembled the team.

"Ready?" I said. This was the usual command for the dogs to pull their lines straight, to prepare to run. It was a long shot; given how tangled they must be, they probably couldn't do much. But the dogs' ears perked up, and, miraculously, they bounded into position. Three perfect pairs, poised to run, stuck at the bottom of a pit.

The lip of the trail was about six feet above us, the wall steep and soft. But the dogs were ready to go. I stared at them, then wrapped my hands very tightly around the handlebar.

"Ready?" I said quietly. "All right."

I'm telling you, it defies physics. But as soon as I said "All right," the dogs ran straight up the wall, their little feet catching hold faster than the snow could collapse around them. And as they reached the packed trail they dug into the ground and leaned into their harnesses and pulled me out, too. And by the time I'd scrambled onto the runners and caught my breath we were running again, not a tangle among us. And they were so *happy*, every muscle in their bodies bounding with excitement, smiles wide, not wolves at all——they were sled dogs, and it was a perfect ten below, and there was nothing in the whole world as fun as running and racing and tumbling into pits and getting out of them again.

"We're okay, aren't we?" I said to the dogs as we careened down a frozen logging road, the sled rattling over bumps in the ice, sending shudders up my bones. "We're doing just fine."

We skidded around a corner, scraping a tree, and nearly ran into another team that was stopped at the side of the trail. Their musher had crashed hard into a rock; her sled was twisted, and her ski pole had snapped in half. "You okay?" I asked, but she waved me on with a grin. When I looked back, her team was running again. She crouched low on the runners, pedaling furiously with her half-a-ski-pole.

The last ten miles were tricky. Lots of road crossings, and spectators, which threw off the rhythm of the long hours. Crowds and campfires emerged from the darkness and fell away again. At one crossing, I heard my parents cheer my name. At another point, somebody had lined a stretch of trail with paper lanterns, which cast flickering, snowflake shadows on the snow. A corridor of light.

We took the last mile at a full sprint, and as we crossed the finish line, in fourth place out of twenty-five, I thought, *Wait—too soon.* We didn't belong here, with the people and trucks and lights. We belonged back on the trail, running. We should turn around. The dogs, of course, knew better. Finishing a run meant time to eat, and finishing a *race* meant especially good food, bear fat and beaver meat from the taxidermist, plus hot kibble soup to wash it all down.

I took off their harnesses and they leaned into me, tails thumping against my thighs. Quince scooped their food into metal dishes. The dogs settled in to eat. Their warm bodies steamed in the night.

ACKNOWLEDGMENTS

I N NORWAY, WHEN STORIES ARE LOST, people say that they've gone into glemmeboka, The Book of Forgetting. The Old Store is a book of remembering, and so is this one. It has come to be with the help of many advisors, experts, and friends. Thank you to Kathy Anderson, agent and dreamer extraordinaire, and to Dan Halpern, Libby Edelson, and Hilary Redmon at Ecco. In particular, thank you to Emma Janaskie, who took on this project with grace and skill.

I want to thank Adrian Nicole LeBlanc for her wisdom and guidance, and Elisabeth Fairfield Stokes for knowing what I was writing long before I did. Jeff Sharlet challenged and sharpened my journalism. Handler Chrissie distracted me when I needed it most. Danica Novgorodoff served as reader and muse. The brilliant Alice Truax served as guardian angel.

I started this book at the Blue Mountain Center and finished it at the MacDowell Colony four years later. That is not a coincidence. The space and energy offered by these residencies is what allowed this project to find its shape. Thank you also to the students and faculty at the University of Iowa, who inspired me and supported my work.

The customers at Johannes Kristofferson's Descendants gave me their time, their welcome, and their friendship. It has been a great privilege to be part of their community. Thank you Christiane, Ragnar, Camilla, Odd Arne, Odd Helge, Marita, Natasha, Torstein, Roald, Leif (both of you!), Geir (all three of you!), Eilif Idar, Elisabeth, Ellinor, Anne-Marit, Anniken, Olav, Walter, Merethe, Bjørn Tormod, Bjorn Arne, Roger, Espen, Håvard, Jan Børre, Katja, Angelina, and Helge Jensen, as well as Gunnhild, Kaia, Lea, Jan, and Christer at 69°Nord. Thank you to Anne for your spinning lessons, Åse for your mittens, and Atle for your wonderful lies. Maria and Anita, thank you for letting me into your family. Anne Lill Gaare, thank you for your warmth, your conviction, and your humor. I think you're the coolest.

Rune died in his home on December 7, 2015. He was 53 years old. I don't know how to thank him.

Historian Arne Pedersen told me hours of stories over many long nights and tiny cups of coffee. Pål Faerøvrig, Bjorn Tore Nøkleby, and Vidar Løkeng shared blazing insights into folk schools and northlanders. Principal Jens Rindal astonished me when I was 18 and still does today. Every student who crosses his path is lucky.

MacKenzie, Maryam, Lawrence, Jana, Tijana, Tine, and Elin: thank you for sharing your memories and sharpening mine. Rebekah Eliasen, you are a brave soul and bright star. I will always be grateful that the glacier brought you and your family into my life.

To my parents, Jana Kay Slater and Marc Braverman: I see myself growing more like you every day, and nothing could make me prouder. Thank you for always being my home, and for supporting me as I make new homes. I love you more than all the grains of sand on all the beaches in all the world.

To Quince: Look under your pillow.

To Arild: Isn't it time to feed your sheep?